SEX IS AS SEX DOES

Sex Is as Sex Does

Governing Transgender Identity

Paisley Currah

NEW YORK UNIVERSITY PRESS

New York

NEW YORK UNIVERSITY PRESS
New York
www.nyupress.org

© 2022 by New York University
All rights reserved

References to Internet websites (URLs) were accurate at the time of writing. Neither the author nor New York University Press is responsible for URLs that may have expired or changed since the manuscript was prepared.

Library of Congress Cataloging-in-Publication Data
Names: Currah, Paisley, 1964–   author.
Title: Sex is as sex does : governing transgender identity / Paisley Currah.
Description: New York : New York University Press, [2022] |
Includes bibliographical references and index.
Identifiers: LCCN 2021025476 | ISBN 9780814717103 (hardback) |
ISBN 9781479812028 (ebook) | ISBN 9781479812011 (ebook other)
Subjects: LCSH: Transgender people—United States. | Transgender people—Identity. |
Gender identity—United States. | Gender nonconformity—United States. | Trangender people—Legal status, laws, etc.—United States.
Classification: LCC HQ77.95.U6 C87 2022 | DDC 306.76/80973—dc23
LC record available at https://lccn.loc.gov/2021025476

New York University Press books are printed on acid-free paper, and their binding materials are chosen for strength and durability. We strive to use environmentally responsible suppliers and materials to the greatest extent possible in publishing our books.

Manufactured in the United States of America

10 9 8 7 6 5 4 3 2 1

Also available as an ebook

For Greta

CONTENTS

I live in New York State. In 2003, when I changed the sex marker on my driver's license, the state required applicants to "submit evidence of medical, psychological, or psychiatric evaluations, with a medical determination that one gender predominates over the other." The only evidence the DMV would accept was a letter signed by a "physician" on official letterhead.[1] I went in person to get the sex marker on my NY driver's license changed from F to M, and I came prepared with a letter from a surgeon attesting to my gender. But the whole thing almost fell apart when the DMV agent at the window disputed the validity of the letter. "The policy says this letter needs to be from a physician," the agent told me, "but this person says he's a surgeon." It took consults with two levels of supervisors and one phone call before the DMV workers could agree that a surgeon's letter would suffice. Once that had been settled, the sex marker attached to my record and on my license was changed.

What happened to me at the DMV could be described as a mundane instance of what T. Benjamin Singer called the "transgender sublime." During this transaction, the gender disorientation my application created was transposed onto confusion about medical credentials. Years ago, the presentation of a transgender figure—in a text, in person—would often induce a certain vertigo. In these moments, people unexpectedly confronted with a gendered figure who confounded everything they thought they knew about sex would find themselves at the edge of a precipice beyond which cognition fails: "The sheer variety of trans bodies and genders exceeds providers' cognitive capacity to comprehend them."[2] To illustrate this point, Singer—who spent years studying the provision of health care to transgender people, as well as training health care professionals about trans issues in the 1990s—recounted an incident involving a medical resident working in the emergency room of a large urban hospital. When a transgender woman with a broken arm came into the hospital's emergency room, the resident took one look at her and announced that he could not set her arm because he hadn't received any medical training on transsexuality. For this resident, who undoubtedly had set and put casts on many broken limbs during his tenure in the ER, the gendered category crisis the patient triggered was so unsettling that it threw all that he knew into confusion, including the most routine of treatments.[3] A broken arm is a broken arm regardless of a patient's gender presentation or genitalia or secondary sex characteristics, but the perplexed MD had lost—one hopes only momentarily—his ability to see that.

Readers habituated to assuming that gender depends on genitals at birth can also have a hard time making sense of accounts of people who move away from their assigned sex. At the very least, keeping track of who is a man and who is a woman can use up a lot of the brain's processing power, power that might be needed to engage with the argument itself. To illustrate: over a decade ago, a colleague in political science told me, over dinner, about an article he had recently reviewed for a journal and had recommended rejecting. He thought I would be interested in the topic since the article was about efforts to reform New York City's policy of issuing amended birth certificates with no sex markers at all to people who had transitioned. "It was impossible to follow," he told me. "From the very beginning, I couldn't keep track of who was a man, who was a woman, if a transsexual woman was a man or a woman." As it turned out, and as I told him, the article had been written by me and a coauthor. It surely wasn't perfect and perhaps it deserved to be rejected by the journal—as it indeed was. (It eventually found a home in a special issue of a feminist philosophy journal.) Our mutual chagrin dissipated after a discussion of the vagaries of academic publishing and more wine. But my colleague's grappling with the most basic building blocks of that particular research piece—individuals whose gender identities do not correspond to the sex they were assigned at birth—meant that he had little cognitive capacity left to allow him to pay attention to our actual analysis. In it, we had looked at the shifts in the legal, medical, and commonsense logics governing the designation of sex on birth certificates issued by the city of New York between 1965 and 2006. Based on archival and ethnographic research, we found that, in the initial policy iteration, the stabilization of legal sex categories was organized around the notion of "fraud"; in later policy discussions, "permanence" was the indicium of authenticity. All that, though, was inaccessible to my reviewing colleague. We had lost him in the first paragraph, when the wheels of his brain began to spin out because of the strangeness of "transsexual woman." (As I explain in more detail in the introduction, I use "sex" to refer to legal classifications.)

In the last few years, however, the gender competency of academics and the general public has improved dramatically. Moments of gender disorientation are becoming rarer. Even transphobic activists know the basic argot, although they may reference it only to dismiss the legitimacy of gender identity as a concept. On the progressive side, there is a veritable industry of diversity trainers specializing in transgender issues; and, as a result, college students, school teachers, social workers, and employees at large corporations are much more likely now to have attended a training session on "what transgender is." In my own history as an activist and educator, I have conducted such sessions and written advocacy briefs. In them, I would carefully and slowly present key terms, provide concrete examples whenever possible, and dispel some of the strangeness of transgender experience by identifying possible moments in audience members' own histories when they transgressed gender norms. In introducing the terms, I would lay the groundwork for "transgender" by first defining "gender identity" as one's deeply held internal sense of being either male or female. (Back in the early aughts, when I was doing this sort of work, non-binary had yet to emerge as a gender identity.) I would explain that most people have a gender identity that is traditionally associated with the sex assigned to them at birth— that is, that infants identified as male develop a male gender identity and those identified as female develop a female gender identity. Then I would cite transgender activist and scholar Jamison Green to explain that "gender expression refers to all of the external characteristics and behaviors that are socially defined as either masculine or feminine, such as dress, mannerisms, speech patterns, and social interactions."[4] Following in the footsteps of so many others, I would say that transgender is usually defined in both broad analytic strokes and in reference to particular constituencies and practices. In its abstract sense, I would explain, transgender describes anyone whose gender identity or gender expression is not traditionally associated with the sex assigned to them at birth. To elaborate further, I might have cited Susan Stryker's influential 1994 definition of transgender as "an umbrella term that refers to all identities and practices that cross over, cut across, move between, or otherwise queer socially constructed sex/gender boundaries."[5] Sometimes, I would add, the terms "gender non-conforming," "gender different," or "gender variant" are used instead of "transgender," or as descriptive terms supplementing it. (I would probably feel compelled to add, parenthetically, that the older term "transsexual" emerged from medical discourses as a label, a pathologizing one, for people whose gender expression or identity is perceived to conflict with the sex assigned to them at birth, and who may want to undergo a process of "gender transition" that may or may not include gender-affirming medical interventions such as hormone therapy and different types of surgery.) Finally, I would talk about "cisgender" and "cissexual." The neologism "cissexual," Julia Serano explains, refers to "people who are not transsexual and who have only ever experienced their physical and subconscious sexes as being aligned," while "cisgender" refers to "people who are not transgender."[6] These terms were introduced to name the previously unmarked normative category of non-transgender—some would use the adjective "accidental" here— men and women.[7] Were I to do such trainings now, there would be a lot more words and definitions.

These excursions into "Trans 101" do much to lessen or even prevent the confusion that can result when the old common senses of sex come unglued. But there are also real disadvantages to making the oddness of gender transition and gender fluidity more familiar. Providing pat definitions of words connected to minoritizing views of sex and gender, perhaps including an extensive glossary of terms in an appendix and containing all of this under the ever-more-domesticated label of transgender, tends to settle meanings that, for some purposes, should be left unsettled. David Valentine argued as far back as 2007 that "transgender" might accomplish too much: "The capacity to stand in for an unspecified group of people is, indeed, one of the seductive things about 'transgender.' . . . Indeed, that 'transgender' can stand both as a description of individual identity and simultaneously as a general term for gendered transgressions of many kinds makes it almost infinitely elastic."[8] No doubt assembling so many particular practices and identities together under the broad concept of transgender provides a certain intelligibility to all kinds of gender non-normativity.

But this contrived boundary drawing comes at a cost. Distinctions related to gender—between men and women and non-binary people, between masculinity and femininity—get erased when transgender and cisgender are set against each other in the ultimate Manichean dualism.[9] One effect of centering the trans-cis divide is to make misogyny and sexism more difficult to see.[10] Another is to inhibit our understanding of more specific transphobic tropes, such as those that circulate in the conservative rhetoric around trans women in women's bathrooms.[11] The reification of transgender also obscures differences of race, ethnicity, class, region, age, (dis)ability, and immigration status. The distinct characteristics of communities that have emerged out of very different contexts; the messy contingencies of history; the specific relations of individuals and communities to larger processes producing hierarchies of race, class, gender, and nation; the endless lexical productivity of language and the proliferation of identities it enables—all that disappears in the service of the conceptual uniformity of the neatly demarcated box.

This book doesn't deliver a "Trans 101." I certainly don't want to befuddle readers unfamiliar with the ins and outs of gender non-normativity and gender transition, but neither do I want to clear up the confusion by providing pat accounts of clearly limned categories like *transgender*, *cisgender*, and *non-binary*. And for those very familiar with transgender issues, I want to make the category's coherence, even intelligibility (the assumptions about community, identity, and the categories of both transgender and cisgender) a bit more strange and unfamiliar. If we decide in advance what male, female, and X (non-binary) mean before turning to the empirical situation—regardless of whether we imagine sex as referring to gender identity or to the sex assigned at birth or to current genital configurations—it becomes harder to concentrate on *why* distinct state actors define sex differently, and to figure out what those differences make possible. Moreover, placing so many different ways of failing to conform to gender norms under a conceptually smooth category of transgender gets in the way of identifying specific forms of exclusion that affect people under the "umbrella" differently.

Similarly, if we begin with the assumptions that there is this singular entity called *the state* and that it often misclassifies transgender people because of transphobia, it will be more difficult to understand at a more granular level the differences between state actors—for example, New

York State's Department of Motor Vehicles and its Department of Corrections. Working on this book has required holding off the move from the specific, apparently anomalous, case to a generalized theory of states and sex classification. An empirical case might be a particular application of a policy on sex definition at a particular agency at a particular moment in time; a general theory might attempt to set out a globalizing account of the relation between the more conceptually coherent categories of *sex* and *the state*. Because coming up with a generalizable theory could get in the way of understanding the policy differences, I stay close to the details and defer turning to these larger analytical categories and coming to theoretical closure for as long as possible.

The work of states is to make distinctions among people, objects, and actions. Governments pass statutes, executive agencies create formal or informal rules and policies for enforcing those statutes, and courts decide if a statute contravenes a state or the federal constitution, or if a regulatory policy adequately adheres to the meaning of the statute. Often, the distinctions seem unfair to some—bailing out banks but not individuals, for instance. But the charge of unfairness depends on assuming that the particular people, institutions, or actions share an important commensurability, or sameness. But that commensurability, that sameness, is not a "truth," but an argument. If justice as equality means, as Aristotle suggested, that like cases ought to be treated alike, the question begs another question.[12] What cases, situations, individuals are alike? Or, as Aristotle put it, "inequality or equality of *what?*" Much of the stuff of politics is taken up with challenging those distinctions, with asserting that two things, people, events share a certain *whatness* in the relevant characteristic, or at the very least an equivalence. Or that they don't.

There is something about sex classification that make different sex reclassification policies seem not just unfair, but contradictory, even paradoxical. Perhaps because sex is thought to be prior to or outside of politics, unearthing its production as a legal classification seems qualitatively different than thinking through the politics of many other sorts of classifications. Or maybe because M and F have been defined in relation to one another, as each other's constitutive opposite, the different rules for classification appear paradoxical. Even people not cognizant of or interested in transgender recognition claims find it absurd that two "alike" individuals—both assigned male at birth, with female gender identities and identical histories of body modification—end up with opposite sex classifications from different agencies. Or when the *same* individual has Fs on some state-issued documents and Ms on others. Most trans rights advocates would argue that it's not only inconsistent but unjust when two individuals who have the same gender identity—regardless of the state of their body or the history of its modification—are assigned different sex markers. In this book, however, I don't center arguments about what the state *ought to do* for sake of consistency and fairness in sex designation. (If we're talking shoulds—*of course*, state actors should classify sex according to gender identity, including non-binary gender identities. *Of course*, governments *should* get out of the business of defining, classifying, and recording Ms, Fs, and Xs. But states are not moral beings, they are mobile technologies for arranging difference, distributing pain and pleasure.) The approach is not to focus on the injustice of the inconsistencies but on why they exist in the first place.

Ultimately, I hope the arguments I present won't just better our understanding of states' decisions about sex, but also inform a politics that challenges these injustices. It's not my intention to fall down the rabbit hole, never to emerge from the fact/right abyss, to permanently foreclose making the impossible and yet necessary jump from the is to the ought on the matter of legal enactments of sex. But it is my contention that we need to understand at a much more historical and granular level what states are, what they do, and the effects of particular rules, laws, and policies on sex. Rather than being a minor matter of housekeeping, an agency's rule for sex reclassification might be more deeply implicated in the agency's specific governance project than is immediately obvious. Failing to apprehend how a state actor's rules for deciding who is M and who is F further its work—for example, tracking the movement of individuals or forging fictions of family and inheritance through the regulation of parenting and marriage—could make it more difficult to recognize its investment in a particular policy. Moreover, calling for uniform criteria for sex classification across all forms and levels of government or for its elimination across the board as a classificatory scheme assumes that sex does the same thing in every location. Grand, large-scale accounts of sex and the state depend on assuming a sameness to sex or a singular rationality to state actors, decisions, and projects. We don't know what a politics of resistance would look like until we understand what it is we're resisting.

* * *

A note on language: in a different monograph, central terms (such as "sex," "gender," "male," "female," "biological") would demand a settled and consistent usage across the chapters. But since much of this book concerns battles over meaning, providing static definitions assumes a consensus that does not yet exist.[13] Additionally, *transgender* is asked to do a lot of work in this book. Transgender as an ever-expanding signifier is discussed at more length in the introduction and conclusion. Because transgender refers to anyone whose gender identity—one's internal sense of oneself as male, as female, as both, as neither—does not correspond to social expectations for the sex they were assigned at birth, I also understand *transgender* to include both binary and non-binary people. In some of the situations I write about, that someone could be something other than male or female was not imagined as a possibility by the policymakers. Sometimes it would be more accurate to replace "trans" or "transgender person" with phrases like, "someone whose gender identity is not traditionally associated with the sex assigned to them at birth," because the individual I am writing about might not identify as transgender. But that is too clunky and so most of the time I use *trans* or *transgender*, interchangeably. Occasionally, I substitute *gender non-normative* as an overarching category. I use *transsexuality* and *transsexual* when discussing twentieth-century medicalized constructions of people whose gender identity is not traditionally associated with the sex assigned at birth and who desire transition-related medical interventions. Transsexuality, later "gender identity disorder" and now "gender dysphoria," pathologizes those whose gender was or is unexpected in one way or another. That medical discourse certainly does not account for those who did not desire to change their bodies and/or who rejected the gender binary. These constructions also marginalized those whose class position, (dis)ability, race, ethnicity, or culture of origin did not correspond with Euro-American white bourgeois gender norms.

What this book is not about: except for the discussion in chapter 5 of the role incarceration plays in mainstream trans rights discourse and in the economy, the book is focused on sex reclassification and related questions. It does not pay a great deal of attention to nondiscrimination law and policy. The analysis is limited to policies in the United States and makes no claim that it can be exported to other places. It is not a handbook for trans rights advocates or policymakers—Shannon Price Minter and I created such a publication decades ago.[14] Nor does it address the question of intersexuality and the law, which has been the subject of excellent scholarship by Julie Greenberg and others.[15] Finally, it makes no attempt to set out a foundation for sex reclassification claims or to justify the existence of transgender people. Generally, publications in the Trans 101 genre and introductions to texts on transgender issues often begin by invoking people born with intersex conditions, various forms of "third sex" and gender non-conforming individuals in non-Western cultures, and/or the social construction of gender and sex. However, I question the perceived necessity of explaining that sex is not always perfectly dimorphic at birth, that every culture has some form of gender crossing, that sex is an effect of gender, in order to justify the acceptance of people who move away from the sex they were assigned at birth. Some or even all or some of these assertions may be right. But what if they're not? If some form of gender crossing at one place and time had no bearing on a different from of gender non-normativity in another place and time; if there were no connections between intersex people and transgender people; if what we call gender identity turns out to have a material foundation in the body for some but not for others—would that somehow invalidate the existence of people whose self-avowed gender identity or gender expression has no bearing on the biological circumstances of their birth? Instead of establishing an ontological foundation for sex reclassification—as if the presence of gender non-normative people requires a justification or even an explanation—this book explores the rationales of governance for deciding when and where what sex you are.

Introduction

"A transsexual fled a Brooklyn courtroom in tears yesterday after recounting how she was menaced in the Barbie aisle by baseball bat–wielding employees of a Toys 'R' Us in Bensonhurst."[1] So opens a 2000 *New York Daily News* story on a discrimination lawsuit brought by three transgender women. In December 2000, the three were harassed and threatened by employees who called the women "fags," "fucking faggots," "homos," and "disgusting transvestites," according to the victims' complaint. A week later they returned to the Brooklyn store for their Christmas shopping. This time about eight employees, including the two brandishing baseball bats, threatened the women with "imminent bodily injury" and tried to chase them off the premises. The women filed a complaint with New York's Human Rights Commission, and the store offered them each a $100 "Geoffrey the Giraffe" gift certificate. The plaintiffs, described by their attorney as "preoperative transsexuals," refused and sued for damages in federal court. They claimed that Toys "R" Us had violated New York City's human rights law by discriminating against them based on sex, gender, gender identity, and perceived sexual orientation.[2] During the jury trial, Toys "R" Us put up a vigorous defense. "Given who they are and what they look like," a Toys "R" Us spokesman said, "comments get passed to them in the rough-and-tumble world of walking around the streets of New York and going about their business."[3] The jury found in the transgender women's favor, but awarded them only one dollar each in damages. One sympathetic juror later said that anything more than that would have resulted in a hung jury. Despite the evidence, some jurors were put off by the "transgenderism" and found the women "sick" and "disgusting."[4]

This story captures the gender crosscurrents of that turn-of-the-century moment. Three people whose female gender identity and feminine gender expression confounded the social expectations for people assigned male at birth were hounded out of a space well-known for its policing of the gender binary. Toys "R" Us, like most retailers of the time, had separate pink and blue aisles for toys—and actually posted signs to designate certain aisles as being for girls and boys—to make it very clear who should be playing with what. The Barbie Bungalow Beach House that one of the plaintiffs wanted to buy for a young relative belonged, according to these norms, in the girls' aisle. The trans women shopping in the store, the company spokesperson's comment implied, did not belong in that aisle, in the store, or really in any public place—or at least they should not expect to be free from harassment should they venture out. The case got very little attention outside of the LGBT press. At that time, only a handful of jurisdictions included gender identity in nondiscrimination ordinances, and most jurisprudence on the subject had yet to recognize that such discrimination is a type of sex or gender discrimination.[5]

More than two decades later, the situation looks very different. Many large stores have gotten rid of the girls' and boys' toy aisles and have even stopped using toy gender categories online. While discrimination against transgender people continues and may even have grown because of heightened visibility, incidents like the one at Toys "R" Us now are likely to result in mainstream news coverage, declarations of solidarity from cisgender people on social media, petitions, even boycotts. Seventy-two percent of millennials support nondiscrimination laws that include transgender people.[6] Toys "R" Us declared bankruptcy in 2018, but many other retailers, including Target, Walgreens, and Barnes & Noble, have policies allowing individuals to use the bathroom corresponding with their gender identity. While polls consistently show the public to be evenly divided on whether or not trans people should be able to use the bathroom that corresponds to their gender identity, women and younger people were much more likely to be in favor of allowing trans people access.[7] In 2014, *Time* magazine ran a cover story proclaiming that the "transgender tipping point" had been reached.[8] In 2015, the *Washington Post* changed its style guide, adopting the singular "they" as its preferred gender-neutral pronoun.[9] Pride Month in 2016 saw Goldman Sachs flying the pink, white, and blue transgender flag outside its Manhattan world headquarters and Pentagon officials announcing the end of the ban on transgender people serving in the armed forces. Although the ban was restored a year later by President Trump, the ban on transgender people serving openly in the armed forces was ended (a second time) in 2021.[10] In 2017, Virginian Danica Roem became the first out transgender person in the United States to take office in a state legislature.[11] By 2019, if any of the plaintiffs in the Toys "R" Us lawsuit had been born in New York City, they would have been able to change the sex designation on their birth certificates to M, F, or X— regardless of whether or not they had modified their bodies through surgery or hormone therapy. (In this book, "sex" refers to classifications of male or female backed by the force of law. I use "gender" when discussing shared, though often contested, norms, narratives, practices, and conventions that arrange bodies, identities, roles, and expressions in hierarchies of difference based on binary notions of male/female, man/woman, and masculinity/femininity. The next chapter will discuss these choices in more depth.) In the 2020 general election, six transgender candidates were elected to statewide offices.[12]

In popular culture, at colleges and universities, in large cities and small towns, and in social service agencies, schools, and state governments, people living in a gender not associated with the sex assigned at birth and others who express gender in ways that fail to conform to social expectations have been transformed from deeply pathologized yet fascinating objects of curiosity to people worthy of toleration, understanding, acceptance, and political equality. Of course, this acceptance is not evenly diffused throughout the population, nor, at the time of writing, has it been translated into nondiscrimination laws in every jurisdiction, the universal reform of sex classification rules, or full-throttled social acceptance. Nonetheless, the transformation in the last two decades has been striking.[13]

Trans and queer institutions, the mainstream media, and many if not most trans people understand this social movement for equality as a new(ish) entrant in the longstanding battle over the politics of identity. Diverse constellations of gender non-normative people who were all but socially illegible in the early 1990s have now been forged into a represented and representable transgender community. One of the mechanisms for this unification has been the concept of *transgender*, which purports to contain all forms of non-normative gender difference. In the 1990s, the term "transgender umbrella" emerged as an educational device to represent all the many different forms of gender non-normativity extant at any one time and place. T. Benjamin Singer recounts seeing an early training document that pictured "a hand-drawn umbrella with an open canopy stretched over a now dated set of terms: 'crossdresser ('drag'),' 'transvestic fetishist,' 'transvestite,' 'transgenderist,' 'transsexual' and 'man/woman.'"[14]

Since then, the transgender umbrella has become a machine of perpetual expansion, generating a seemingly endless proliferation of practices and identities. Susan Stryker uses "transgender" to "refer to people who move away from the gender they were assigned at birth." That includes people who "feel strongly that they properly belong to another gender through which it would be better for them to live" as well as those who "simply feel the need to challenge the conventional expectations bound up with the gender that was initially put upon them."[15] The category thus brings together, at times uneasily, both ascriptive and performative notions of identity/subjectivity: people who understand themselves as having been born in the wrong body find themselves working alongside those who reject the gender binary altogether.[16] Certainly, the transgender umbrella hides fundamental disagreements among those it shelters—about sex, gender and the gender binary, transition, the ontological status of the body, the fixity of gender, and the effects of a medical model of transgender identity. But the political benefits of aggregating cannot be denied. When the Centers for Disease Control allowed the question "Do you consider yourself to be transgender?" to appear on large-scale state health surveys, the responses led to an estimate of 1.4 million adults in the "transgender population" in the United States.[17] Earlier estimates had put the trans population at about half of that.[18]

It is the politics of identity that makes it possible for this "myriad of alterities" to be seen as a coherent political force—a cacophonous crowd, to be sure, yet one that is still imagined as moving forward together under the protective carapace of transgender.[19] In this way, the transgender community becomes visible against the backdrop of the civil rights tradition in the United States. While political organizing under the rubric of trans became visible to community members in the 1990s with the emergence of grassroots groups such as Transsexual Menace and Transgender Nation, a successful movement organized around identity needs to be seen by and intelligible to an outside audience. The accelerating usage of "transgender" in major newspapers attests to its growing recognition after the turn of this century: "transgender" did not appear once before 1995; it appeared nine times by 1999 and two million times by 2003. Similarly, a Google search for "transgender" in March 2004 generated over eight hundred thousand hits; my search in August 2021 generated over 170 million.[20] Without the transgender nomenclature, the jumble of uneven advances in a wide variety of settings (different agencies, different branches of government, different jurisdictions) addressing very different legal areas (identity documents, discrimination, family law, incarceration, immigration, etc.) and involving different sorts of gender non-normativity (hewing to or rejecting the gender binary, for example) would not have hypostasized into a larger phenomenon. But with the term, these successes are written into a new chapter in the story of progress that underwrites the liberal worldview in the United States: a previously disdained social group's slow but (in hindsight) inevitable triumph over an oppression enforced by the state and made possible by widespread social animus.

However, it would be a mistake to assume the (relative) success of the trans rights movement was entirely—or even mostly—a result of self-generating momentum. My proposition, counterintuitive though it may seem given the dominance of the identity politics narrative recounted above, is this: the achievements of the movement organized under the political category of *transgender* do not justify using that category as its own self-explanatory tool. Notwithstanding the genesis stories of new social movements and the rhetoric of activists, in fact the transgender movement did not pull itself up by its own bootstraps—especially on the question of states and sex classification. Over the course of the twentieth century, the law's use of classification regimes to treat people differently diminished as a result of the civil rights movement and of the expanding capacity of apparatuses of domination to manage inequality outside the formal sphere of the law. Gender had been gradually *disestablished* from the state during this period, culminating in the *Obergefell* decision in 2015 when the Supreme Court ruled that state bans on same-sex marriage were unconstitutional.[21]

Sex Changes

In 1994, Idaho resident Jane Jones was arrested and briefly imprisoned for the crime of "false personation." The police had come to her home with a search warrant in the course of investigating her husband for writing bad checks. When the officer looked over her papers during the search, he discovered a contradiction between the identity information on her driver's license ("John," male) and her marriage certificate ("Jane," female). Her husband might have been writing bad checks, but it was Jane, the officer decided, who had committed fraud. She was charged with "marriage under false personation," an assault, according to her arrest warrant, "against the peace and dignity of the State of Idaho."[22] Who was this person—Jane or John? For the Idaho deputy sheriff, Jane was John. As a man, John was in a same-sex marriage, which meant in 1994 it wasn't a marriage at all: at the time, the state of Idaho did not allow an individual to marry someone of the same sex. Jane, the woman who answered the door and let the officer into her home, lacked the identification documents she needed to support her claim to being a member of the female sex. Despite identifying as a woman and consistently being perceived by others as a woman, despite using a different name and presenting herself as a woman—despite, in fact, modifying her body so that it aligned with her gender identity—she had an M printed on her ID by the Idaho Department of Motor Vehicles, which became the pivotal fact in this unfortunate incident. Once her husband's alleged check kiting drew legal attention to the couple, the awareness of a gap between her identity documents and her self (her "personation") could be explained only as some sort of fraud.[23] Jane—or rather John, in the eyes of the police officer—was pretending to be someone she wasn't.

Who gets to decide whether the woman who spent the night in an Idaho county jail is a man or a woman? The individual who identifies as a woman? The individual who signed the marriage certificate attesting to her status as female? The police officer who sees the "M" on the driver's license he's holding in his hand? In one sense, everyone is free to decide what gender they are, and to make judgments about the gender of others. Just as the police officer who arrested her is free to think of himself as male, Jane is free to think of herself as a woman, to present herself publicly as a woman, and to change her name through a court order or, in states that honor the common law tradition of using the name one "goes by," by taking on a new name. In a different context—were he to pass Jane on the street, say—the sheriff's deputy might have concluded, based on an almost unthinking microsecond-long reading of the cultural insignia of gender Jane presented, that she was female.[24] While both Jane and the deputy can make judgments about Jane's status as a man or a woman, it was the deputy's decision that was backed by the force of law. Jane might identify as a woman and exist as a woman socially. But in this case, the sex classification on her driver's license, a state-issued identity document, trumped her presentation and self-understanding as a woman. She spent a night in jail because of the discrepancy.

The conundrum I take on in this book is this: sex changes. By "sex changes," I am not speaking of the less-than-respectful label for those who have transitioned, or the old-fashioned term for gender affirmation surgery. I mean, instead, that an individual's *designation* as F or M can shift. When some individuals cross borders, walk into a government office to apply for benefits, get a driver's license, go to prison, sign up for Selective Service, get married, or have any interaction with a state agency, their sex classification can switch from male to female, from female to male, and even, in a handful of jurisdictions and situations, from M or F to non-binary. Even within a single jurisdiction, almost every particular state agency—from federal to municipal—has the authority to decide its own rules for sex classification. And, to complicate matters even more, both state and federal judges have found that one's sex classification for some social functions may not hold for others. The lack of a universal standard for classifying people as male or female means that some state agencies will recognize the new sex of people who change it while some will not. For most people—those many refer to as "cisgendered"—this lack of uniformity doesn't present a problem.[25] For others, it does. In New York City, for example, the policy of homeless shelters is to house people according to their gender identity. The state's corrections system, on the other hand, usually bases the distinction between men and women on external genitalia. Most people who identify as a sex different from the one assigned to them at birth do not have surgery to change their genitals. If a transgender woman housed in a women's shelter were to be arrested, in jail she would be housed with women but possibly in a special transgender unit.[26] If she were convicted and sentenced and sent upstate to a corrections institution, she would very likely find herself in a men's prison.[27] While a Republican Party resolution holds that sex begins at conception, even a Republican president could not make that position the uniform law of the land across these United States.[28] There has never been a consistent, universal policy regarding reclassifying the sex of the people who move away from the sex they were assigned at birth.

For people whose deeply held internal sense of themselves as male or female does not align with the sex assigned to them at birth, how their sex is designated depends on criteria for sex classification used by the particular government agency in question. And one of the central arguments of this book is that those criteria often depend on what the particular agency does—regulate marriage and families, make decisions about property, track births and deaths, provide residents with identity documents, house the homeless, regulate the professions, ensure the security of air travel, or incarcerate populations. Sex classification becomes a malleable instrument of governmentality, threaded through an apparently endless number of apparatuses at every level of government, from department of motor vehicles policies, to case law on marriage, parenting, and inheritance, to rules regarding incarcerated prisoners. For transgender people, the immense number of state institutions defining sex in the United States has ensnared us in a Kafkaesque web of official identity contradiction and chaos. In Idaho, for example, Jane could have changed the sex classification on her driver's license if she had wanted to negotiate the bureaucracy and give officials at the Department of Motor Vehicles a letter from a physician documenting the history of her body and her gender identity. But until 2018 the Idaho Office of Vital Statistics would not change the sex classification on the birth certificates they issue.[29] So an Idaho resident who was also born in the state might have, for the majority of her life, carried a driver's license with an F on it in her wallet and kept a birth certificate listing her as M tucked away in a drawer in her home.

In the past, people who presented themselves as a sex that was not the one assigned to them at birth have been cast as frauds by the mainstream media, by policymakers, and by perpetrators (and their defenders) of violence against transgender people (and their defenders). In

1965, officials in New York City decided that the "public interest for the protection against fraud" justified a policy pronouncement against sex reclassification on birth certificates issued by the city.[30] In this report, the possibility that a transsexual woman—a male in the eyes of its authors, as well as in the eyes of physicians and psychiatrists—would find an unwitting man to marry stood out as the most worrisome possibility. In the case of murder and assault, the "transgender panic" defense—e.g., "I didn't know she had a penis until we started having sex"—is meant to amplify a jury's impression that transgender people are frauds.[31] In 2008, two candidates who lost a primary election in Georgia to a transgender woman, Michelle Bruce, went to court to contest the results. "Mr. Bruce misled the voters into believing that he was a female," argued their attorney.[32] However, while the idea of fraud continues to circulate in the popular imaginary, transgender people have rarely been arrested for "false personation" or "fraud," as Jane was. Instead, the *disjunction* between the sex one believes oneself to be and the sex a state institution says one is has been the vehicle for taking away rights and privileges that are distributed based on sex: before bans on same-sex marriage were declared unconstitutional, for example, such marriages were declared invalid and wills were voided. Parental relationships were, and in some jurisdictions can still be, permanently severed and jobs have been lost as a result of transitioning. In addition, incarcerated trans people are segregated according to genital status in the vast majority of state and federal prisons and municipal jails, causing untold danger, discomfort, and distress.

Much of the debate on state sex classification appears to depend on identifying which is the most objectively true definition of sex: (1) sex is the physical state of the characteristics associated with sex and identifiable on or in the body at the time of one's birth; (2) sex is genitals; (3) sex is gender identity. The working definition of sex used in this book, however, is this: sex is whatever an entity whose decisions are backed by the force of law says it is. In short, in examining state decisions on sex classification, in this book I focus not on *what sex is* but on *what it does*. This means not starting with the claim that sex has been misclassified or that the rules of sex classification are contradictory. It looks like a contradiction when one individual is simultaneously classified as M and F by different government agencies. It looks like a contradiction when a bearded, balding, only slightly paunchy middle-aged man like myself is classified as F, while the bearded, balding, paunchy middle-aged man standing in line next to me is M. But in letting go (at least provisionally) of the assumption that there is any *there* there, any whatness to (legal) sex apart from what the state says it is, the contradiction evaporates. The official sex designation—more precisely, the M, the F, or more recently the X—stamped on documents or coded in records becomes the only true thing we know. Then, an analysis can focus not on what sex really is, or what it should be, but on what it does, what it accomplishes, what it produces.

Sex Reclassification Is Not Just for Transgender People; Gender Equality Is Not Just for Feminism

The issue of sex reclassification might appear to be of interest only to people who disagree with the M or the F stamped on their identity documents. Certainly, the number of people who find their sex misclassified by state actors is a very small proportion of the general population. In utilitarian logic the problems of bigger groups usually matter more than those of smaller groups. Perhaps the single most common question that journalists and policymakers ask transgender rights advocates is "Just how many transgender people are there?" That is an impossible question to answer accurately both for reasons of methodology (how do researchers identify people in this position when coming out as transgender carries great risks?) and epistemology (what are the metrics of "transgender"?).[33] Yet, because policymakers and journalists demand an answer, transgender advocates try to provide one. If the legal regulation of sex appears to affect only a tiny (but vocal) segment of the population, why should it be of concern to the vast majority of the (non-transgender) public who live in the commonsense world of gender, where fetuses have gender reveal parties and infants are easily labeled male or female at birth and inevitably grow up to be men or women? In terms of scholarship, how could looking into state decisions and policies on sex reclassification possibly add to the pressing research agenda of the critical/theoretical left, which includes investigations of popular sovereignty and constitutive exclusions, the nation and narratives of cultural reproduction, surveillance and the securitization of risk, apparatuses of governmentality and biological citizenship, the neoliberal political project, and the escalation of income inequality?

With a little category shifting, queer theorist Eve Sedgwick's work can help explain the connection between the sexually misclassified and everyone else. Examining the divide between homosexuality and heterosexuality, Sedgwick identifies two contradictory ways of understanding the distinction. The "minoritizing" approach constructs the problem as one of "active importance primarily for a small, distinct, relatively fixed homosexual minority." In contrast, the "universalizing" view sees this divide "as an issue of continuing, determinative importance in the lives of people across the spectrum of sexualities."[34] If we transpose the terms of Sedgwick's analysis so that *transgender/non-transgender* takes the place of *homosexual/heterosexual*, the minoritizing view would understand state rules for sex classification as harmful only to a very small and distinct population of people. It's only the peculiar anomaly of transgender people—the disjunction between the sex we think we are and the sex that state actors say we are—that puts us in the unlucky position of having to carry around a piece of government-issued paper that might have the wrong sex marker written on it. In this approach, the plight of transgender people is an unanticipated remainder of processes that are unremarkable in every other way. According to this framework, the policing of sex definitions does not pose problems for the vast majority of people: those who develop and hold fast throughout their life course to a gender identity that conforms to expectations for the sex stamped on their birth certificate. The minoritizing perspective, understandably adopted by many transgender rights advocates, thus takes on the vernacular of identity politics.[35] A specific subset of people comes forward to claim that their group has been denied equal treatment under the law and to seek redress.

From the universalizing perspective, however, the problem is not limited to the particular situation of transgender people—though our situation highlights it. Its effects reach people whose sex designation is and has always been "traditionally associated with" their gender identity, whose classification as M or F is consistent across all government agencies, and who cannot imagine that the accuracy of their sex classification might ever be vulnerable to future state decisions. Identity documents that do not *mis*classify the sex of individuals and that allow access to sex-segregated institutions are also products of state systems for classifying sex. Indeed, the barriers to sex reclassification that transgender people face reinforce the credibility of sex as a metric of identity for everyone. The legitimacy of the majority's sex classifications, which most have probably never questioned, is made possible by erecting obstacles to others' requests for reclassification; the vulnerability of "transgender" individuals subtends the perceived invulnerability of everyone else on that score. This elementary point—that there is no "us" without a "them"—is the organizing principle of many genres of critical scholarship, including disability studies, race and ethnic studies, colonial and postcolonial theory, feminist theory, queer theory, and sexuality studies. But in examining state constructions of sex, it's important to underline this point as explicitly as possible. While scholarship and teaching have shown that the binaries of masculinity/femininity, able-bodied/disabled, heterosexuality/homosexuality, and white/nonwhite result from social, legal, and ideological processes rather than inherent differences, when it comes to M and F classifications it can be particularly difficult to displace the idea that male and female really do mean something and are not primarily words with legal effects.

For a long time, analyses of state constructions of sex have tended to stick to either the particular or the general framework. Rarely did thinking about sex and states cross these boundaries. The particularistic approach centered the details of sex definition; the more general approach focused on how states use gender to distribute rights and resources. One could, with a little wedging, suggest that most transgender work in legal studies exemplified the former approach while feminist scholarship mapped onto the latter. Like the proverbial ships passing in the night, investigations into states and sex definition had not been in conversation with research on gender and distributive justice. Scholarship and advocacy about transgender rights (including some of my own previous work) have hewed closely to the language of recognition, focusing on the special case of sex misclassification. A little bit of tinkering with the rules—perhaps the adoption of a uniform standard for all jurisdictions and state functions, or even the disestablishment of sex altogether—and the unfairness is reformed away. While it is essential for transgender rights advocates to seek short-term fixes to the problems of sex classification, in the longer term we need to advance a critical framework that identifies the scale of the problem and the historical formations that have produced it.[36]

Feminist scholarship, by comparison, is all about understanding how gender operates as a foundation for a host of other social arrangements—not just marriage, but the family, private property, and citizenship.[37] But almost all that scholarship has traditionally taken the categories of M/F as given a priori when examining how states use them to distribute rights and resources.[38] The situation faced by transgender people becomes, once again, an anomaly. Rather than understand how the deviant case of the sexually misclassified might actually structure the normal situation, the issue devolves into the problem of sex misclassification suffered by a small band of gender nonconformers, or "transsexual menaces."[39] What's more, the differing criteria for sex definition from agency to agency, from court to court, from jurisdiction to jurisdiction, and from one social function to another, which should be recognized by scholars as a wellspring of data, have either been overlooked or examined as only illogical discrepancies in the classification of transgender people. Examining those differences in sex definition could do much to help us understand how gender works in particular contexts to distribute inequality. Such an understanding might also support, and occasionally challenge, theories of gender justice and histories of state-sponsored gender discrimination. Thus far, neither research on the ins and outs of sex classification policies nor work on gender as a distributive mechanism for states has examined how these issues are not just connected but mutually constitutive. In this book, my aim is to show the necessity of integrating the minoritizing (transgender) and universalizing (gender) approaches to the study of state constructions of sex and the politics of trans politics. What sex turns out to mean, legally, will often depend on what it has done or what it continues to do for particular state projects, and how that work is imbricated in other processes involved in the giving and taking of money, pleasure, liberty, health, and life. This slippage should be of interest not only to scholars. If the trans political movement fails to challenge the larger asymmetry of power in gender relations that is responsible for cementing sex into the legal structures in the first place and is now responsible for continuing gender subordination outside the legal sphere (such as pay disparity and the structures of work and family life) that disproportionately affect women, it will indeed turn out to have been nothing more than a minoritizing, single-focused, limited political project.

Undoing Transgender

It may seem untimely to fold up the proverbial transgender umbrella at the very moment of its accession into the storied history of social movements in the United States. Indeed, *transgender* convenes most, though not all, of the legal phenomena under examination in the following chapters. But it doesn't explain them. Though *transgender* may be at a moment of heightened legibility in popular culture, *transgender* itself is not a coherent object of analysis for an investigation into sex classification policies. Historically, these rules were not put in place to target transgender populations. Nor were they an expression of transphobia. Rather than taking *transgender* as the rubric for policies that negatively impact transgender people and examining many different policy positions—both the wins and the impediments—together as metrics of the progress of this group, this book turns to the granular, the nitty-gritty, the particular legal constructions over any generalized trend. In doing so, other fault lines are made visible. Instead of seeing these changes as necessarily part of a drama that climaxes in a decisive thematic moment—the transgender tipping point reached, the last legal obstacle downed—the focus turns to discrete elements, which are not assumed to simply be gears meshing to propel the putative trans rights movement to its goal. Though they may seem counterintuitive at first, the readings of the case law, administrative policy, legislation, and movement strategies do not always treat the trans-vs.-cis analytic paradigm as key to understanding how policy differences between trans and cis have emerged and to identifying solutions to end this formal inequality. Identifying transphobia as the global explanation for policies that harm people whose gender identity doesn't correspond with the traditional expectations for those of their birth sex makes it more difficult to see these policies in light of distinct histories and governing rationales of different regulatory realms: marriage, parenting, and family law; identity documents and the surveillance state; incarceration and criminal justice.

Given the centrality of the trans-cis paradigm at the present moment, then, there is a good case to be made for adopting a less familiar approach, as others have done. For example, in his work on blackness and "transness," C. Riley Snorton avoids defaulting to the cisgender-transgender binary; indeed, his project is to show "how the condensation of transness into the category of transgender is a racial narrative."[40] In this book, a close study of government rules for sex reclassification reveals how sex has been operationalized differently and how those policies produced different effects. Reading these tangled rules about sex with and against each other reveals incongruities that disrupt the notion that the policy issues affecting sex reclassification should be thought of as a single problem with a single trajectory. Rules and policies regarding definitions of M or F classification that are thought to be about "transgender people" often have had much more to do with the specific context, with the role of the person being classified—worker, incarcerated person, parent, spouse, voter, social service client—than with any larger scientific or philosophical position on what "sex"—as in male or female—really is. More fundamentally, the precise way "sex" is regulated in each of these contexts has often been deeply connected to the distribution of economic, racial, and social inequality, though those connections are not always obvious. Identifying the exclusions wrought by states' police power to define sex as a problem of *transgender* exclusion obscures the work that sex has done, and in some cases is still doing, to produce inequality in concert with other social and economic markers such as race and class.

It is undeniable that the political category of transgender brought the rights claims of gender non-normative people into public consciousness. Its successes in the first two decades of the twenty-first century in making compelling arguments for state recognition have been remarkable. As the rationales for the necessity of distinguishing between men and women have fallen away, and continue to do so, arguments based on the new identity category of transgender have filled the void—so much so that earlier feminist understandings of the effects of that distinction seem quaint, or even unrecognizable to progressive millennials and Gen Zers. But if the effects of the category and of the new social movement it constitutes are seen from a different angle, the work the category does in obscuring economic inequality as well as other forms of social inequality becomes more visible. *Transgender*, as a unifying yet abstract appellation, projects a clarity that does not account for the differences in how sex classification and gender are made to matter in different concrete situations. In fact, its widespread usage may obscure the fact that sometimes transgender status per se is not the sole or even primary cause of the physical, social, and economic vulnerabilities many gender nonnormative people experience. As longtime trans rights advocate Shannon Minter suggests, the impetus in trans activism to understand "so many issues, like incarceration, violence, workplace discrimination, and schools, through a trans-only lens has obscured much more determinative and systemic inequities, mostly around race and gender, and led trans advocates too often to miss the forest for the trees."[41] This book takes a harder look at the role that *transgender* is now beginning to play as a political category unto itself.

In queer and trans studies, revealing the traditions, institutions, and practices that make gender normativity and heteronormativity seem natural is now considered fundamental to any serious project outside of the hard sciences. But proponents and theorists of transgender movements for justice have generally paid much less attention to denaturalizing states and markets.[42] *The state* does not spring fully formed out of the heads of classical liberal theorists and the men who put those ideas to paper as materializations of the idea of popular sovereignty and the rule of law; it is not the benevolent night watchman who has unfortunately neglected to keep up with contemporary theories and enactments of gender identities. Nor does *the state* come into being in a singular extraordinary declaration that marks a collision between fact and right. In fact, in the territories that constitute what is now known as the United States, the institutions of government and the legitimacy that appears to saturate them take shape through the slow accretion of regularized practices of governing. The fictions that underwrite essentialist understandings of gender and resistance to transgender rights claims—that everyone is either male or female, that gender cannot or should not change, that an individual's gender is easily known by the insignia of genitalia—are now widely recognized as such in trans activist circles.[43]

But the fictions that have helped create the current situation of vast disparities in the vulnerability of individuals to early death and severe income inequality—that laissez-faire is not planned, that free markets are self-regulating, that social relations are fundamentally economic relations, that colonial power relations are a thing of the past, that work justly reflects one's value as a citizen, and that to be self-actualized is to be an ever-improving productive employee/innovator, an "entrepreneur of the self"—are much less likely to be challenged in these same circles. This constricted vision on the part of many trans advocates is likely a consequence of larger political shifts in the late twentieth century. Transgender rights advocacy and scholarship began to flourish at a time when broader visions of social justice were being eclipsed by representational politics. The rise of the US culture wars of the 1980s, which centered on the morality of changing sexual and gender norms, largely coincided with the dismantling of the Great Society programs, the marketization of social goods, and the political project of neoliberalism.[44] In the fog of the battle for the "soul of America," demands for distributive justice and the quest for recognition have become more disconnected than ever. In its pure form, the latter reinforces the status quo rather than challenging the morality of the maldistribution of vulnerabilities to poverty, disease, violence, and early death.

Precisely how demands for economic justice should be linked to desires for full inclusion in the body politic is contested. Leftist critics of identity politics suggest that its very logic—that identity-based groups are the "fundamental units of political consciousness and action"—leads it to devolve into nothing more than a kind of interest-group pluralism. Sectoring the population based on difference prevents the formation of a collective political movement that could, in Adolph Reed's words, unite to "directly challenge the current power relations." Identity politics, he suggests, "is not an alternative to class politics; it is a class politics, the politics of the left-wing of neoliberalism."[45] Indeed, making representation the metric of fairness and equality (Goldman Sachs flies the transgender flag!) propels inclusion in a way that dovetails neatly with the diversity, equity, and inclusion industry and the corporate culture that sustains it, and puts questions of larger structural transformation to the side. A diminishing number of stern leftists decry identity politics altogether, especially that practiced by sexual and gender minorities, as only epiphenomenal to class struggle, a distorted byproduct of the oppressive social relations of production that wrongly directs attention to securing equality in law, politics, and culture. Others on the left see the naming of identity-based exclusions as a necessary corrective to the false universalism of past leftist projects. Such an approach insists that identity-based oppressions and socioeconomic status cannot and should not be analyzed as separate phenomena, that structures such as racism and patriarchy are not secondary to class, and that all are woven so deeply together—but differently, depending on the historical context— that no grand theory of the relations among them is possible. Given the many sites and kinds of power structures, the study of sex reclassification requires jettisoning assumptions about what the state is. It's also imperative to look more closely at the effects of a politics organized around transgender identities. In both efforts, we need to understand how these phenomena link with state and nonstate processes that allocate inequality.

From Residual Category to Proxy in the Gender Wars

That so many different agencies have overlapping jurisdiction on the matter of sex classification is not the only problem. The lack of consistency also stems from the impossible purity of categories themselves.[46] First, the abstract and apparently simple distinction between male and female conceals the history of colonial violence embedded within it. María Lugones identifies the biological dimorphism of the gender binary as a nonuniversal product of the "light side of the colonial/modern organization of gender": the modern European binary constructions of male/female that replaced older narratives around the beginning of the early modern era developed against and through colonial processes of racialization. Gender itself, then, is a "colonial concept."[47] As a technology of power, the gender binary reflected what we now recognize as emergent white supremacism. Similarly, Kyla Schuller points out that "binary sex does not exist in parallel or intersecting dimension with race. Rather, the rhetoric of distinct sexes of male and female consolidate as a *function* of race."[48] The analytic neatness of a putatively universal M-F binary is belied by history.

It is also undone by the concrete empirical messiness warranted, ironically, by the flowering of the science of sex in the last half century.[49] In the present moment, any one of many properties associated with gender could be chosen as the definitive one in sex classification in law and policy. Moreover, even those attributes—sex chromosomes, gonadal sex, sex hormone patterns, internal nongonadal sex organs, genitalia, secondary sex characteristics, gender of rearing, and gender identity—tend not to be binary but either continuous or non-binary. While the science of sex has historically played a fundamental role in securing a wide range of social and biological attributes to a natural M/F dualism, it's also true that the science undermining the neatness of the distinction was never entirely dismissed. In recent years, such work has moved to the forefront. Although it has yet to dislodge completely the older binary paradigm, its trajectory is clear: the more the science of sex advances, the less unitary and untroubled sex becomes.[50]

In the thousands of policies and laws that draw distinctions between men and women, however, that uncertainty vanishes. The M-F systems of sex classification in administrative apparatuses have a rigidity never entirely supported by the science, and now increasingly less so. While, in the past, mainstream medical discourse could be reliably counted on to justify the state's employment of binary sex difference in furthering particular ends, there is now a growing tension between the law and the science of sex. This tension is perhaps most visible in court cases on the matter of sex classification. More and more, the expert witnesses on the side of the trans party, arguing for the malleability of sex or the adoption of gender identity as the criterion for sex classification by the state, are better credentialed and have a higher status in the medico-scientific social world than the experts on the other side, arguing that the sex assigned at birth should be one's legal sex for life or that transition is not complete without genital surgery. Before the latter half of the twentieth century, objections to the classifications were generally limited to intersex individuals.[51] But with the innovations in hormone therapy and gender-affirming surgery in the twentieth century, an increasing number of people began to seek identity documents and state recognition of their new gender.[52] Initially, officials responded to these requests on an arbitrary and case-by-case basis, but as the numbers grew, agencies and then courts—when individuals challenged agency denials—had to come up with definitions for male and female for the purposes of sex reclassification. For example, in 1965 New York City's commissioner of health noted that the department had had four requests for sex reclassification on birth certificates; two had been denied and two had been approved. With the fifth request, this official decided the city needed a more systematic approach and sought the advice of medical experts.[53]

Across the United States, government actors filled these definitional voids with a range of responses. Some held that the M or F assigned at birth could not be changed in these records and on identity documents. Others based reclassification on proof of gender-affirming surgery, chromosomes, and, more recently, gender identity as vouched for by a medical professional.

From the vantage point of the transgender political movement, obstacles to sex reclassification are at worst symptoms of ill will toward trans people and at best intentional neglect of our needs. However, the transphobia animus argument needs to be supplemented by an account that takes a longer historical view. That there has never been a uniform policy governing who is male and who is female is not the result of intentional hostility toward people called transsexual in the twentieth century or transgender in the twenty-first. Instead, those groups inhabited, and still continue to inhabit in many jurisdictions and agencies, what Susan Leigh Star and Geoffrey C. Bowker call residual categories, "that which is left over after a classification is built."[54] The borders of categories come into sharp relief in response to an unanticipated or abnormal situation not imagined in the first instance. Initially set out in the abstract, a category is fully defined only ex post facto, when its interior is made visible after a particular case troubles its assumptions and becomes its constitutive outside, a remainder that turns out to have been necessary to maintain the neatness and order of the classification system. Of course, the occupants of this residual category produced by a binary sex classification scheme are not entirely outside the system. Those whose gender identity is not traditionally associated with the sex assigned to them at birth do have sex classifications on their identity documents—but it may not be the desired classification.

Until recently, the obstacles that trans people faced with regard to sex classification were effects of gender-based oppression. In European and, later, American legal traditions, gender difference was codified in laws designed to limit the rights and resources available to white women. From coverture to inheritance laws to the inability to vote to exemptions in the criminal sphere for marital rape, the law's distinctions illustrated how deeply patriarchal norms were incorporated into state structures.[55] With regard to some laws, such as those governing divorce and child support—requiring husbands or fathers to provide for ex-wives and children—the distinction did disadvantage men, though for the purpose of protecting the public fisc, not redistributing wealth to women. For enslaved people in the United States, state-mandated gender difference operated differently, functioning in the service of slavery and white supremacy.[56] With the end of slavery and the slow and uneven dismantling of laws that used racial categories to further white supremacy, the administration of state-sponsored race discrimination shifted to operate through facially neutral social and economic policies that had racially disparate effects, usually intentionally so.[57] As a result, formal sex classification systems are now race neutral on their face, even as the effects of bad sex reclassification policies disproportionately harm Black, Indigenous, and other people of color, those living in poverty, and undocumented migrants.

Over the course of the twentieth century, the machinery of state-sanctioned gender discrimination was slowly and unevenly dismantled in the United States. By the turn of this century, states still distinguished between men and women in registration for Selective Service, in combat roles in the military, in facilities traditionally segregated by gender, in restrictions on abortion rights, and in laws that limited marriage to heterosexual couples.[58] But in the first decades of the twenty-first century, all combat roles in the armed forces had been opened to women by 2015, and a bill introduced in the Senate in 2016 mandating that eligible women also register for Selective Service garnered a considerable amount of bipartisan support.[59] In 2015, the Supreme Court decided that the state institution perhaps most responsible for maintaining gender subordination, marriage, could no longer be limited to opposite-sex couples—though the rationale for the decision focused on sexual orientation discrimination rather than gender discrimination.

It's no accident that claims for recognition put forward by those outside the traditional gender binary entered the mainstream as state-mandated gender inequality was in its death throes. Certainly, a minoritizing identity politics neatly packaged as transgender rights is partly responsible for these successes. In a larger sense, however, the achievements so far (and those yet to be realized) have also been made possible (and will be made possible, as barriers to reclassification still in place fall in the future) by feminism. Over the course of the twentieth century, the now much-maligned classically liberal branch of feminism succeeded in lowering the stakes for sex reclassification. Although governments continue to classify people as M or F, the consequences of sex classification now matter much less because an F designation can no longer be used to curtail civil and property rights, to deny equal access to education and the professions, or to enforce heteronormativity through bans on same-sex marriage. It is precisely because there is so much *less* at stake in sex classification than there used to be that, by the third decade of this century, policymakers and judges have less reason to deny reclassification requests and reforms, or to erect obstacles, such as genital surgery requirements. (That said, in chapter 5 I will show how, even now, decisions about sex designation still depend to some degree on the particular state project at issue.)

Social constructionist feminist contributions to the transgender rights project are more widely acknowledged, possibly because where those in the millennial generation have encountered feminism it has likely been of the Butler variety. By loosening the ties between bodies and identities and by showing that gender norms are effects of power, not of biology, these theoretical insights made various forms of gender nonnormativity legible as a failure to comply with the gender binary. Many of those who see themselves as born in the wrong body have not signed on to this particular theoretical project, but even arguments based on the medical model of transsexuality now describe gender identity—to be sure, still a scientific concept, though grounded in psychology rather than biology—as the primary indicator, rather than any material aspect of the supposedly sexed body. Obstacles to sex reclassification have historically been the result of the imbrication of gender subordination with state structures, and the headway made so far has been partially the outcome of feminist work to dismantle those legal barriers—to disestablish state-supported, historically normative gender arrangements. The defenders of traditional gender arrangements have lost the ability to use government to enforce the exclusion of women from the public sphere and their relegation to second-class status in family life. To be clear, this is not to suggest that gender subordination is a thing of the past—far from it. This particular structure of authority and domination, however, no longer finds formal support in the law—with the exception of laws governing abortion rights, which are discussed in the conclusion.

However—we now find ourselves in a new political moment, one in which transgender rights have been enrolled in the newest eruption in the culture wars, which some had hoped had been brought to an end with *Obergefell*. By the second decade of this century, transgender had shifted from a largely off-the-radar residual category, bobbing along in the wake of a much larger movement for gender equality before law, to the newest proxy in the arguments over culture and belonging. While the *formal* allotment of rights and resources based on gender has ended, its precondition—the ability of governments to distinguish between men and women, and to use their police powers (the sovereign capacity to ensure the safety, health, and welfare of the population) to classify sex in order to decide who is a man and who is a woman—remains part of the legal architecture. From a spate of bathroom bills in state legislatures—none of which passed or stayed passed—to a new round of anti-trans bills in 2021 aimed at preventing medical professionals from providing gender-affirming care to transgender teens and trans girls from participating in girls' sports, transgender people have become a focus of ire from the conservative movement, increasingly vulnerable in red states though seemingly protected in blue ones.[60] As part of this on-slaught, at the federal level the Trump administration reversed many of the transgender-friendly administrative rules and regulations instituted by the Obama administration. Under Trump, the Department of Education withdrew Obama-era interpretations of Title IX allowing access to bathrooms and locker rooms based on gender identity. It also challenged the Obama administration's inclusion of gender identity in provisions against sex discrimination in health care and insurance coverage. And of course, President Trump announced, via tweet, that transgender people would no longer be able to serve in the military.[61] Within the first months of his administration, President Biden began to reverse these Trump administration policies.

While trans advocates across the United States engage in battles over sex definition, access to sex-segregated spaces, and medical treatment, their opponents see themselves as also resisting much broader social forces. Conservative opposition to reforming sex classification policies reflects animus against transgender people, to be sure. But it also indexes a much larger anxiety about the changes feminism has wrought and the effects of what many of those on the religious right are beginning to call "gender ideology." Outside of restrictions on abortion, it's no longer politically feasible for conservatives to contest the victories of liberal feminism in ensuring equality before the law. Still, gender subordination remains one of the organizing principles of domestic life, the workplace, and cultural production. The persistence of that form of domination— what political theorist Corey Robin calls "the private life of power"— outside the equalizing gaze of the state is something conservatives and all those who benefit from it are eager to maintain. Ventriloquizing this position, Robin writes: "Cede the field of the public, if you must, stand fast in the private. Allow men and women to become democratic citizens of the state; make sure they remain feudal subjects in the family, the factory, and the field."[62] Debates about sex reclassification and access to gender-segregated spaces, alongside laws restricting abortion rights, give conservatives the opportunity, increasingly rare after the gains of liberal feminism, to make arguments that resonate both ways. It allows them to re-prosecute the gender wars in the legal arena. It also uses the institutions of government to put state actors' imprimaturs on traditional visions of normative gender, from deputizing individuals to dispute someone's gender in public spaces to using the bully pulpits of state legislatures to instruct the public on womanhood and manhood. Sex classification policies, while most certainly public, are also intrusions into the innermost sanctums of the private sphere. Indeed, what could be more intimate than being able to use the bathroom without fear of harassment? Even as one's status as male or female or non-binary no longer carries distributive consequences—in that states cannot deny a right or responsibility based on it—the police powers of the state can still be wielded to decide precisely what sex is and, in so doing, enforce traditional gender norms.[63]

Book Overview

First, a word about the framework. The book adopts what is a heterodox method for transgender studies, which, despite a collective antinaturalism, is nevertheless an identity studies field and as such has consolidated around the category of *transgender*. First, it toggles the focus from those harmed to the institutions doing the harming. Second, it abandons the default assumption that transphobia is the cause of policies that harm trans people. Third, it does not assume that the misrecognition of transgender people constitutes a singular phenomenon. Instead I examine the policies and decisions that constitute these injustices separately. The method in this book is to start with apparently contradictory sex reclassification policies or decisions and then, instead of amalgamating them into a global explanation of transphobia, to separate the strands and push on them to reveal the particular rationalities at play. By decentering animus against gender transgression as a cause of injustices, this approach suggests an alternative "history of the present."[64] Instead of exposing unfair decisions and policies as appendages of an imagined hydra that is transphobia, I turn my attention to the inconsistencies between decisions and rules for sex reclassification at one time, and try to figure out what accounts for them. Why are some institutions more open to sex reclassification than others? Why for some purposes, and not others? What accounts for so many different metrics for sex reclassification? Unlike a true Foucauldian genealogical investigation that traces discontinuities and the effects of contingent events over time, my analysis is more synchronic than diachronic. For the most part, I do not narrate transgender quest for justice chronologically. I do not explain discrepancies between policies as the result of differences between early adopters or holdouts, of lags in the acceptance of changes in the hegemonic medical model of transsexuality and gender identity in particular places. Instead, I hone in on the period when these inconsistencies in sex classification were at their extreme. But rather than simply seeing an individual classified as both male and female as representing a contradiction, a paradox, a bureaucratic mistake, and calling for that injustice to be rectified, I suggest such a situation seems paradoxical only if one assumes that state decisions about sex index something outside or before the decision itself, something that should be consistent regardless of the particular governing apparatus that decides. For the purposes of understanding these rationalities, it's necessary, at least provisionally, to let go of any notions about what M/F/X actually are, or how they *should* be defined. This is not to suggest that there aren't injustices in the here and now to be rectified. But it is to suggest that replacing a conceptual apparatus that centers the harms suffered by *individuals* to one that centers different technologies of governance might make visible the historical formations that factored into their production.

Chapter 1 sets the stage for these analyses. Because much of the debate on state sex classification appears to depend on identifying the most objectively true definition of sex or gender—both words are used in legal classification systems—this chapter presents an overview of the possibilities: sex is the physical state of the characteristics associated with gender and identifiable on or in the body at birth; sex is genitals; sex is gender identity. It then presents a justification for the working definition of sex used in this book: sex is whatever an entity whose decisions are backed by the force of law says it is. In examining state decisions on sex classification, it might be more useful to direction our attention not to what sex *is*, but what it *does*.

Chapters 2 and 3 turn our attention to the state. Just as the singular motif of the wronged transgender subject is displaced in this project as the analytical starting point, so too is a too-singular notion of the state. Turning the state into a thing, as we have turned sex into a thing, makes us oblivious to the messiness of the phenomena under discussion and masks how states come into being through the accretion of practices, conventions, and citations. This twinned approach to sex and states makes it possible to trace how apparently contradictory classifications in fact advanced different state projects. Chapter 2 focuses on the story of the traditional version of popular sovereignty and the civil rights tradition, distilled into something resembling a civics lesson account of sovereignty and the power to classify and exclude. This approach comes with a built-in justification for rejecting individuals' challenges to sex misclassification: sex is cast as an inalienable property of the individual, before and outside of politics and therefore not subject to revision. But the internal logic of this pre-political justification for exclusion eventually becomes the basis for inclusion. The abnormal characteristic that defined the exclusion in the first place—having a gender identity that does not conform to expectations for the sex one was assigned at birth—becomes, over time, the basis for inclusion. Much transgender rights advocacy and doctrinal legal analysis of the problem are pinned to the popular sovereignty story and depend on asserting that gender identity is inalienable, immutable.

Chapter 3 presents two alternative ways of understanding the politics of sex classification. The first alternative, enunciated in the theoretical register of deconstruction, reads the momentous yet arbitrary decisions on sex classification as exemplars of the paradox of law. M or F is a decision underwritten by violence, not an announcement of a fact. ("It's a republic," the Founders declare; "It's a boy," the doctor announces.) Rather than the perfect correspondence between the people and the governing authority they erect described in the story of popular sovereignty, the state comes into existence only through exclusions present at recurring founding moments. Classifications backed by the force of law are understood as the outcome of political processes of exclusion and distribution, not external to them. Decisions about sex classification are not the result of a rule being applied to a particular case, but moments in which the particular case generates the exception that constitutes the rule. The paradox of law approach reminds us of the impossibility of securing M or F to a person except through constitutive violence. It also illustrates the centrality of the anomalous case, in this case the occupants of the residual category created by the sex binary, to understanding the presumable universalizing categories of M and F. The second alternative approach to the popular sovereignty narrative accounts for contradictory decision-making on sex classification at different agencies, in different jurisdictions, and at different levels of government. Because there are many distinct state actors creating rules for defining sex, it's not that useful to direct all our attention to *the* state; instead, understanding sovereignty as encircled by, or folded into, processes of governmentality might be more useful. Rather than focusing mostly on a singular constitutive exclusion, this approach considers sex classification in relation to traditional police powers and administrative apparatuses.[65] This approach also decenters the primacy of the state. The second alternative account reflects a Foucauldian disposition; what I'm calling the deconstructive account tends to center a single big-bang moment of violence, when force takes on the mantle of right.[66] Of course, it's not a matter of either/or. Issues of sex classification and reclassification show how both accounts matter: every time a sex is assigned and written on a birth certificate form, every time visible genitals determine a prisoner's placement in a sex-segregated prison, it's both an example of the slow drip of dispersed and plural disciplinary powers abiding in a wide range of governing apparatuses—and the constitutive violence of naming, backed by the force of law.

Chapter 4 unpacks one of the apparent contradictions in the sex classification policies of the recent past: why were some people who were allowed to change their sex classification on their identity documents found to have a sex "fixed at birth" for the purposes of marriage? This chapter suggests that this is not so much a perplexing contradiction as an expression of different projects: one centered on recognition and the other on distribution, or, to understand it another way, one enunciated in the register of states and spatial logics of control and the other in the language of narrative, nation, property, and temporality. Incongruities in sex designation help us understand the larger processes that marry territory to people, link state with nation, and connect the administrative imperative to recognize the individuals inhabiting its territories with national distributive projects organized around the family, private property, and race. This chapter also addresses the purported antagonism, asserted by some left critics, between identity politics and economic justice.

In chapter 5, "Incarceration, Identity Politics, and the Trans-Cis Divide," I turn my attention back to the movement that grew (partly) out of the residual category created by the sex binary and solidified into an identity politics organized around the transgender umbrella. This chapter looks at the situation of transgender prisoners in the United States. The analysis here centers on the "freeze-frame" policy, which mandates that prisoners be maintained at the stage of gender transition they were in when they became incarcerated. It reads that policy in relation to the temporal flows of civil society and to the novelistic trope of heterosexual romance. The chapter then shows how trans rights discourse on nondiscrimination and inclusion resonates with the neoliberal emphasis on work, productivity, and market rationality. Ultimately, it suggests that the transgender-cisgender binary, the grid of intelligibility that so dominates trans studies and advocacy, in many cases obscures more than it reveals, including differences of class, race, and even gender. By working through this question at a more granular level, it shows these policies connect to other forms of displacement and how they nestle into the larger operations of power and the distribution of violence and inequality.

The conclusion considers the political juncture in which we now find ourselves. On the one hand, the loose coherence that once defined transgender is giving way to a more universalizing gender chaos—and I use "chaos" here approvingly—because of the seemingly innumerable ways of moving away from the sex assigned at birth and the growing number of people disinclined to attach strongly to one side or the other of the gender binary. We are very close to the moment when the gender binary will be disestablished from most projects of governing. On the other hand, transgender no longer occupies a liminal space left over from the legal disenfranchisement of women: it is now a specific target of those who traffic in moral panics. The right-wing attack on transgender people is increasingly articulated as objections to the de-binarizing "gender ideology" it sees as providing a foundation for the separation of bodies from gender roles, expressions, and identities. The attacks on those who have succumbed to "gender ideology," however, are not limited to transgender people—we are just the most obvious manifestation of the disorder it has wrought.

1

"If Sex Is Not a Biologic Phenomenon"

In 1965, a woman petitioned New York City's Bureau of Records and Statistics to change the M on her birth certificate to an F. "Anonymous" had done everything she could to function socially as a woman: she had had her gender identity affirmed by a medical professional; she had passed the "real life" test, required at the time, to live as a woman for two years; she had undergone gender-affirming medical care.[1] But the M remained on her birth certificate. With an M on her birth certificate, Anonymous's ability to move through the world as a woman would inevitably be compromised.

This was not the first time the city had been asked to change an M to an F on a birth certificate. The director of the Bureau of Records and Statistics had responded positively to three earlier requests, basing his decision on lab tests (later described as "very tenuous") that had been submitted, indicating hormone levels in what was thought to be the appropriate range for women.[2] At the fifth request from a transsexual individual, however, the official balked. What had been a few odd cases, mere bureaucratic blips, now seemed to augur a larger trend. The director asked for policy guidance from the Board of Health, which has jurisdiction over the New York City Health Code, including rules for birth certificates. Members of this appointed board were confused about what to do. According to their head, George James, the commissioner of health, the members "felt rather strongly that they were getting involved with a very deep and serious situation." James decided to commission "an exhaustive inquiry into the subject" by asking an ad hoc committee of medical experts, convened by the New York Academy of Medicine, to investigate the problem and to recommend how to respond to requests like these. Should the city change the sex classification on the birth certificates of transsexual individuals? If the M or F on a birth certificate is a "biologic fact and represents the situation at the time of birth," James asked in his letter to the physicians' committee, why change it? But, he went on, "if sex is not a biologic phenomenon, then what would the implications be if the Board of Health permitted a psychological determination of sex to be the compelling issue. On what basis would it hear testimony along this line and how make [sic] a decision?"[3] In other words, what evidence would be required to ensure that suspicious bodies, or bodies with suspicious histories, would not confound various state projects organized around gender? Over the next five decades, the initial "sex cannot change" policy was amended four more times.

This chapter uses these discussions about sex reclassification on New York City birth certificates—spanning five decades—to limn one of the central arguments of this book: while ideas about what sex is may appear to guide sex reclassification policies and proposals for reforming them, considerations about what sex does for different governing apparatuses have often played a far bigger role in determining the rules. Because so much of the debate on state recognition has been thought to center on the definition of sex, however, I review a series of "what sex is" positions—sex is attached permanently to the body at birth; sex is genitals; sex is gender identity; sex is nothing but a proxy for gender, which is itself an effect of power arrangements—and their corresponding approaches to the problem of sex reclassification. The chapter then counters these positions with the argument that fixating on what sex "really is" hinders our ability to understand why it is operationalized differently in particular circumstances. Thus, for the purposes of *this* project, F and M and X do not designate properties. They do not signify gender identity, or the sex assigned at birth, or the configurations of a "post-transition" body. They are simply what is recorded after a decision has been made by state bureaucracies and judges. They are ink shapes on paper, the electrical on/off pulses of binary codes in administrative records. Although they are arbitrary, they are backed by the force of law. Certainly, in many sex reclassification debates, as we will see in the following chapters, judges' and policymakers' arguments have usually been clothed in the mantle of sex definition. But making sense of the apparent contradictions between these policies requires looking at the effects of particular rules for sex reclassification. The chapter's last section suggests that sex is better conceptualized as plural, rather than as singular because questions of sex classification cannot be disentangled from thinking about states and governance; this chapter focuses on sex, while chapters 2 and 3 focus on states.

New York City: Five Decades of Debates over Sex Classification

Back to 1965: the committee met twice that year before deciding to recommend that the sex classification on birth certificates should not be changed. Significantly, the committee, composed entirely of medical doctors, spent most of its time considering "the legal aspects of a change of sex." The legal implications, the committee found, would include allowing marriage between a transsexual woman and a nontranssexual man, changing draft status, denying or providing access to benefits, and enabling individuals to obtain passports with the new sex classification.[4] The committee concluded its report—widely cited in many court decisions on the issue of sex classification in the following decades—with the assertion that "male-to-female transsexuals are still chromosomally males while ostensibly females." It went on: "The desire of concealment of a change of sex by the transsexual is outweighed by the public interest for protection against fraud."[5] The commissioner of health followed the committee's recommendations: as a matter of policy, transsexual people would not be able to have their sex changed on birth certificates issued by the city. Anonymous's petition was denied, and that decision was affirmed by an appellate state court.[6] In 1971, this policy was somewhat reformed: instead of outright denial of these requests, the city would issue new birth certificates with *no* sex designation.[7] This change came about because the New York Civil Liberties Union had pushed the Board of Health to allow the new sex designation to appear on the certificate. But since birth sex was "a matter of record," eliminating it altogether, declared one member of the Board of Health, was "as far as we can go."[8] To be eligible for this "no sex" certificate, an individual would need to submit a psychiatric evaluation affirming that he or she represented a "true case of transsexualism," a report of the "convertive surgery" that had taken place, a "post-operative examination signed by the surgeon," and a court order granting a name change. Individuals would have to prove not only that their genitals had been reconstructed (phalloplasty for men or vaginoplasty for women) but also that they had been sterilized through surgery (a hysterectomy for those assigned as female at birth, an orchiectomy for those assigned male at birth). Only after satisfying all these conditions would they be eligible for this new "no sex" certificate.[9] At the time, the policy was among the most liberal in the United States.

By the turn of this century, however, most US states had changed their sex reclassification policies for birth certificates. If individuals could supply evidence of "sex change surgery," most states would issue new birth certificates listing the reclassified sex.[10] (New York City sets its own policies on birth certificates separate from the rest of New York State. For other jurisdictions, birth certificate policy is set at the state or territory level.) The city was again an outlier, but this time its policy lagged behind that of forty-six state jurisdictions. By the early 2000s, its "no sex" birth certificate was only one step ahead of the three jurisdictions that outright refused to change the F or M on birth certificates: Ohio, Idaho, and Tennessee. Even more ostensibly conservative states such as Alabama, Missouri, Virginia, and Arkansas would reclassify an individual's sex provided they satisfied the surgery conditions. In 2005, finding itself in the rearguard of sex classification, the New York City Bureau of Vital Statistics revisited the policy, convening a second panel of experts. This time, the committee included transgender health care experts and transgender rights advocates, as well as surgeons and psychiatrists not considered allies. I was a member of that committee. Of the committee members not on the city's payroll, most worked hard to convince policymakers to drop the requirement for genital surgery— indeed for any modification of the body at all. (It was not a surprise that the two urologist surgeons on the committee did not, preferring a genital surgical standard.[11]) We argued that transition was an individualized process and that gender identity, not genitals, should determine sex classification. Initially, the Board of Health appeared willing to adopt the recommendation and went so far as to promulgate it for public comment. But after other city agencies weighed in against the proposal, it was withdrawn by city officials. Instead, the policy adopted matched those of most other jurisdictions at the time: only those who could prove they had had genital surgery could change the sex marker on their birth certificates.[12]

Transgender rights advocates sued the city a few years later, claiming that its policy requiring individuals who want to change the sex classification on their birth certificates to submit evidence of genital surgery is "arbitrary, capricious, discriminatory, and otherwise unlawful." The Transgender Legal Defense and Education Fund contended that sex is "the sex of their brain—an immutable, intrinsic sense of being physically male or female." The brief drew on a host of medical, scientific, and psychological findings, including the American Psychological Association's statement contending that identity documents should be consistent with an individual's "gender identity and expression."[13] The city's stated reasons for keeping the policy in place were "irrational," the advocates argued. In 2014 the lawsuit was made irrelevant when the New York City Council passed legislation, with the support of a new Democratic mayoral administration and the Board of Health, that made it possible for people born in the city to change the sex marker on their birth certificate to have it correspond to their gender identity. Individuals requesting these changes would not be required to have undergone medical treatment of any kind, though they would have to provide an affidavit from a physician, nurse practitioner, or physician's assistant attesting to the change. (By March 2017, more than seven hundred people had changed the sex marker on their birth certificate since January 2015, the effective date of the 2014 legislation. When the surgery requirement was in place, only about twenty people did so per year.)[14] In 2018, New York City also added a non-binary gender category of X and removed the requirement for a medical affidavit.[15] Now those born in New York City need only submit their own affidavit to change the sex marker on their birth certificate to F, M, or X.

From this account, one might think that trans advocates and the city spent five decades arguing over the most accurate definition of sex. But while the former group was marshalling evidence about what sex "really is," representatives of the latter were concerned with the consequences of changing the rules. The debate over sex took place in two different registers—the advocates' register of expertise and truth, and the bureaucrats register of governing and politics. The assumption that sex reclassification policies should be based on the correct definition of sex (whether that definition indexes common sense or contemporary medical knowledge) was belied by policymakers' stated concerns about the effects of changing the definitions. During the 1965 policy deliberations, the director of the city's Bureau of Records and Statistics wrote to the National Center for Health Statistics, a division of the federal Department of Health, Education, and Welfare, asking for guidance on the question of sex classification. In researching a response to this question, the recipient of the letter, the chief of the Registration Methods Branch, consulted "a number of security and non-security agencies in the Federal Government for their viewpoints." This official found that "this has been a long-term and difficult problem for them as well." The federal government could not provide any guidance to the city on the question, he concluded, "since various agencies carry out differing responsibilities the problems which confront them vary." In fact, "the more we delved into the problem, the more the ramifications that cropped up."[16] Officials at some agencies were more concerned with identity management and ensuring a perfect correspondence between an individual and their records over their life span; officials at agencies that distributed benefits based on gender were worried about how individuals who changed their sex would unsettle their work. In other words, there could be no unified policy on the matter of sex reclassification because each state agency would have to investigate the effects of sex reclassification polices on its own work. Similarly, when in 2006 city officials decided against making gender identity the effective criterion, it was because the "potential impacts of these proposed changes would be more complex and far reaching than we anticipated." Worried about "ramifications beyond its intended purposes" in schools, housing, workplaces, and prisons, they left a surgery standard in place.[17] In response to claims made in the 2011 lawsuit that the surgery requirement was irrational, city lawyers noted that while other documents, such as driver's licenses issued by the state of New York, United States passports, and even other jurisdictions' birth certificates may use different criteria to classify people as F or M, "the existence of different approaches to similar problems does not render an agency's rule irrational."[18] In other words, the rationality of each agency's approach to sex classification depended on its remit, not what sex is in itself. In the syntax of the city's structures of governance, sex was a mobile property—dependent not on what it is, but what it does.

By 2014—the year that body modifications were effectively removed as requirements for sex reclassifications in both the city and the state—sex had been decommissioned in some matters of governance. This victory, which made gender identity the effective standard for birth certificate reclassification, was not simply the result of an agreement between advocates and the city about the ontological foundation of sex. Instead, contingent events made it possible to override some of the particular governing rationalities of the different agencies with regard to reclassifying sex: the election of a progressive mayor in 2013, the growing visibility of the transgender rights movement, and, most importantly, the legalization of same-sex marriage in New York State in 2011. Indeed, the issue of same-sex marriage had been raised in discussions several times at the city level. In 1966, the possibility that a transsexual person might use a new birth certificate to marry—and hence "fraudulently" enter into an opposite-sex marriage—was a constant worry, as documented in the meeting minutes of the New York Academy of Medicine's ad hoc committee.[19] By 2006, without the requirement of body modification, which policymakers had almost universally taken to be a guarantee of a transition and its permanence, they worried that one half of a gay or lesbian couple—presumably both of whom were cisgender, though that assumption was only implicit—would simply change the F or M on their birth certificate and present that when applying for a marriage license.[20] But the question of ersatz heterosexual marriages was rendered moot when the ban on same-sex marriage was ended in New York State in 2011. Now sex could take on a new role in the political algorithms of governance. Instead of functioning as a large-scale technology for the management of distributive injustice through institutions such as marriage, sex reclassification policy could evolve into a vehicle of contemporary identity politics. It has now become a political tool in blue states for recognizing the particular needs of the constituency identified as transgender and in red states for inciting an ugly culture war. Indeed, in New York City the rhetoric in support of making gender identity the only necessary condition for changing one's birth certificate highlighted the needs of a particular group; it did not mark this change as a step in the universal dismantling of the system for sex classification. For example, the mayor at the time, Bill de Blasio, announced his support of the change this way: "Transgender and gender non-conforming New Yorkers deserve the right to choose how they identify and to live with respect and dignity."[21] In other parts of the United States, transgender identity politics has been operationalized by the right wing very differently. Transgender people have been targeted as frauds, potential sex offenders, and dupes of "transgender ideology."[22]

Certainly, the reforms addressed the very pressing needs of both binary and non-binary trans people, people whose inability to negotiate identity bureaucracies, unnoticeable and quotidian to cisgender people, creates barriers to their participation in social, economic, and civic life. But meeting the needs of transgender people born in the city did not constitute a fundamental reimagining of what M, X, or F is meant to signify. If the operative definition of sex had been revisited, no newborn would have an F or M or X on their birth certificates; sex markers would be added later, when children were old enough to have and to know their gender identity, whether it be F, M, or non-binary.[23] Or there would be no sex designation for anyone. But as a vestige of the original governing architecture, traditional notions of sex remain baked into the system. No longer a tool for allocating rights and resources, it serves as the "common sense" universalizing backdrop against which the seemingly particular claims of self-identified trans and non-binary people—estimates suggest that 0.58 percent of the US adult population identifies as transgender[24]—are played out. While the universalizing and largely unexamined biopolitical technologies of sex classification have long been a necessary mechanism for the state-sponsored oppression of women, the issue of sex reclassification had appeared to be a concern limited to transgender people.

I've been using the old-fashioned and awkward word "sex" to talk about government decisions to classify individuals as male or female. Why use "sex" and not "gender"? Among feminist theorists, since the 1980s "gender" has won almost universal acceptance as the most apt term to describe the norms that govern relations between men and women. When one sees "sex" and "gender" used together, often the former signifies bodily difference and the latter refers to the social norms that make those differences matter.[25] The use of "sex," especially when it's not accompanied by "gender," can signal the worldview that understands sex as a naturally occurring attribute of the body that accounts for differences in the identities, roles, and expressions of boys and girls, men and women, masculinity and femininity. But that's not my intention here. While lay conceptions of sex assume there's no gap between the word and what it signifies, there is no clear agreement among feminist and transgender scholars and activists, and among policymakers and judges, about what sex means or what the terms of the binary that subtends it (male and female) mean. In the past I've used "gender" to describe the laws, rules, and policies relating to M/F classifications. In this book "sex" is used—partly because "sex" appears more often than "gender" in policies and decisions (because they were created before "gender" was in wide usage), and partly because its outmoded awkwardness makes it stand out as a placeholder word.

With that stipulation, I can assert this: the working thesis of this book is that the only thing we can say for sure about what sex means is what a particular state actor says it means. Unlike the definitions put forth by individuals or circulated by activists and researchers, state declarations of sex are backed by the force of law. When you're arrested for "false personation," when your parental relationship with your children is permanently severed, when your marriage is declared void, when you arrive at your polling place only to be denied the right to vote, when you lose your benefits as a surviving spouse—all because of what a judge or a policy or an identity document says your sex is—then the definition matters. For my purposes here, sex is not a thing, a property, or a trait, but the outcome of decisions backed by legal authority. And its meaning changes. This is not to say that the actual body does not come into it. In state rules on sex classification, evidence of material characteristics— penises or vaginas, XX or XY chromosomes, breasts or beards—can still determine whether one is male or female for state purposes. But, leaving aside for a moment the materiality of letters and affidavits, *which* material is material is not consistent. In adopting *for this particular project* the methodological axiom that sex does not exist in itself, as an already given thing, I am not saying that sex does not matter. Indeed, its very production as a legal category is all about making it matter—a lot.

To understand how sex is brought into being and made to bear a lot of weight for state projects, we might think of it as a "transactional reality." Foucault identifies civil society, madness, and sexuality as "transactional realities" that, "although they have not always existed are nonetheless real, are born precisely from the interplay of relations of power and everything which constantly eludes them, at the interface, so to speak, of governors and governed." Because sex has been so thoroughly naturalized and for so long, for many it may be harder to suspend one's disbelief and think of sex as a transactional reality than it would be to think of civil society or madness or sexuality that way.[26] But that there are different iterations of this particular transactional reality—for example, one institution decrees a person is M, another decides the same person is F—might make the proposition a little easier to accept, at least provisionally. I also opt to deploy sex as the shifting placeholder instead of gender because gender *does* mean something: decades of scholarship and activism have created a shared, though not uncontested, body of historical knowledge about the ways norms, narratives, practices, conventions, and laws have arranged bodies, identities, roles, and expressions in hierarchies of difference. I want to reserve the use of gender for thinking about these processes. As I will show in the chapters that follow, ideologies of gender certainly undergird state determinations of "male" and "female." The effects of gender, however, are not contained within legal architectures. They exceed, even envelop, them. By now there has been a great deal of thought on the relationship between gender and sex, from early second-wave feminism's understanding of sex as a biological status and gender as a set of social arrangements and practices to Judith Butler's observation that sex "will be shown to have been gender all along."[27] Instead of looking at the ways gender brings sex into being, this work centers the relationship between sex and states. This is indeed a partial project: legal enactments of sex are still enclosed within the architectures and narratives that regulate gender outside of the law. But moving the spotlight from the *gender/sex* relation to the *state/sex* relation may bring to light aspects of state formation, sovereignty, and governmentality that a too-quick dismissal of the juridical-political realm might overlook.

Sex is a legal effect. Were I a positivist political scientist, I would posit sex as the dependent variable and the state as the independent variable. It would not be a problem that sex is not known in advance, outside of the circumstances in which it's generated. As the independent variable, however, the state should be operationalized with a clear account of what it is and what it is not. After all, it's impossible to solve an equation without *any* absolute values; something has to be known. But the proposition that sex is manufactured in and through regulations, formal and informal policies, judicial decisions, and legislative enactments does not actually mean that the state is fixed in place, still and hard as a monument. To naturalize is to characterize a product of social or political process as existing prior to them—in short, to describe an effect as a cause and to place that cause before or outside human culture. The idea that sex is natural, for example, is still relatively hegemonic in the popular imaginary. In denaturalizing sex, however, it's important to resist the temptation to renaturalize something else, in this case the state, by putting it on the same foundational footing that nature used to occupy. Sex may be a product of state actions, but that does not require us to think of the state as an edifice with absolute values and clear boundaries limned in advance. Nor, as Mariana Valverde suggests, does it require us to treat state actors like the proverbial closed "black boxes" of social theory: institutions as closed machines that produce outputs—in our case, decisions about what sex is—but that conceal from view what went into making them.[28]

The "What Sex Is" Approach to the Problem of Sex Classification

The last five decades have seen radical shifts in the common sense of sex. The position that it is not possible to change from M to F, from F to M, or from either to X, was taken as uncontestable as recently as the 1960s. In an article published in 1967, ethnomethodologist Harold Garfinkel coined the phrase "the natural attitude" to describe the view that "members of the normal population . . . are essentially, originally, in the first place, always have been, and always will be, once and for all, in the final analysis, either 'male' or 'female.'"[29] That attitude was evident in the categorical denial of the possibility of changing one's sex by the New York Academy of Medicine's ad hoc committee on birth certificates. To do so, these medical experts opined, would constitute fraud.[30] Since that time, however, the social consensus that sex is fixed forever at birth has unraveled and it is not likely to reconsolidate around a single metric, given the diversity of views on the matter. Indeed, even social conservatives tacitly admit that the criteria for assigning the categories of M or F is now a political question when they seek laws that would settle the question of sex classification. Most state entities that classify people according to M/F now allow one to amend the sex assigned at birth, though many still require body modification as surety. Even as social conservative groups reignite the culture wars with the specter of "men" in women's bathrooms, by 2015 half of the millennial generation, according to one poll, agreed that gender is a spectrum, not a binary.[31] The once-undeniable public fact of sex as easily and objectively knowable has lost its authority; the common sense of sex will never be made whole again, if it ever was. In its place, some positions establish the body as the basis or verifier of M/F, while others attribute that role to the mind. And some see the M/F distinction as inherently groundless. In the table below, I've aligned each understanding of sex with a particular policy preference on sex reclassification. This table reduces a fluid range of positions enunciated across a number of discourses in very different contexts to four bare-bones categories. With apologies for the violence this boundary drawing does to nuance, this heuristic is meant to orient readers who are not in the relatively small population of people who spend a lot of time thinking about sex reclassification policies.

TABLE 1.1. Theories of sex and their corresponding positions on sex (re)classification

What sex is	Sex is determined at birth, sex is determined at conception, and/or sex is defined by reproductive capacity	Sex is constituted by or verified by genitals	Sex is gender identity: male, female, or non-binary	Sex is an effect of gender norms
Position on sex reclassification	No re-recognition after initial sex assignment	Recognition should follow evidence of gender-affirming surgery	Recognition of F/M/X should follow declaration of gender identity	F/M/X classification for all should be ended
Held by	Social conservatives; "traditional common sense"	Postwar twentieth-century sexology	Mainstream transgender rights advocates; contemporary medical experts; liberal/doctrinal approach	More gender-radical trans advocates; constructionists

Over time, the consensus represented in the first column has come apart, supplanted by newer ways of conceptualizing M and F. This is not to predict a trajectory that ends with trans communities moving beyond the liberal framework of recognition to the position that all governments' systems for sex classification should be abolished. Older common senses of sex as set at birth or by current genital configuration continue to resonate and justify some policy choices on sex classification.[32] For example, in 2016, a Texas judge blocked the Obama administration's rules allowing trans students to use the bathroom associated with their gender identity, with this justification: "It cannot be disputed that the plain meaning of the term 'sex'" in Title IX was meant to refer to "the biological and anatomical differences between male and female students as determined at their birth."[33] In fact, it can be disputed, and it is. Indeed, in the adjacent area of sex discrimination law, in 2020 Justice Neil Gorsuch found that an employer who summarily fired a transgender woman when she announced her intent to transition had violated a statute banning sex discrimination.[34] But despite intense conflicts about chromosomes, genitals, gender identity, and the impossibility of securing the relation between signifier and signified, all four positions are enunciated as conflicts about what sex is or what it is not.

The next position in the "what sex is" chart holds that one's genitals anchor the distinction: a man will possess a penis, a woman a vagina. As Suzanne Kessler and Wendy McKenna demonstrated in 1978, genitals are taken as "the essential sign of gender."[35] This logic underpins the second approach. Indeed, it was so hegemonic that it was unremarked upon outside sexology and related sciences of sex—that is, until questions about sex reclassification were thrust into the popular imaginary. When that happened, suggestions that genitals might not be the most apt metric for sex classification were initially met with ridicule—and continue to be in some precincts. For example, when the New York City Board of Health invited public comment on the 2006 proposal for amending sex classification on birth certificates—with no requirement for genital surgery if it passed—one member of the public asked, "How might it be possible for someone with male genitals to now be listed as being female? Is everyone expected to be blind?"[36] In Congress, a bill that would ban discrimination based on gender identity, among other things, has been consistently blocked by Republicans. Yet even when Democrats controlled both the houses, the bill repeatedly faltered on the rocky shoals of sex as genitals. Should transgender women be able to change in the women's locker room if they haven't had genital surgery? Even the House's onetime champion of gay rights, Massachusetts Democrat Barney Frank, had in 1999 objected to classifying people other than by the shape of their genitals. "Transgendered people want a law that mandates a person with a penis be allowed to shower with women," Frank said, explaining his objections to legislation supported by transgender communities.[37]

Significantly, gender-affirming surgery as a metric does not always reflect the preferences of or economic constraints on trans people. Numbers are difficult to come by, but it appears that a minority of those in the United States who move from their assigned sex at birth into another gender have the genital surgeries often taken in popular discourse to be the litmus test for sex—vaginoplasty or phalloplasty.[38] While many trans people did not want such surgeries, and others could not have them because of medical conditions that make surgical intervention risky, the vast majority of people simply could not afford it. Until state Medicaid policies, private insurance companies, and providers governed by the Affordable Care Act began to cover transition-related health care in the second decade of this century, a body modified through "sex change surgery" was one also mediated through class. When prohibitively expensive genital surgery was required, as it was and still is in some contexts, access to large sums of money effectively became a prerequisite for change of sex classification. This argument, however, did not prevail during the era when surgery policies were dominant. Most policymakers preferred to isolate the attributes chosen for classifying F/M from the social conditions that determined whether or not one could access the technologies necessary to produce them. The discussions were limited to "what sex is," putting socioeconomic status outside the boundaries of those deliberations.

By the mid-1990s, most transgender advocates in the United States had largely coalesced around the third position: that the state's referent for F or M should be gender identity, not any characteristics of the body. The "International Bill of Gender Rights," a document drafted by a handful of transgender women in the United States in the mid-1990s, called for the right to define and express one's own gender identity, "regardless of chromosomal sex, genitalia, assigned birth sex, or initial gender role."[39] The "sex is gender identity" argument begins by explaining that most people develop a gender identity—a deeply felt sense of oneself as male or female—that conforms to social expectations for assigned sex at birth. An infant assigned male at birth based on a physician's visual examination of the genitalia will most likely develop an identification as a boy/man. But some people turn out to have a gender identity *not* traditionally associated with their birth sex. In that case, gender identity ought to trump the sex assigned at birth. Neither the body nor any of its constituent parts should be the criterion for sex reclassification. If people assigned male at birth modify their bodies to align with a female gender identity, for example, advocates stress that those changes are made *because of* gender identity.

These arguments developed incrementally over time, and with heavy reliance on the expertise of medical professionals sympathetic to the community.[40] When the goal was to reform policies that did not allow any change from the M or the F assigned at birth, arguments grounded demands for sex reclassification in the classic transsexual narrative introduced in the United States with the press coverage of Christine Jorgensen's "sex change" in 1952: that sex can change, with the efforts of surgeons and endocrinologists, supported by proper (and heterosexual) gender comportment. But even the medical professionals who in the twentieth century had jealously guarded the morphological gates to gender transition eventually came to realize that the "fierce and demanding drive" of transsexual men and women for recognition meant that "psychological sex"—what we now call gender identity—was more intransigent than biology. In her history of transsexuality in the United States, Joanne Meyerowitz explains how psychologists and psychiatrists came to recognize the relative immutability of gender identity: "the mind—the sense of self—was less malleable than the body."[41] Penises and vaginas, beards and breasts, cannot be the basis for M and F classifications—they can be created or made to disappear, after all. Medical interventions such as genital surgery become "gender-affirming," not gender changing in themselves. Even policymakers' rhetoric justifying the requirement for genital surgery oscillates between understanding genital reconfiguration as *verifying* that change and *constituting* that change. Individuals may want to modify their body to bring it into alignment with their conception of themselves, but what one *thinks*, not the body one *has*, is most fundamental and sets in motion any other changes that might follow. Jennifer Germon aptly summarizes the psychological position on the primacy of gender identity that is now hegemonic in the field: "Where there is a mismatch between identity and morphology the body must always give way to the psyche, to identity, to gender."[42]

In the specialized realms of the medical sciences, then, having a gender identity not associated with the sex assigned at birth—which had been the necessary condition for the surgical and hormonal interventions that were thought to begin the transition process—eventually became the sole attribute that should be the basis for one's classification as male or female, regardless of body modification. Indeed, as medical gatekeepers moved away from the position that surgical interventions are necessary, transgender advocates were able to rely on these experts more and more to advance the case for gender identity as the metric for sex classification, the third column in the above chart. Advocacy arguments are now saturated with this type of authoritative discourse. Indeed, it has become commonplace in trans legal advocacy and education to explain that "gender is what's between your ears, sex is what's between your legs." For example, the ACLU argued in one case that "it is well established in the scientific community that gender identity is the most important among the nine factors making up a person's sex."[43] The force and history of cultural scripts that present gender as an effect of a naturally sexed body once made exporting gender identity from its origin in psychological discourse to the realm of public policy a hard sell. For example, in 2001 the constitutionality of a local law in Kentucky banning discrimination based on gender identity was challenged as "inherently unintelligible" and "unconstitutionally vague."[44] Now, of course, along with "gender expression," the term "gender identity" is ubiquitous in nondiscrimination laws and jurisprudence, and easily rolls off the tongues of judges and progressive elected officials.

While the link between biological sex and social/psychological gender was being severed in the psychological sciences,[45] earlier generations of feminist scholars were engaged in the related project of decommissioning biological sex from its role as authorizer of women's subordination. Because the putative existence of natural sex differences had justified the inequality of women in the domestic, economic, and public spheres for millennia (what Engels referred to as "the world historical defeat of the female sex"), the crucial contribution of much feminist research in the 1970s and 1980s was to demonstrate that the traffic between nature and culture flowed in the other direction. The acceptance of inequality between men and women had required smuggling contemporary gender norms into accounts of natural sex difference. Exposing gender roles and norms as social artifacts and identifying the foundational role that those norms played in institutions from marriage to the military gave the women's liberation movement the footing it needed to demand an end to culturally and legislatively mandated limits to women's rights as self-governing subjects. But even as the domain of biological sex shrank, the immutability of the F/M binary went largely unquestioned. In her genealogy of the concept of gender, Germon notes that "feminism's ambivalent relation to the category of sex and its seeming reluctance to critically engage with the matter of matter meant that the binary logic so central to sexological and medico-scientific understandings of gender, sex, and sexuality was reinforced."[46] As a result, most liberal feminist projects called for an end to any number of gendered social and legal codes, but challenging states' powers to police the boundary between male and female through sex reclassification policies was usually not among them. While there were more points of agreement between feminism and the incipient transsexual rights movement in the 1970s and 1980s than has generally been acknowledged,[47] mainstream feminist organizations did not begin to call for reforms to sex reclassification until the early aughts—and at the time that signaled ally-ship with trans communities more than a rethinking of sex classification as a technology of governing.

The fourth position holds that, since sex is an effect of gender, the government should simply get out of the business of classifying it at all. Propelled by the claim of deconstructionists that language does not represent the world we know but creates it, eventually sex is understood as an artifact of gender—or at least as knowable only through gendered discourse. Historians such as Thomas Laqueur, biologists such as Anne Fausto-Sterling, and psychologists such as Suzanne Kessler—and, of course, Judith Butler—have all argued that the meanings we attach to sex do not, indeed cannot, reflect the materiality of the phenomenon. Laqueur summarizes this position: "The nature of sexual difference is not susceptible to empirical testing. It is logically independent of biological facts because already embedded in the language of science, at least when applied to any culturally resonant construal of sexual difference, is the language of gender."[48] For Judith Butler, the question of whether there is "a physical body prior to the perceptually perceived body" is unanswerable. Butler argued that the repeated acts of gender performance—dress, movement, voice, affect—taking place in a context of constitutive constraint do not reflect the ontological truth of sex as a fixed, stable, natural, or a priori fact, but in fact produce it. She explains, "This production of sex as prediscursive ought to be understood as the effect of the apparatus of cultural construction designated by *gender*."[49] If sex is an effect of systems of gender norms and arrangements, the classification of sex—based on bodily characteristics or on gender identity—has no foundation outside the milieus that give rise to the norms.[50] Some liberal feminists viewed the denaturalizing of sex as undermining political projects organized in the name of women.[51] But many feminist and trans thinkers and activists, coming of age during and after the poststructuralist revolution, saw it as emancipatory: no longer could—or rather, should—the strictures of science or nature be used to dictate how women ought to behave. Nor should they be used to police the border between F and M, and feminine and masculine. For example, as far back as 2003, trans activist Dylan Vade suggested that because "sex is gender pretending to be objective scientific truth," it should be displaced. Vade offers the term "gender galaxy" instead: "The gender galaxy is not a cute fanciful construct that leaves in place 'sex' as truth. It displaces sex. Sex is gone. All that is left is the gender galaxy."[52] Similarly, Heath Fogg Davis argues that "lack of an "objective, socially agreed-upon test for determining who is male and who is female" means that "we should do away with the vast majority of sex classification policies."[53]

Injustices and Inconsistencies

To be an advocate for people seeking sex reclassification is to necessarily adopt the ontological givens of the classical liberal ethos that sustains the mainstream American political imaginary—the individual, the neutral umpire state, and the social contract that binds the two. On this view, the problem to be fixed inheres in the relationship between the individual and their government, which has failed to correctly identify one of their attributes. Sex misclassification is seen as an injustice of misrecognition. Not only does this framework underwrite most advocacy done on behalf of transgender people in general and individual plaintiffs in particular, it also animates a great deal of research on gender identity and the law, and was instrumental in developing the doctrinal framework hegemonic in law reviews, which will be discussed in the next chapter.

This approach has been subject to sustained and rigorous critique by those who argue that a certain domesticated form of selfhood is produced when states address individuals and when individuals recognize themselves in this addressing—"interpellate" is the term used in social theory to describe this relationship. From this perspective, those seeking to reform sex reclassification policies are merely insisting that the addressing be more accurate. Aren Aizura observes that the focus of traditional trans rights advocates begins and ends with a "critique of the legal mechanics of fixing the 'truth' of gendered bodies."[54] Dan Irving recommends that we question "the theoretical and political implications of putting forward individualistic strategies of sex/gender self-determination, especially within the contemporary neoliberal context, where the minimalist state and a free-market economy demand individual self-sufficiency."[55] Dean Spade describes "formal legal equality as a window dressing for harmful and violent political and economic arrangements," and suggests we "move from demands for recognition and inclusion in law to demands for material changes to our lives."[56] In short, the quest for inclusion through recognition might constitute "political emancipation," but that is not, Marx reminds us, the same as "human emancipation."[57] Critics of a politics centered on individual rights understand that it's necessary to do two things at once: to support liberal demands and to acknowledge their limits. Trans people, especially those lacking the privilege that economic security and whiteness bestow, do not have the luxury of not having the identity documents they need to work, to consume, to access public services and benefits, and even to protest their own disenfranchisement. Yet, over the medium and long term, what disadvantages the majority of trans people the most is not transphobia but the structures and processes of late racial capitalism: the use of incarceration as a system of social control, a minimum wage lagging far behind a living wage, a privatized health care system, and government policies bent on maintaining a carbon-based infrastructure, among other things.

In some trans publics, the critique of the liberal approach has been conflated with the constructionist position. What is taken to be a revolutionary or at least subversive stance on gender is falsely equated with a more radical stance toward the state, capital, and the racialization of vulnerability. Rejecting gender norms is assumed to index a broad spectrum of radical positions; adhering to them is assumed to reflect an attachment to status quos of all kinds. But being "against" gender normativity doesn't *necessarily* entail a broader radical politics. It's a historical and logical error to assume the unmooring of sex is necessarily part and parcel of resistance to the escalating inequalities that make life increasingly miserable for greater and greater segments of the population. In the same vein, the assimilationist charge made within queer and trans communities has been directed at those who understand their identity as something they were born with and whose gender politics—apart from transitioning from one gender to the other—is thought to be fundamentally normative.[58]

Certainly, the move away from facile analogies (for example, sexism is "like" racism) or the cumulative framework (for example, oppressed as queer *and* as poor) toward an understanding of gender, race, class, and other social locations as mutually constitutive has been important and necessary to identity-based studies. But that doesn't mean, for example, that processes of gendering and racialization are identical. Or that the system that produces class differences is the same as, or operates perfectly in sync with, the formation of hierarchies of sexuality-based difference. As Wendy Brown points out, "Not simply the content but the modalities of power producing gender, race, or caste are specific to each production—the mode of production and dimensions of state power that produce class, and the discourses and institutions of normative heterosexuality that produce gender, are largely noncomparable forms and styles of power."[59] Certainly, race, gender, class, sexuality, and present-day coloniality should not be made abstract, each term extracted from its contingent enmeshment with others. Sometimes, however, that analytical starting point devolves into an assertion of equality between forms of oppression and a default mutuality, which is not borne out by history. For example, as I will suggest in chapter 5, the gradual and piecemeal unmooring of the categories of male and female might well be a sign not of the political potency of purportedly radical gender politics but of the diminishing salience of gender as a mechanism for maldistribution, at least for white people.

Since any single binary definition (e.g., genitals at birth, chromosomes, gender identity) cannot account for everyone, some who hold the constructionist position argue that the state should just end the practice of classifying people as M, F, or even X, altogether. With no consensus on what sex is, the logic goes, it shouldn't be recorded or listed on documents. Undergirding this is the assumption that states classify only that which is "objectively" there. But distinguishing between kinds of people or kinds of activities and backing up those distinctions with the force of law makes those distinctions very real, at least in their effects.[60] Indeed, legislating difference is the central activity of the accretion of laws, rules, institutions, norms, and forces loosely sedimented together and commonly thought of as "the state." One could say—and indeed some have—that establishing all manner of differences is what brings states into being.[61] Merely pointing out that sex lacks an objective foundation will not bring about the collapse of the classification system or the power of states to establish and maintain categories. Of course, calling out states for what they *should* and *should not* do can be a rhetorically powerful and movement-building incitement to justice. Reinforcing that gesture, however, by looking at how particular sex classification policies might further different state projects, from surveillance to incarceration to nation-building, can deepen our understanding of how sex classification has been enrolled in governance. The task at hand, then, is to disaggregate what's been cast as the *singular* issue of sex reclassification policy, as if all bad policies ultimately sprung from the same monstrous (and transphobic) hydra and all good ones from pure, untethered, objectively true reason. Any analysis that assumes sex reclassification is one problem with one solution will not be able to identify the logic of different, even contradictory, rationalities at play. Such an approach hypostasizes the state as a conceptual and ahistorical unity. Recall, from earlier in the chapter, that trans advocates in the birth certificate lawsuit claimed that the contradictory rules for sex reclassification among city agencies rendered them all, collectively, "arbitrary" and "capricious." Attorneys for the city responded by pointing out that "the existence of different approaches to similar problems does not render an agency's rule irrational."[62] Each agency's policy for deciding who was male and who was female depended on the particular agency's work, not on some abstract notion of sex itself.

One way to distinguish injustices and inconsistencies is to see them spatially. The vector of inconsistency can be imagined as vertical: it concerns the relation between an individual and a state actor. Here the inconsistency—the injustice—inheres in the mismatch between the M or F on a person's identity papers and their gender identity. In those cases, even everyday transactions can lead to moments of vulnerability.

As one woman explained to New York City legislators in 2001: "I do not suffer from gender dysphoria. I suffer from bureaucratic dysphoria. My ID does not match my appearance. I worry every time I apply for a job, every time I authorize a credit card check, every time I buy a plane ticket, every time I buy a beer at the corner deli. I have changed my name but my gender continues to be officially and bureaucratically M."[63] The transgender rights movement's advocacy has been largely oriented around this vertical axis, attempting to resolve the injustice of sex misclassification by particular government agencies. The movement has made real progress in the first two decades of the twenty-first century. The departments of motor vehicles in most states have created policies that allow people to change the sex classification on their driver's licenses. As a result of court rulings or policy changes at the administrative level, by 2021 only one state, Tennessee, does not allow individuals to change the sex on their birth certificate. The US Department of State rules for US passports now require only an affirmation of gender identity accompanied by an affidavit from a physician, although the language is intimidating: "Had appropriate clinical treatment for gender transition to the new gender of either male or female."[64] But there have also been some tremendous losses, most notably when the sex classification issue has been raised in the context of incarceration or parenting. Before the Supreme Court's decision in *Obergefell v. Hodges*, several appellate courts had ruled that, for purposes of marriage, sex is determined at birth or by external genitalia. (This will be discussed in chapter 4.) And many penal institutions remain resistant to any suggestion that prisoners be segregated according to anything but external genitalia, as discussed in chapter 5.

The second vector of inconsistency is horizontal: it refers to a lack of uniformity *between* state policies and decisions on sex reclassification. Here the inconsistency inheres not in a clash between an individual and the government agency that misclassifies them, but in the differences between entities that make decisions backed by the force of law with regard to the criteria they rely on for sex designation. (And even with agencies that have the same policies, what must be provided as evidence to meet the policy's criteria can differ.[65]) For the purposes of this analytical framework, I am not particularly interested in the individual—or the "subject." Rather than centering on the differences between the individual and the state, I focus on the differences between state actors. From this perspective, individuals fade into the background, figuring not as actors but as the acted upon. As the individual recedes, so does sex itself. In its place, state actions—rules, regulations, decisions, policies, laws—take center stage: the focus becomes not what sex is, but how states produce it, and what effect those decisions have. Second, rather than understanding the problem as one of injustice and prescribing a solution for how states "ought to" define sex, or "ought to" refrain from classifying sex at all, I defer shifting, as much as possible, from describing the current situation to prescribing the solution for it. Moving too quickly from the "is" to the "ought" means that we don't spend enough time trying to figure out what particular systems of sex classification do. Instead of positing the differences as discrepancies, I try to understand how they're not. The different metrics for sex are telling, and much is lost when those differences are summarily portrayed as irrational vestiges of social structures long past or as effects of transphobia. The project here is not to resolve the disorder of sex classification, but to pull it apart even more and use it to figure out at a very molecular level what these different sets of criteria accomplish.

2

Sex and Popular Sovereignty

For years, I had put off changing my sex designation in my Social Security records. I had changed my sex classification and my name on my old passport and driver's license, from Paisley Ann Currah to Paisley Alan Currah. But word on the transgender digital street had it that under President George W. Bush, the Social Security Administration (SSA) had tightened requirements for changing the sex marker in one's record. (It had.) I had also procrastinated because this was not a bureaucratic transaction I could accomplish through the US mail. Unlike residents of, say, Nebraska, residents of Brooklyn, Queens, and five other municipalities across the country, at that time, had to show up in person at a "Social Security Card Center" to "strengthen the integrity of the Social Security Number."[1] The idea of outing myself in a face-to-face transaction with a government bureaucrat was not appealing to me. (I had already had that experience at the New York Department of Motor Vehicles.)

But by the time President Bush left the Oval Office, I had decided to get my ducks in a row and get the record changed. I had developed a slightly paranoid fear that I would be denied my Social Security benefits in the future because of a mismatch between the SSA's record associated with the number assigned to me and (what I can only describe as) myself. A few years earlier, I had read, in a dusty archive of a medical association, a letter written in 1965 by a federal official at the Department of Health, Education, and Welfare. He was responding to an inquiry from New York City's Bureau of Records and Statistics, which had asked for input on a policy for applications for a "change of sex" on a birth certificate. The federal official had found that the "crucial problem" raised by the question concerned the connection between two different files, with different names and sex markers. "Assuming that 'x' has undergone medical treatment [operations for 'change of sex'], how do we link 'x' with the birth certificate?"[2] As a researcher, the discovery was exciting; here was a letter from the last century in which a federal bureaucrat reflected on one of the central problems of modern state formations—how to *recognize* its citizens—and tied that to the question of legal sex classification. But from the perspective of someone who hopes to receive Social Security benefits upon retirement, the idea that the SSA might not be able to connect me to my records instilled in me a sense of vertigo. What if the government said the Paisley Currah in their records was not *me*? What if "I" was not sufficiently linked with the Paisley Currah who would receive Social Security benefits?

In 2009, the SSA explained what forms and documents one must tender for an ordinary "change of information" request, including changing one's name and correcting one's date of birth. Change of legal sex presumably fell under this "change of information" category, but there weren't any instructions for that. In the SSA's online manual for its field officers, under the heading "Changing Numident Data for Reasons Other than Name Change," I found what I needed. "Sex-Operation: Applicant must submit a letter from his or her surgeon or the attending physician verifying that the sex change surgery was completed. All documents must clearly identify the NH."[3] NH is the acronym for Numident Holder; Numident is a short form of Numerical Identification System. "My" number, my file, is the Numident; I am the Numident Holder. If my request is successful, the regulations state, "a new record showing the new data is appended to the prior record(s) on the Numident." My identity in this federal database would not be erased but augmented—the records of the male "Paisley Alan Currah" would be appended to the prior records of the female "Paisley Ann Currah." While the SSA had not yet resolved (and still hasn't) the epistemological uncertainty about the link between my SSA files and me[4]—the link between the Numident and the presumptive Numident Holder—at least "my" different records would be connected administratively.

I filled out Form SS-5, "Application for a Social Security Card," which is used for new cards as well as for changes of information, checked the box marked "Male," wrote in my new name and my old name, and went to 625 Fulton Street in Downtown Brooklyn to get the deed done. About fifty people were in line, waiting to get through metal detectors en route to the card center on the sixth floor. Three armed guards from a private security firm periodically broadcast directives to us Numident Holders and would-be Numident Holders: no food, no drink except for water or infant formula, no alcohol, no weapons of any kind, no tools.

The wait was shorter on the sixth floor. When I was called to window 21, I passed my SS-5 through the slot. "Is this for a new card?" the field officer asked through the window's intercom system. This was the moment I had been dreading. "I'm just updating the information on the card, the gender and the name," I responded, wondering if any clients at nearby windows could hear me. I was instructed to slide my documents over, which included my passport, proof of my name change, and a notarized letter from a surgeon. The clerk looked at the order from the Civil Court of the City of New York granting me "the right to assume the name of Paisley Alan Currah." After she'd skimmed it, she ran her hand over the last page to feel for the court's seal. She turned to the next document, the doctor's letter. It stated, "Psychological and medical testing has been carried out to determine the patient's true gender. In the case of Paisley Currah, this was determined to be male." It also stated the patient had undergone "surgical procedures . . . to irreversibly alter his anatomy and appearance to that of a male." This document, which is only five sentences, took the field officer what seemed like a long time to read.

The officer finally looked up, smiled, and said, "All right, I'm just going to check this out, verify it, and we're good." She went in search of a supervisor, or at least someone who knew what to do with my request. After wandering from one end of the long glassed-in area to the other at least three times, she found someone to advise her—the field officer at window 25. They consulted for a few minutes, looking over my documents together. Before she returned to the window, she photocopied my documents. "Okay, it's all checked out, and we're good." She started making changes at the computer. She looked up once to inform me that my immigration status had never been updated. "I can fix that right now." The friendliness had ratcheted up significantly. She was now super helpful and I was super appreciative. When the officer was done, she had me sign a form consenting to all the changes to my record and returned all the originals and a receipt to me. I thanked her and skedaddled out of there.

But for the long wait, security checks, and suspense at window 21, it was a relatively painless exercise. I had done what conscientious Numident Holders are supposed to do. And since recognition involves mutuality, the federal government, at least this particular agency, had assented to my request for recognition. My sex classification had been changed, my name had been changed, even my citizenship status had been updated. (I was born in Canada.) Despite my fears about encountering transphobia, my white privilege and my class position had made completing this bureaucratic not only possible, but uneventful. I was not treated with suspicion. I had been able to pay for transition-related care, which wasn't covered by insurance back then, and could produce the doctor's letter required at the time. My future Social Security payments were safe.

* * *

The last chapter was about sex, while this chapter and the next look at the state—though there's no easy demarcation between them. In what follows, I present three approaches to thinking about sex classification by the state. Each approach offers a different account of the state. First, I offer the traditional version of popular sovereignty, which is favored by transgender advocates. In this version of the story, the force of law derives from the rule of law, which is underwritten by the consent of the people. It's true that this first story comes with a built-in justification for rejecting transgender individuals' challenges to sex misclassification: sex is cast as a natural property of the individual, something that cannot be changed and as such is before and outside of politics. But the logic of this pre-political justification for denying challenges to sex misclassification eventually becomes, in the hands of advocates, the basis of the remedy. The characteristic that defined the misclassification in the first place—having a gender identity that does not conform to expectations for one's assigned sex at birth—eventually becomes the basis for reclassification. Over the course of the twentieth century, the psychiatric establishment joined transsexual people in believing that "psychological sex" (now called gender identity) was more intransigent than biology. Most transgender rights advocacy and doctrinal legal analysis of the problem are pinned to this story. This approach has had some success. Since my foray into the SSA office in 2009, both the SSA and the Department of Homeland Security have made it possible for individuals to change the sex listed on their records and passport based on gender identity alone. At times, however, the claim that gender identity should be the basis for sex reclassification has failed. In these cases, even after hearing evidence about the persistence and immutability of gender identity, the government simply decides that your sex is not what you believe it to be.

In the following chapter, I present the other two approaches. The second approach to the question of sex misclassification by the state, which is favored by academics of a particular theoretical bent, challenges the axioms of popular sovereignty. Rather than positing a perfect correspondence between the people and the government, this second approach argues that the state only comes into existence through exclusions present at the moment of its founding. The distinction between what is illegal and what is legal rests upon that initial exclusion. That distinction is thus to some extent arbitrary, wrought not by right but by violence. Classifications, including sex classifications, backed by the force of law are not external to these political processes of exclusion; they are the outcome of those processes. Decisions about sex classification are not the result of a rule being applied to a particular case, but rather of moments in which the particular case generates the exception that enacts that rule. The advocates' approach helps us understand advances in state recognition, and the more academic approach provides a way of thinking about the limits of appeals to justice. Neither approach, however, can make sense of all the contradictions in sex classification policy, nor of the way that sex classification has been deployed for different distributive ends—and, more recently, overtly political ones. Thus, I offer a third reading of police powers and classificatory systems. Going back to the central problem—that sex changes depending on where, when, and why—I suggest that contradictory decision-making on sex classification at different agencies, in different jurisdictions, and at different levels of government are parts of a convoluted web of overlapping state projects. Pluralizing sex and the state in this way makes room for a much more granular analysis, although also a much messier one, since contingencies and historical variations fail to produce the conceptual neatness of a singular authority making a singular (good or bad) decision.

None of these three accounts of the authority for state acts of sex classification is wrong and none tells the whole story. These accounts tend to circulate largely in isolation from each other, but advocates and scholars invested in one explanation might benefit from a reading that commingles these different ways of thinking about sex classification and law. Those who discount the story of rights and popular sovereignty as naïve might be reminded of the resonance of appeals made in that register, that those appeals already have led to decisions that endow some transgender individuals with the dignity and respect and capacity to negotiate bureaucratic life that others take for granted. Those who see the second approach as an unnecessary, abstruse analysis of the relation between language and power or as a simplistic, ahistorical explanation might be reminded of the finality of a judge's decision, the obstacles that policies on sex classification seemingly present, and the intransigence of the gap between legal authority and justice. Finally, those who imagine "the state" and its sovereign power as absolute, as exhibiting a unity of purpose and execution, might consider that the capacity and power of the federal government, relative to local state actors, is often overstated. Most of the laws that govern our lives are state laws. Complex social formations and distributions of privilege—including the power to categorize and distinguish—predate and enfold particular constitutional enactments of authority and myths of popular sovereignty. Rather than presenting successive accounts as improvements over what preceded them, these two chapters unfold more like a fugue, with counterpoints embedded in each of the main narrative themes.

Popular Sovereignty

"What does the Constitution do?" That is one of one hundred potential questions on the naturalization test that one must pass to become a US citizen. The guide the US government provides to prospective citizens to help them study for the test says: "With the words 'We the People,' the Constitution states that the people set up the government. The government works for the people and protects the rights of people. In the United States, the power to govern comes from the people, who are the highest power. This is called 'popular sovereignty.'" Later, the study guide explains how the rule of law guarantees equality. In creating what John Adams, the second president, described as "a government of laws, and not of men," the Founding Fathers ensured that "the rule of law helps to make sure that government protects all people equally" and that "the individual rights and liberties of each person are better protected."[5] No doubt there are other ways to relate the plotlines of the story of popular sovereignty in the United States, but distilling the essence of the story from the naturalization test study guide published by the US government seems appropriate. The facts presented in that pamphlet are backed by the force of law: one does, after all, have to get six out of ten randomly chosen questions right to pass the naturalization test.

Recalling that slavery was also codified in the Constitution, an attentive reader of the study guide takes issue with the statement that "people are born with natural rights that no government can take away," and that "the government protects all people equally." It does not seem that "the good People" in whose name and by whose authority the nation is declared independent in the Declaration, and "the People" who "do ordain and establish" the US Constitution, referred to *all* the people in what was claimed as US territory at the time. However, exclusions based on race and sex, the study guide explains, show that the United States is a work in progress, not a done deed: "For more than 200 years, the United States has strived to become a 'more perfect union.' Its history has been one of expansive citizenship for all Americans."[6] Over time, those not originally deemed part of "the people" were included through "changes and additions" to the Constitution.

Of the three accounts of the relationships between sex classifications and the state, it is the popular sovereignty narrative that has been capacious enough to justify both misclassification and reclassification. The story of sovereignty encountered in naturalization tests, in high school civics classes, and in rights advocacy clearly identifies the origin of the law's authority outside of, and prior to, the law. In these iterations of the story of popular sovereignty, people are said to exist prior to the government they bring into being. They voluntarily consent to live under the rule of law—which applies equally to everyone—because it's in their interests to create a system of laws that will protect their fundamental and inalienable rights of "Life, Liberty, and the Pursuit of Happiness." From various vantage points in the future, omissions and mistakes may turn out to have been made: genocide, slavery, segregation, referring to the right to vote of "male citizens" in the Fourteenth Amendment and not including "sex" in the Fifteenth Amendment, disparate treatment of people with disabilities, the criminalization of migrants, state laws that criminalized same-sex sexual intimacy, state bans on same-sex marriage. At the founding, the gap between "the People" (those invoked as the authorizers of the Constitution and fully endowed with rights) and all the actual people on US territory was vast. For "at least two-thirds of American history, the majority of the domestic adult population was also ineligible for full citizenship," Rogers Smith points out, "because of their race, original nationality, or gender."[7] But as the study guide suggests, the instrument created to set up this system of laws has an endlessly iterative self-correcting mechanism: the amendment process. Additionally, there is a second corrective mechanism: judicial review.

Because of the amendment process and judicial review, the one thing we know for sure about the Constitution is that the work of creating a more perfect union is never done. The Court's evolving stances on the question of same-sex sex and same-sex marriage are only the most recent demonstrations of the inexorable march of expansive citizenship conveyed in the story of popular sovereignty.[8] For trans people, it's possible that the constitutional wrong of sex misclassification, and the injustices that happen because of that misclassification, will one day be seen as a violation of the US Constitution. For some, it may seem audacious to set transgender civil rights claims alongside the campaigns led by Frederick Douglass, Martin Luther King Jr., and Susan B. Anthony, and to argue that transgender people as a group have been wrongly excluded from the political community of "the People."[9] How could challenges to rules for sex reclassification be part of the same story that chronicles the end of slavery, segregation, coverture, and the disenfranchisement of women? Even describing the more established and widely supported modern gay rights movement as an extension of the civil rights revolution used to regularly draw ire from some quarters. Injustices of the present, however, are often not widely recognized as such until time has moved us to the vantage point of the future's common sense. As even Justice Scalia once observed, "every age is [closed-minded], including our own, with regard to matters it cannot guess, because it simply does not consider them debatable." But "our ancestors . . . left us free to change."[10] From the perspective of the classes of persons whose gender identity is not corroborated by the M or F printed on the state-issued ID they carry, the story of popular sovereignty and the expansion of equality suggests a future in which non-normative gender identities are not misrecognized. Laws and regulations that treat some individuals differently because of an arbitrary characteristic or difference that has no bearing on legitimate matters of public policy will be found to have violated the most fundamental principles of popular sovereignty.

In a 2016 speech, the US attorney general appeared to move trans people closer to that future moment. Announcing a federal lawsuit challenging a North Carolina law that restricted bathroom access in schools and public buildings to the sex classification on one's birth certificate, Loretta Lynch drew on this story of expanding progress. The lawsuit, she declared, is "about the founding ideals that have led this country—haltingly but inexorably—in the direction of fairness, inclusion, and equality for all Americans." Lynch situated the rights of trans people firmly within the civil rights tradition: "This is not the first time that we have seen discriminatory responses to historic moments of progress for our nation. We saw it in the Jim Crow laws that followed the Emancipation Proclamation. We saw it in fierce and widespread resistance to *Brown v. Board of Education*. And we saw it in the proliferation of state bans on same-sex unions intended to stifle any hope that gay and lesbian Americans might one day be afforded the right to marry." Lynch pointed out that it is wrong to discriminate against our "fellow Americans . . . for something they cannot control." Lynch ended with a promise to the transgender community: "This country was founded on a promise of equal rights for all, and we have always managed to move closer to that promise, little by little, one day at a time. It may not be easy—but we'll get there together."[11] For many trans communities, it was a watershed. Mara Keisling, the head of the National Center for Transgender Equality, explained why: "To see the [attorney general] come out and speak the way she did to humanize us, to say the federal government had our backs, that the president of the United States was watching and cared. . . . We've never seen anything like that."[12] In 2016, it seemed as if trans people were on the cusp of full inclusion.

The precedent for this vision may be found in the effort to end states' differential treatment of men and women in the twentieth century. The courts have used the Equal Protection Clause of the Fourteenth Amendment, which prohibits states from denying "to any person within its jurisdiction the equal protection of the laws," to overturn most laws that discriminate on the basis of sex and to limit the ability of governments to treat men and women differently.[13] Of course, governments make distinctions between people all the time—between people who drive too fast and those who do not, between people who score higher on tests and those who score lower, between people who own cars and those who own bikes, between people who are licensed as pilots and those who are not. What equal protection means, in the words of former chief justice William Rehnquist, is that "states must treat like cases alike but may treat unlike cases accordingly."[14] Any government effort to differentiate, classify, order, and regulate people, accordingly, must have a "rational basis." If a law is challenged by an individual who stands to lose something because of its classification, and the state cannot explain how the classification is "reasonably related" to a "legitimate" government interest, it won't pass muster with the courts.[15] This is a low bar: normally, courts defer to legislatures' decisions about classifications related to government interests. Requiring drivers to be at least sixteen years old, for example, makes the roads safer.

But courts review statutes that affect some particular classifications with more care. In the lexicon of constitutional law, laws that treat people differently because of particular "accidents of birth," such as race (or skin color in the language of earlier cases) and national origin, are "suspect" and require much closer scrutiny by the courts. According to equal protection doctrine, if groups described in a 1938 decision as "discrete and insular minorities" have suffered a history of discrimination and are politically powerless and thus unable to rectify the problem through the political process (via legislation), a heightened level of judicial review will be triggered.[16] In a landmark 1973 decision, a plurality of Supreme Court justices agreed to add sex to this list of suspect classifications. Laws that treat men and women differently would trigger a stricter review by the courts. The Supreme Court explained that "sex, like race and national origin, is an immutable characteristic determined solely by the accident of birth.... [T]he sex characteristic frequently bears no relation to ability to perform or contribute to society. As a result, statutory distinctions between the sexes often have the effect of invidiously relegating the entire class of females to inferior legal status without regard to the actual capabilities of its individual members."[17]

Over time, the jurisprudence of equal protection settled into three tiers of review. The highest tier of review involves laws that target people based on their race, ethnicity, or national origin, or laws that impinge on activities interpreted as fundamental rights (e.g., marriage, voting). These should be subject to "strict scrutiny" by federal courts. It's difficult for these laws to pass constitutional muster: they must be narrowly tailored and the government need that they serve must be compelling. The second tier is an intermediate standard of review: the classification must be substantially (rather than narrowly) related to an important (rather than compelling) government interest. Retreating a bit from a 1973 landmark decision regarding sex discrimination, the Court has decided that laws involving "gender classifications" should be subject to intermediate review; laws making distinctions based on the accident of birth of sex may be constitutional if they are substantially related to an important government interest.[18] This standard of judicial review is lower than the standard applied to distinctions based on race and national origin, but higher than those applied in the third and final tier of review: the rational basis test. In recent decades, a Republican-dominated Court has tended to avoid, whenever possible, invoking anything other than rational basis review. The Court has banned most sex-based classifications, from different drinking ages for men and women to denial of spousal benefits to husbands of military personnel. Other sex-based distinctions, including those related to sex-segregated facilities and institutions (most importantly jails and prisons, examined in chapter 5), naturalization laws, and statutory rape laws with different ages of consent for men and women, remain in place because the Court identified an important government interest in those policies. In the case of statutory rape laws, for example, "young men and young women are not similarly situated with respect to the problems and the risks of sexual intercourse."[19] Distinctions based on sex do not just organize the distribution of inequality based on gender. They have also made discrimination against gay, lesbian, and bisexual people possible because state-sponsored discrimination against lesbian, gay, and bisexual people depends on the existence of a system of sex classification. Indeed, without the power to classify individuals as male or female, it would not have been possible for states to ban same-sex marriage or same-sex sex. Many laws that have discriminated against gay, lesbian, and bisexual people—for example, bans on same-sex marriage, adoption, military service, and government employment—have been justified by the argument that they served important state interests.

Challenges to sex classification are more recent than challenges to racial classifications, which have long been contested. Since the colonial era, racial classifications have secured the "color line" necessary to slavery, segregation, and other race-based institutions. Individuals who thought themselves racially misclassified have fought to cross to the privileged side of this line. For example, the use of race to exclude non-whites from being naturalized as citizens between 1790 and 1954 gave rise to "racial perquisite" cases in which would-be citizens from Armenia, Burma, China, Hawaii, Japan, and Mexico, among other countries, fought their classification as "not white." As Ian Haney López has documented, some individuals won, but most lost.[20] Before antimiscegenation laws were ruled unconstitutional in 1967, individuals challenged their or their spouses' racial designation—sometimes to argue in criminal proceedings that the marriage did not violate the miscegenation laws of their state, other times to have the marriage declared invalid.[21] After the Court decided that governments must generally not treat people differently because of their race, challenges to the racial classifications assigned to individuals fell off dramatically. In addition to challenges to state-sponsored discrimination based on race, and to challenges to particular racial classifications attached to an individual, there have even been challenges to the very ability of the state to make racial classifications in the first place. For example, Albion Tourgée, Homer Plessy's counsel in *Plessy v. Ferguson*, in challenging Louisiana's Jim Crow laws, argued in his brief to the Supreme Court that "the question is not as to the *equality* of the privileges enjoyed, but *the right of the State to label one citizen as white and another as colored*."[22] In its 1896 decision finding the Jim Crow law did not violate the US Constitution, the Supreme Court did not deign to address Plessy's argument about the state's right to make racial classifications and attach them to individuals.

Of course, governments still rely on the category of race to distinguish people. Affirmative action policies and nondiscrimination laws, designed to rectify the past injustices of slavery, segregation, and discrimination generally, require racial classifications. Policymakers and scholars have not yet come to a consensus as to how one's claim to racial minority status should or could be verified. Moreover, some jurists, Chief Justice John Roberts among them, understand race as skin color. Armed with that definition, Roberts rarely sees any compelling reason to make distinctions based on such an arbitrary characteristic, even in race-conscious affirmative action or diversity programs. Others understand race as a historically constructed social and legal identity, and are more likely to support use of the category to right past wrongs. As Jennifer Hochschild and Vesla Weaver explain, "the same classification system that promotes inequality may also undermine it. Once the categorization generates groups with sharply defined boundaries, the members of that group can draw on their shared identity to mobilize against that subordinate position."[23] Race also remains a central element of statistical data gathered to measure and track populations. Like sex, the metrics for classifying race, and the racial categories themselves, vary from jurisdiction to jurisdiction, from agency to agency, and they change over time. As legal scholar Reginald Oh points out, "different approaches to race and equal protection have had enormous doctrinal and political consequences."[24] In this sense, like sex, race is (defined) as race does.[25]

Unlike racial classification, however, decisions about sex classification were rarely challenged before the latter half of the twentieth century. No doubt that is largely due to the fact that the segment of the population assigned a sex at birth that did not comport with their gender identity or lived gender experience was minute. But quantity can't entirely explain the disparity. Appellate courts are more likely to hear and publish decisions on cases of first impression, which these cases would have been. Their paucity is more likely due to the fact that the pre-political naturalness attributed to sex is more firmly embedded in law than is that of race. Antimiscegenation laws, historian Peggy Pascoe reminds us, "had depended on hierarchies of sex and gender as well as hierarchies of race." Even so, Pascoe tells us, "although lawyers, judges, and juries spent an enormous amount of energy debating the race classification of the partners to a marriage, the issue of sex classification only rarely entered their minds."[26] Racial categories have long been understood to be products of legal and social norms, and race itself has been so contradictory in its definition and application that, according to W. E. B. Du Bois, the notion that race was a concept implied too much coherence: "perhaps it is wrong to speak of it at all as 'a concept' rather than as a group of contradictory forces, facts, and tendencies."[27] Of course, racial embodiments cannot be separated from gendered ones.[28] Yet in the terrible efficiency of US *legal* architectures, systems of sex classification strip out cultures and histories: the heterogeneity of ways of living gender in particular locations evaporates into the deracinated binary abstraction of sex. Like the most successful ideological inversions, that move is as effective as it is false: in severing the categories from the contexts that give them meaning, systems of legal sex classification present particular configurations of the binary—and the binary itself—as universal.

The recognition of the plasticity of sex, therefore, is a more recent phenomenon. The presumed tight correspondence between the *what* that is classified and the classification itself had long rested on rather intractable assumptions about the body: it is a simple matter to tell the difference between a male and female—just look at them. The tenacity of the idea that sex is an attribute of the body, not the mind, made the M or F on an identity document seem like a completely unremarkable description rather than a decision that could potentially be contested. But when greater numbers of people started coming forward in the last third of the twentieth century to contest the sex they had been assigned at birth, a dissonance was created between the perception of the physical body, imagined as a priori, and the reality of an unexpected gender identity inhabiting that same body.[29] Suddenly, the question of sex classification achieved a new visibility in the courts and in the realm of politics. Once there, requests for reclassification made by individuals or by advocates looking to change policy were initially adjudicated vis-à-vis traditional commonsense ideas about what male and female bodies should look like, or, literally, dictionary definitions of sex. Over time, however, the doctrine that an individual is—or rather, must be—bound for life by the sex assigned at birth has lost its infallibility.

By the end of the second decade of the twenty-first century, the older conventional knowledge of sex is fast unraveling; indeed, one might say that at the level of policy it has been reconfigured into three distinct positions. Though the emergence of these positions is chronological, at the present moment all are in circulation. The first view is the one that preceded, yet persists amid, the unraveling: that sex at birth is sex for life. This school still resonates in the popular imaginary because it remains one of the most widely shared assumptions held about human animals, visible in almost every realm of human activity transmitted through language—from children's books to wedding vows to the "transgender panic" defense, invoked by individuals accused of killing someone whose genitals provoke rage. But many now agree with the proposition that sex can change, and consequently those changes should be acknowledged by state agencies. This second position holds that it is the body that determines whether sex should be reclassified. The question then becomes: *what* has to have changed or become different from the situation that existed at birth to change the designation to M, F, or X? At this point, most agencies in the US make it possible for individuals to change their sex classification. But because of the tenacity of the view that the body provides the objective grounding for what sex is, attributes of the body still matter in a great many policies. From the first media representations of Christine Jorgensen in 1952 to still-prevalent understandings of transgender people today, the assumption is that sex changes when the body does: the addition or removal of breasts, penises, and vaginas through surgery, and feminizing or masculinizing changes to characteristics associated with sex (facial hair, musculature, voice in some cases) through hormone therapy. Of those changes, it was genital surgery that for a very long time mattered the most to policymakers who supported sex reclassification. Certainly, people choose—or would choose, if there were no barriers to transition-related surgeries—to modify their bodies in small or large ways to make them appear more congruent with their gender identity.[30] Indeed, the ontological status granted to the body as the teller of the truth of sex shows that this position (that sex can change, and that the change is marked by the body) has much in common with the first (that sex can't change). Both assign the body the task of identifying sex; what distinguishes them is a temporal metric. Either the sex is assigned at the time of birth (based on a visual check of the infant's body) and the classification is fixed for life, or sex can be reassigned later in life. Documents describing changes to the body become the verifiable indicator for a change of sex.

The third position, which is advanced by most transgender rights advocates and that each year gains more traction with policymakers, holds that gender identity should be the basis for sex classification. For the vast majority of people, the sex assigned to them at birth will turn out to have accurately predicted the gender identity they develop and maintain over their lifetime. But some people develop a gender identity that doesn't conform with social expectations for the sex assigned to them at birth. If one's sense of one's self as male or female—or as not solely one or the other—is distinct from the sex classification assigned at birth, gender identity, not the body, should be the metric for resolving that difference. In current litigation about sex classifications, the argument for the primacy of gender identity circulates as boilerplate in brief after brief. For example, in a case brought by an individual challenging the Illinois Department of Motor Vehicles policy requiring gender-affirming surgery, advocates in an Illinois DMV case explained to the court that "sex reassignment does not change a person's gender, which is determined by their gender identity." Surgical changes to the body do not change one from M to F or F to M, but instead should be understood, advocates explain, as simply gender-affirming.[31] Advocates often cite statistics showing that a majority of transgender people in the US have not had genital surgery.[32] People who eschew both M and F are non-binary, and that is also a gender identity, which more and more policies are acknowledging by allowing individuals to change their gender on their driver's licenses to "non-binary," or to "X," with no medical affirmation of any sort.[33] Making gender identity the basis for sex reclassification provides a much-needed escape clause for transgender people, but it does not disturb the larger system of sex classification at birth. Sex classification registers as a matter of politics and policy only for those whose gender identity conflicts with social expectations and who seek reclassification. The sex classifications of those whose gender identity conforms to social expectations—the invisible norm—rests on an apparently less contestable foundation: the particular attributes of the body associated with one sex or the other.

The long campaign to end the exclusion of transgender people from the promises of "expansive citizenship" has, as its goal, the substitution of gender identity for the sexual attributes recognized on the body. That goal has been achieved, effectively, at the SSA and the Department of State. For years, the Department of State had required individuals requesting to change the M or F on their passports to provide "supporting evidence for a change of surgery in the form of an affidavit from a surgeon." In 2010, at the urging of advocates, the Obama administration changed what would count as evidence. Under the new policy, applicants could submit identity documents listing the new sex or a certification from a physician attesting that "you have had appropriate clinical treatment for transition from male to female or female to male." The guidelines note that what constitutes appropriate clinical treatment is up to the physician.[34] While these rules do not explicitly state that the affirmation of a gender identity not associated with one's birth sex (supported by evidence from a medical provider) is sufficient, the absence of the surgical requirement effectively accomplishes that.[35] In 2013, the Social Security Administration also changed its policy. Had I waited a few more years to request that the F in my Numident record be replaced by an M, my physician's letter would only have had to state that I had had "appropriate clinical treatment for gender transition."[36]

From the perspective of those whose gender identity is not traditionally associated with the sex marker on their birth certificates (e.g., a person identified as male on their birth certificate, but whose gender identity is female), sex classification should not be set in stone, forever fixed by the M or F on the birth certificate originally issued to them. The central principles of popular sovereignty that invigorate political rhetoric in the US—that individuals are prior to the state they create, that "the government exists because the people think it should," that it's generally wrong to treat people differently because of some (though not all) "accidents of birth"—are used to justify equality for transgender people. Gender is an essential attribute of an individual's identity.[37] In fact, as a feature of one's self that can't be transferred or taken away, it could be cast as inalienable. That the Declaration explicitly lists some inalienable rights (life, liberty, and the pursuit of happiness) as "among" those with which the Creator endows us does not rule out the possibility of other unenumerated inalienable rights, such as the right to particular religious convictions. Francis Hutcheson, a thinker of the Scottish Enlightenment whom many believe was an important influence on the drafters of the Declaration, described "unalienable" rights as those that would be impossible to change on demand: "no man can really change his sentiments, judgments, and inward affections, at the pleasure of another; nor can it tend to any good to make him profess what is contrary to his heart."[38] Conceivably, the inalienable rights not listed might include the right of individuals "to define, and to redefine as their lives unfold, their own gender identities," as the authors of the International Bill of Gender Rights declared in 1996.[39] While one's gender identity might change over time in this tradition, it's not something that can be changed at the command of another. As an essential aspect of one's self, gender identity falls outside the purview of the state; the role of government is only to catalog it. And so the inalienability of gender identity, construed as trumping the sex assigned at birth, effectively becomes the rationale for including gender identity in the legal order established on the basis of popular sovereignty.

Ironically, both supporters and opponents of trans rights agree that an individual's sex classification is a fact that should not be up for debate. In 1977, Tennessee legislators voted to prohibit individuals from changing Tennessee birth certificates to indicate their new sex.[40] A bill to reverse this and make it possible to change the sex marker on birth certificates issued by Tennessee was introduced in 2011 and was considered by the Tennessee House Health and Human Resources Subcommittee the following year. Because rules for sex classification are usually decided at the administrative level—as commonsense "housekeeping" rules that require no public comment or, more recently, as publicly promulgated policies—it's a rare thing for legislators to expound publicly on the parameters of sex. The exchange between Republican Joey Hensley, then a member of the Tennessee House, and two of the bill's advocates—LGBT rights attorney Abby Rubenfeld and Tennessee Transgender Political Coalition president Marissa Richmond—captures the points of disagreement.

Rubenfeld ends her remarks to the committee by comparing changing gender to changing one's name.

> RUBENFELD: There is no problem with changing birth certificates in this way, to change somebody's name or to change their gender designation. . . . And changing this law . . . will do a great service to the few people that need to do this whose lives are prejudiced and are damaged in significant ways because they can't make this vital correction. . . . Birth certificates are routinely changed and there's never a problem about that. We change names on birth certificates. You can go to court here in Nashville and get your name changed for any reason that you want and change it on your birth certificate, any reason that you want and you'll have a new birth certificate that has that name with no record of your old name.
>
> HENSLEY: So you say that you can change the name, but can you change the date or the place of birth on your birth certificate?
>
> RUBENFELD: I don't think so. I don't know why anybody would want to.
>
> HENSLEY: Well, I would think that would be the same way this is. That's a fact when someone is born, they're born at a certain time,

they're born at a certain place, and they're born a certain gender. And the birth certificate is just designating that.

RUBENFELD: But they're also born with a certain name and it's changed easily.

HENSLEY: Names can be changed. Names are something given to a person after birth.

RUBENFELD: But gender designation I would respectively suggest is also just given to a person at birth. . . . But for people who take this extraordinary step to correct their physical gender to match what they really are, that is a fact for them, it's a fact from birth.

HENSLEY: We just disagree about that.

The bill would not only have reversed Tennessee legislation on the question and aligned the state's policy with those of the vast majority of other US jurisdictions that allow one's sex designation to be changed on birth certificates. Because the requirements in the bill did not include surgery or body modification of any kind, passage of this legislation would also have catapulted Tennessee, at that time, to the forefront of policy on the issue. The rule in Tennessee would have been essentially the same as the Department of State's passport rule, as well as that of a handful of other jurisdictions with the most liberal criteria for changing sex on birth certificates at the time. While advocates and sponsors of the bill couched their argument in terms of physical transition—the traditional narratives most intelligible to elected officials and the public—the bill required as evidence for sex reclassification only a sworn statement from a physician, psychologist, or social worker "that the gender of the person had been changed." Below, the questioning turns on what evidence would be appropriate for a change of sex:

HENSLEY: But what exactly has to determine someone's gender? I notice this amendment lists several different people that can have a sworn statement. Physician, and then it goes ahead and I don't know why you list all of these, but a surgeon and an endocrinologist and a gynecologist and internist, a neurologist and psychiatrist. Those are all physicians. And then you go to psychologist or a social worker. How can a social worker have a sworn statement about someone's gender?

RUBENFELD: I would just point out that in this time when we're trying to have limited government I don't know why legislators can make that decision, either.

RICHMOND: Those categories are based on what the US State Department picked for the gender change policy for the passport, and so all of those categories are professional categories who treat and deal with transgender people. And that's why those specific categories were selected.

HENSLEY: Is this someone who has gone through all the physical changes to change their gender or is this just someone that cross-dresses, they can change their gender?

RICHMOND: Cross dressers are not defined as someone who has changed their gender, so they would not fall under this particular law, if this bill becomes a law.

HENSLEY: What does designate when someone has changed their gender?

RICHMOND: . . . That is a definition determined by the medical community, and in consultation between that care provider and the patient and to determine what procedures and steps are necessary. And for certain people, for instance in a wheelchair, they would not be allowed in certain cases to get certain procedures but nonetheless their gender change would have actually occurred. But yet the medical profession may not be willing to take it a full step. But they would still have transitioned, changed their lives, they would assume a new gender, and this bill would allow them to have a document which then they can take out and carry on with the rest of their lives and matching up all their other documents at one time.

HENSLEY: But you're adding social worker as somebody that can have a sworn statement. Even if this bill passed it would seem like adding someone who was a social worker is a stretch.

RICHMOND: We can remove that particular category.

HENSLEY: I don't support it anyway, but adding a social worker is a stretch.

Representative Hensley simply doesn't believe sex can change. As he puts it, "We just disagree about that." But, he advises the advocates, even if sex can change, that change shouldn't be based on the sworn statement of a *social worker*. At that moment in the hearing, the bill's sponsor, Jeanne Richardson, Democrat from Memphis, stood up and offered to remove "psychologist" and "social worker" from the bill. She then made a final statement:

> For someone to have surgery or to change their lives, this totally is a very, very serious, thoughtful process. This is not something that's done lightly. . . . It has to do with the person and their personhood and what they are, it's as essential as anything could be about them. There are very few people in our society that make this decision, but I respect those people that do. . . . So when they make that decision, and we have medical professionals who will back them up, I see no reason why the rest of us should challenge that.[41]

Despite Richardson's plea to her legislative colleagues to think of gender identity as a central aspect of personhood that they should refrain from interfering with, the bill was voted down a few minutes later.

By 2021, the Supreme Court had yet to hear a constitutional case regarding the right to have one's sex reclassified on an identity document, though cases are working their way up through the courts. For example, Tennessee's policy has been challenged by four transgender people born in Tennessee who argue that the statute violates the Equal Protection and Due Process clauses of the US Constitution.[42] From the broad outline of US constitutional law laid out earlier, we can see that there are several potential avenues for such a claim: via equal protection (of an identity, like race or sex), as expressive activity (analogous to speech or manifestations of religious belief), or as a fundamental right based on a liberty interest (emerging out of the Constitution's implicit guarantees of privacy and meant to limit the majority's ability to alienate an individual from deep-seated properties of the self that should not be subject to others' decisions). The back-and-forth in the testimony quoted above encapsulates some of the paradoxes raised in thinking about popular sovereignty and sex reclassification. Provided with the opportunity to revisit their earlier statutory decision to not allow sex to be changed on birth certificates, Tennessee legislators decided not to. In this case, arguments about the centrality of gender identity to personhood came up against the hard wall of legislative incredulity. In Tennessee, that incredulity wasn't just due to a difference of opinion about what should count when it comes to sex classification. The view of legislators such as Hensley, who apparently represented the majority, is backed by the force of law. As a result, the state of Tennessee still will not change the sex classification on the birth certificates of transgender people born in that state, even though sex reclassification is a matter of great importance to this particular population. A survey of transgender people found that having "gender incongruent identification exposes people to a range of negative outcomes, from denial of employment, housing, and public benefits to harassment and physical violence."[43] Just as the time and place of birth are construed as facts outside the realm of politics, so, for these legislators, is the sex (assigned) at birth. While advocates explain that it is gender identity, not birth sex, that should be outside of politics, decisions about the rule for sex classification depend on the common sense of the time, the hegemonic ideas in circulation. Sex classification, whether it is based on the "facts" of birth or an "inalienable" gender identity, will always be a matter of politics.

In the story of popular sovereignty, through fits and starts, the people get closer to justice through the ongoing recognition that constitutional principles have been wrongly interpreted in the past. But another way of thinking about sovereignty, one with a distinctly more theoretical provenance, shifts our focus away from the people and toward power. In this story, regardless of whether the decision is deemed good or bad, sex classification is an effect of sovereignty. This account, the subject of the next chapter, provides another way of thinking about precisely what happened when the Social Security Administration changed the F to an M in my records.

3

Sex Classification as a Technology of Governance

When the great adventurer Baron Munchausen had to save himself from sinking in a swamp, the story goes, he pulled himself up and out by his own pigtail. Eventually—perhaps as men's hairstyles got shorter—the pigtail morphed into bootstraps in English-language retellings of the story.[1] That's one account of the origins of the bootstraps metaphor, anyway. What is interesting is how, over time, the meaning of the metaphor shifted from being a description of a quintessentially impossible task to representing what's best about American capitalism: the self-made man or woman who lifts themselves up by their own bootstraps. This mythic origin story of auto-generation is, writ small, a reprise of the founding story of the United States. But, just as one cannot lift oneself off the ground, a people cannot call itself into being. Traditional renderings of popular sovereignty identify the source of constitutional authority as the consent of the people; critiques of the concept of such self-generation point to its Munchausen-like impossibility. How can a legal order be instituted by the very thing—in this case, the people—that the legal instrument calls into being ("the People")? Hannah Arendt captures the conundrum faced by anyone who would found a new political community: "Those who get together to constitute a new government are themselves unconstitutional, that is, they have no authority to do what they set out to achieve."[2] From Plato to Agamben, political theorists have wrestled with this paradox: the force that creates the law cannot be justified by a law that has not yet come into being. Sovereignty's foundation requires a moment of "fabulous retroactivity" in which time is warped: the apparatus of constitutional principles, the legal architecture set in place by violence, can be legitimate only if it comes before the violence that makes possible its use.[3] But until a time machine appears, or a deus ex machina descends from the heavens to sort this out, the law can't come before the force that institutes it. Violence, then, precedes and is constitutive of the founding act. And that violence produces exclusions:

for example, the remainder left after "the People" endowed with rights by the US Constitution are subtracted from the total of all people inhabiting the territories of the thirteen founding states, including enslaved people (the "all other Persons" of the Constitution).

Feminists and gender studies theorists have shown sex classification to be another sort of constitutive violence in which the effect (M or F) stands in for its cause. Judith Butler explains, "Sex becomes something like a fiction . . . retroactively installed at a prelinguistic site to which there is no direct access."[4] While the assumption is that the linguistic markers M or F have a direct and transparent relation to the essential biological phenomena of differently sexed bodies, the meanings attached to M and F are produced (horizontally) through the differences between those terms, not (vertically) between a direct and simple relationship between the term and what we imagine its real referent to be. The act of attaching labels produces the classifications themselves. When the preamble to the US Constitution identifies "the People" as the agents and authorizers of the US government, the document actually brings that "People" into existence; similarly, the act of attaching the word "male" to describe a material condition is what in fact constitutes the category. The meaning of both is secured not through a link with reality or nature but through establishing what the term does not contain, which is the term's constitutive other: "all other Persons" for the former, "female" for the latter. Whatever the pre-social, pre-linguistic, pre-political reality might be—that would be impossible for us to apprehend—it begins to matter politically only after it's named, differentiated, distinguished through language. Both the self-legitimating discourse of popular sovereignty and the status of sex difference as an unassailable fact, then, depend on an apparently transparent relationship between language and nature.

It's difficult to find a verb to describe the connection between someone and the M or F on the piece of paper in their hand that gets to the crux of the relationship between sex and the state. There are words like "indicating," "describing," "listing," and "stating" that suggest an easy correspondence between the thing that is to be known—the body—and the sex marker on the identity document. Or one might want to use words such as "certifying," "verifying," "attesting," "affirming," and "authenticating" that suggest a looser relationship. These actions imply that the person is tethered to the document that purports to describe them through the imprimatur of the authorizing power: individual X is female. Finally, "creating," "designating," or "enacting" convey the sense that the relationship between the body and the document is inaugurated by the declaration of M or F. Sociologist Claudine Dardy uses a range of words to describe what identity documents do: "[Identity] papers are at one and the same time papers of constraint and control, including control by the state, but they are also purveyors of identity. For each and every one of us, our identity—at least a certain kind of identity—is enacted and reenacted, stamped, affirmed in these papers."[5] Suggesting that sex is a property not of the body but of the government-issued document, phenomenologist Gayle Salamon argues, "Sex is something that the documents themselves enact, and sex becomes performative in the sense that the 'm' or the 'f' on the document does not merely report on the sex of its bearer but becomes the truth of and bestows the bearer's sex."[6]

The paradox-of-sovereignty account is less than convincing to those who live outside its theoretical precincts. The idea that categories are not already "out there" but are made real through their naming seems counterintuitive, at the very least. But if that's the case, perhaps we can consider Patricia Williams's economical (and humorous) explanation of language and difference:

> Walking down Fifth Avenue in New York not long ago, I came up behind a couple and their young son. The child, about four or five years old, had evidently been complaining about big dogs. The mother was saying, "But why are you afraid of big dogs?" "Because they're big," he responded with eminent good sense. "But what's the difference between a big dog and a little dog?" the father persisted. "They're big," said the child. "But there's really no difference," said the mother, pointing to a large slathering wolfhound with narrow eyes and the calculated amble of a gangster, and then to a beribboned Pekinese the size of a roller skate, who was flouncing along just ahead of us all, in that little fox-trotty step that keep Pekinese from ever being taken seriously. "See?" said the father. "If you look really closely you'll see that there's no difference at all. They're just dogs."[7]

As the child in this story might have wondered, how is the Pekinese the same thing as the wolfhound? The signifier "dog" seems like an arbitrary convention; for the four year old who is still being initiated into culture, it's not intuitive. But as he moves further into language, he will become more and more fluent in the adult currencies of names, categories, and classifications. (It's probably no accident that toddlers and young children are generally more open to gender non-conformity, gender transition, and the like than are adults.)

The arbitrary and conventional character of language in general and classifications in particular can be properly described as violent—in the sense of creating meaning and imposing order by cutting one thing off from another, by foreclosing the possibility of other combinations of things. This is no less true of the kind of violence that underpins legal decisions. From the extraordinary moments of constitution-making to quotidian administrative rulings, legal decisions are backed by the force of law. Robert Cover explains, "Legal interpretation takes place in a field of pain and death. . . . A judge articulates her understanding of a text, and as a result, somebody loses his freedom, his property, his children, even his life."[8] When legislators, policymakers, judges, and writers of constitutions enact laws, make rules, and hand down decisions, those acts are enforced with state-sanctioned violence. What's essential to this difference is the finality of the sovereign decision: there is no higher power, no greater logic, no foundational text beyond it to appeal to. In this sense, the foreclosure of plural possibilities through the application of force is precisely what constitutes sovereignty.

That brings us back to the peculiar alchemy of a sovereignty's founding moments, which transmute some inhabitants of a given territory into citizens; some into owners of people and others into property; some into free "passive citizens"—such as women who lack the right to contract—and others into workers toiling outside the social safety net. The people who are not "the People" are denied the basic guarantee of the rule of law (its generality, its impartiality) even as they suffer its force. Agamben calls this state of internal exclusion "bare life." Butler describes it as "highly juridified," a dispossession that is "both expelled and contained . . . saturated with power precisely at the moment in which it is deprived of citizenship."[9] Between the rhetoric of an "indivisible" popular sovereignty that comprises "each" and "all" and the arithmetic of a regime's incorporation, the putative generality of the rule of law is belied by the partiality in and the particularity of its application.[10] The very generality of the rule itself, Carl Schmitt points out in an important restatement of the paradox of law, is made possible only by a sovereignty that he defines as the decision to create an exception to the rule. In the decision to suspend the law in relation to a particular event or group, the chaos "outside" gets contrasted with the law's inside, turning the latter into a "'homogeneous medium,'" a regular "situation in which judicial rules can be valid."[11]

In this twinned account of sovereignty and sex, the classifications ("the People," M/F) are the effects of decisions, not simple and transparent descriptions of something already there. "The People," as the authorizers of sovereignty, are not wandering around in some state of nature, ready to draw up the social contract; they are brought into being through the decision to exclude other, particular peoples.[12] And similarly, sex classifications are not a priori but are produced through the very decision that results in the classification. What gives the act of putting an M or an F on a record its performative power is the contrast between describing the world and creating it, the very contrast that gives the law its productive force. Decisions about legal sex are best understood not as the result of a rule being applied to a particular case but as moments in which the exception consolidates the normative categories.

Rules for sex classification become explicit when it becomes necessary to account for the anomalies of transsexuality, intersexuality, and gender deviance. The mistaken case serves as the condition of possibility for the entire edifice of sex classification.[13] If there were no possibility of anomaly, for infelicitous or deviant cases, there would be no need for a classification system. It would not be subject to debate, evaluation, or measurement; it would be prior, really outside the social. Writing about sovereignty in general, Bonnie Honig puts it thus: "In every system (every practice), whether linguistic, cultural, or political, there is a moment or place that the system cannot account for. Every system is secured by placeholders that are irrevocably, structurally arbitrary and prelegitimate. They enable the system but are illegitimate from its vantage point." This undecidability is the paradox of sovereignty. Honig continues, "No signature, promise, or performative—no act of foundation—possesses resources adequate to guarantee itself . . . each and every one necessarily needs some external, systemically illegitimate guarantee to work."[14] Legal scholar Karl Llewellyn's remarks on statutory construction ("to effect its purpose a statute may be implemented beyond its text");[15] de Man's reading of Rousseau, noting that "every text generates a referent that subverts the grammatical principle to which it is owed its constitution"; Derrida's argument about the centrality of the anomalous case, the accident, the marginal, the deviant, and the parasitical to the "structure called normal or ideal"[16]—all suggest that purportedly anomalous cases/particulars are central to the construction of the general, the rule.

J. L. Austin's speech act theory provides another way of describing the paradox of sovereignty that has so troubled (yet constituted) the political theory tradition. Some statements are said to describe something, others to do something. The former type, which Austin named "constative," can be evaluated as true or false; the latter, which Austin named "performative," refer to utterances that do something, that carry out an act, or attempt to. An example of a constative statement would be, "They are married." An example of a performative statement would be, "I now pronounce you man and wife." According to Austin, a performative utterance like this one, "spoken seriously" as part of a conventional procedure with the appropriate people taking part, is an example of a case "in which to say something is to do something."[17] Performative speech acts cannot be evaluated as true or false, but rather as successful or unsuccessful, felicitous or infelicitous.[18]

Common sense tells us that a doctor's identification of an infant's sex at birth as male or female is a simple description of the world as it is, albeit a very tiny piece of it. In the lexicon of Austin's speech act theory, the assignment of sex to an infant would be a constative statement: it's assumed that the statement "It's a boy!" can easily be evaluated as either true or false. It turns out, however, that distinguishing statements of fact from utterances that perform an action is not so simple. In fact, in working through the implications of his original typology, Austin decided that all constative statements are actually special cases of the performative: "The issuing of the utterance is the performing of an action . . . not just saying something."[19] As Jonathan Culler explains, "In English the sentence 'The cat is on the mat' is for some reason the stock example of a simple declarative sentence, your basic constative utterance. But 'The cat is on the mat' could be seen, rather, as the elliptical version of 'I hereby affirm that the cat is on the mat,' a performative utterance that accomplishes the act of affirming to which it refers. . . . Constative utterances also perform actions—actions of stating, affirming, describing, and so on. They are a kind of performative."[20] In this way, the idea that language simply and transparently represents the world is radically undermined by the fact that, in saying things, our statements are doing things. The SSA field officer's decision to reclassify my sex and a doctor's announcement of birth sex are both performative. A successful performative must follow "an accepted conventional procedure," must involve the appropriate persons, and must be executed completely and correctly.[21] Susan Stryker, writing about the scene in the hospital when her lover's child was born, provides a viscerally powerful and theoretically apt description of the violence of sex classification: "Gender attribution is compulsory; it codes and deploys our bodies in ways that materially affect us, yet we choose neither our marks nor the meanings they carry. This was the act accomplished between the beginning and the end of that short sentence in the delivery room: 'It's a girl.'" [22] After such a declaration (a shortened version of "I hereby affirm that it's a girl"), "female" or "F" gets recorded by the doctor on a form for the hospital registrar, who then submits the infant's vital statistics to the state.

States of affairs imputed to be outside of political conventions turn out to be internal to them. Saying something is natural is a command that it be so. While all constative statements are special cases of performative statements, while saying is doing, it's the claim that there is a difference between the two that matters. Indeed, the generative power of language to make something new depends on both the distinction between describing a state of affairs and effecting an action *and* the impossibility of maintaining that distinction. Significantly, Austin excludes literature, poetry, and plays from the notion of performative speech: "Surely," he writes, "the words must be spoken 'seriously' . . . to be taken 'seriously.'"[23] There is, he suggests, a real difference between a religious or civil official saying, "I now pronounce you man and wife" in a public ritual, and an actor saying it on a stage. Not taking place in "ordinary circumstances," these utterances are "hollow or void."[24] Utterances backed by the force of law—properly executed legal instruments that convey property, judges' decisions, legislative acts, administrative rulings—figure as paradigmatic serious performatives. By way of contrast, Austin repeatedly invokes the joke, alongside the poem, as an example of a nonserious utterance that must be set aside in discussions of statements that effect an action. These speech acts, Austin says, do not reflect the use of language in "ordinary circumstances": they are "aetiolations, parasitic uses . . . 'not serious' and 'not full normal' uses" in which "the normal conditions of reference may be suspended."[25]

By excluding these utterances as "citational" or "parasitical," Culler points out, Austin greatly limits the significance of his theory about the generative effects of language, its performative power to make the world. Even as he undoes the distinction between speech acts that describe the world and those that make it, Austin installs a new opposition—between the original and citational, the normal and the parasitic, the ordinary and the anomalous, the act of importance and the joke, the inaugural moment and its etiolated copy. Derrida, de Man, Butler, and, by this point, generations of literary theorists have rejected this setting aside of some speech acts as nonserious. Moreover, just as Austin worked through the opposition between saying and doing in speech to arrive at the conclusion that announcements of facts are really actions—actions that may fail or succeed—so have these theorists found the distinction between the serious and the nonserious to be untenable, but productively so.

It's not only nonserious utterances that are citational; statements that are serious, statements that "do things," are also citational. For a serious statement to be able to effect an action, it must be intelligible. And its intelligibility rests on its status as a repetition. Serious statements, such as promises, orders, and commands, are themselves iterations of previous statements, categories, linguistic conventions, and the long historical accretion of words already written and statements already said. Defining the serious in opposition to the nonserious puts the latter firmly within the realm of the former, "an essential, internal, and permanent part" of the "so-called 'standard case.'"[26] What Austin calls the abnormal or anomalous case, in which an original performative is "quoted" in a future derivative performance, gets contrasted with pure (or purer) acts of inauguration that do not cite but yet are somehow intelligible, which produce something new. For Derrida, the anomalous case—the accidental, the marginal, the deviant, the parasitical—is actually central to the "structure called normal or ideal."[27] Limiting performative utterances to the serious is an attempt, Derrida suggests, to install a regulatory ideal that would rule out the possibility that serious performatives also have quotation marks around them.[28] In the language of popular sovereignty and the social contract, this regulatory ideal purportedly structures the move from nature to political society. In that moment something new is said to be created through the serious utterance: the People. Getting rid of the quotation marks—insisting on the originality of the serious moment—becomes another way of smuggling convention back into an idealized nature, which operates as a regulatory principle of some sort of pre-political purity. And the assertion of seriousness, of originality, I suggest, also organizes the distinction between sex classification at birth and sex reclassification later in life. The former, even as it depends on a confusion between saying and doing, gets casts as an original moment, while sex reclassification becomes derivative, an anomalous citation, a monster, a joke, a rare accidental residual product of the gender binary, perhaps even a gesture of appeasement to a vocal but tiny identity politics group—but not really real. Why else continue with the system of sex classification at birth?

Accounts of sex reclassification circulate as jokes, as anomalies, and most definitely as "not full normal."[29] Indeed, what used to give stories of transgender individuals changing identity documents, marrying, or giving birth such charged valences—what propelled them to circulate so widely, even going viral—is that they were so out of the ordinary, so much so as to be almost, but not quite, unintelligible. Although Christine Jorgensen's very public transition took place in the middle of the last century, stories of gender transformation were seen as weirdly new well into the twenty-first century: brain teasers confounding our settled assumptions. So we have jokes, parasitism, citations, and etiolated copies on the one hand, and on the other we have serious performative utterances. Austin's examples suggest that if serious/nonserious were a continuum rather than a binary, the most serious would be those utterances backed by the force of law. How then do we account for the legal joke? The law's anomaly? Cases that are most definitely "not full normal"? What happens with a serious anomaly, a joke upon which laws act? What, in short, might be happening when state actors make decisions about sex reclassification?

It may seem that this theoretical discussion has wandered far from the issue before us: sex classification at the SSA. But, as it turns out, figuring out what is going on with the addition of an M or an F to a Numident Holder's record requires thinking through the relations between the general and the particular, the rule and the event, the classification decision and the force of law that makes M or F mean something—or rather, as this book argues, do something. A doctor announcing "It's a girl" in a hospital birthing room appears to be stating a fact, while an SSA field officer changing one's sex classification seems to be making a decision, evaluating the evidence presented to her in light of the agency's rules. According to this view, sex classification at birth is a simple fact: sex is already there, easily identified, not a matter that would need to be settled through policy negotiations. The anomalous event of someone requesting a change of sex, on the other hand, seems to belong to the category of things that have to be figured out, decided; if not a joke, it is at least some sort of freakish oddity. With the emergence of individuals who contested their legal sex classification, agencies had to come up with policies to handle such cases. Certainly, when the Social Security Act was first passed in 1935, legislators had not imagined that the agency would ever need to reclassify the sex of individuals. (That legislation motivated people to get birth certificates for themselves and their children.) But once enough individuals came forward requesting that the M in their records be changed to an F, or the F to an M, and once those claims had been made legitimate by the authority of medical discourse, a rule was developed: "Applicant must submit a letter from his or her surgeon or the attending physician verifying that the sex change surgery was completed."[30]

Reclassification of one's legal sex is a clearly political matter, not prior to policy, decisions, or interpretation. So too, however, is the edifice of sex classification. The after-the-fact hacks to accommodate the anomalous situation, the nonserious, and the residual "none-of-the-above" individuals illuminate the constructedness of the system. Sex classification in general, then, is, among other things, an effect of language, and legal sex classification in particular is an effect of sovereignty. That is, it's not just the anomalous cases of individuals who want to change their legal sex classification that's at issue here; it's all the law's sex classifications, even ones that turn out to never change over a lifetime. The Ms and Fs on everyone's records and identity documents don't refer to an original pre-political state, an uncontestable already-present truth, analogous to "the People" in the traditional story of the founding; the classifying is itself a product of decisions that create the authority they depend on for their legitimacy. Sex assignment, as an effect of sovereignty, is yet another paradox of that fabulously retroactive moment of inauguration, where the indeterminacy between facts and decision, nature and convention, might and right, is and ought, combusts to generate something new. Taking the argument further, Ms and Fs on all our identity documents are effects, as wrapped up with the paradox of sovereignty. When state actors classify one's sex, they are not simply making a statement, a constative statement to be evaluated as true or false. Sex classification is also a performative statement—it is doing something. In designating an M or an F to be attached to the individual, states are making a decision that becomes true by virtue of the state's power to make a classification, as per Hobbes's dictum: "Authority, not truth, makes the law." This is not just a matter of applying a rule to a particular case, but a matter of creating the rule, making the law. For each individual, each body and particular constellation of sex characteristics, one's sex assignment is an inaugural decision—though these inaugural decisions are endlessly repeated.

Many Paradoxes, Many Sovereignties

The paradox of sovereignty analysis, coupled with the recognition that sex classification partakes of similarly arbitrary exercises of power, provides a necessary critical counterpoint to the popular sovereignty narrative. Butler's invocation of the performative and the citational, and Derrida's identification of the centrality of the anomalous, are meant to show there is no pre-political truth to gender or the sex binary. I don't disagree with that conclusion. But pointing out that such decisions are not the product of God or nature, that they are buttressed through repetition and citation, should not be the end of the analysis. That sex classification is arbitrary does not entirely answer the question before us *because there is not just one decision about sex classification, but many.* How can we account for the contradictory decisions? How can we account for situations in which state actors make *different* decisions about the *same* individual?

The third approach to understanding the relation of sex classification to politics—the approach that animates this book—focuses on contradictory decisions about sex classification at *different* agencies, jurisdictions, and levels of government. Because there are many distinct state actors creating rules for defining sex, it's not all that useful to direct all our attention to sovereignty and "the State"; instead, understanding sovereignty as encircled by, or folded into, processes of governmentality might be more useful. Rather than focusing mostly on the inauguration of sovereignty and its constitutive exclusions, this approach considers sex classification in relation to traditional police powers and administrative apparatuses. Unlike the political categories that are thought to preexist the moment of sovereignty's creation, traditional police powers *really were* "always already" there—even before the constitutive moment of a founding. Here I read the tropes of sovereignty and the exception regarding lesser noticed (and much less sexy) apparatuses and domains of governmentality that even Foucault found too dull to look into:[31] administration, unenumerated police powers, the population, norms of classification that precede inaugural moments, texts as dull as the Domesday Book, regulatory decisions and interpretive rules, and the US Social Security Administration's manual for field personnel. This approach also decenters the primacy of the idea of the state as singular.

While the idea that the exclusion of a class of people labeled "transgender" subtends the general class of normatively sexed people may be analytically and politically compelling, it's also mistaken. Certainly, general rules and hegemonic norms are shaped by what they expel, dismiss, prohibit. But it's important that we not generalize about particular exclusions by suggesting, for example, that the situation of all "transgender people" in relation to sex classification is the same. Individuals whose gender identity differs from what is traditionally associated with the sex assigned to them at birth may be included or excluded from systems of sex classification (that is, their sex may or may not be designated as they would choose) based on their birth sex or current genital configuration or any number of contingencies—even the credentials of the professionals proffering evidence of their sex change can matter. Nor should we oversimplify by positing that a norm or rule in one place is necessarily the same as norms or rules in other places, and that all these rules reflect a single organizing principle for all sex-based classification. Such meta-level conclusions are not borne out by the analysis of the many state rules and decisions defining male and female. Configurations of "what sex is" change, often depending on the actual policy in question, and can be buried deep inside the "cracks and crevices of the administrative state."[32] The exclusions are not global—mandating that all "transgender people" step to the side, becoming strangers, equally, to every kind of law and state decision—but specific to particular state projects.

I've been using "the state" in the singular to refer to it as an idea and in the plural to refer to enacted laws, administrative policies and rules, and judges' decisions. I also use "state actor" to refer to the particular legislatures, courts, and agencies that issue these decisions, though perhaps "actor" implies an intentionality that I don't mean to suggest. As a concept, the modern state is thought to be rational, hierarchically ordered, and structured with clear divisions of territorial and institutional jurisdiction. In the United States, "the state" is characterized by a division of authority between the federal and state governments and between the various branches of government at all levels. All those powers, however, are ultimately thought to be made legitimate by the US Constitution. Justified in its various forms by political theorists of different stripes, narrated in foundational documents like the Constitution, and evoked by individuals and movements seeking redress against perceived wrongs it commits, this conceptual state becomes the target of and the solution for arguments for justice. Should it ensure free markets or erase poverty? Should it promote morality or guarantee the rights of individuals to pursue their own ideas of the good? Should it regulate business or let the market police itself? Should it educate the illiterate or incarcerate them? Should it kill or rehabilitate? Should it act like a nanny or an umpire? In popular debates, the state is portrayed as some sort of Platonic ship—steered by a leader, all hands following the orders of the captain, and always headed toward a destination, though the ship may change course when a different crew takes over.

Perhaps what underlies assumptions that sex definition should make sense is our belief that "the state" expresses an underlying coherence, that it knows what it's doing. The ataxic disarray of state actors in the United States results from the uncountable number of norms, institutions, and processes across all jurisdictions—from legislatures, courts, departments, and agencies to elected officials, political appointees, and civil servants working under the "color of law," to constitutions, laws, regulations, administrative rules, and informal norms and practices. What makes this hard to fathom, Timothy Mitchell has suggested, is that while in actuality states are messy, diffuse, and ambiguous, the "public imaginary of the state as an ideological construct is more coherent."[33] As Wendy Brown explains, "Despite the almost unavoidable tendency to speak of the state as an 'it,' the domain we call the state is not a thing, system, or subject but a significantly unbounded terrain of powers and techniques, an ensemble of discourses, rules, and practices, cohabiting in limited, tension-ridden, often contradictory relation with one another."[34] The very use of the phrase "*the* state" expresses and reinforces this misconception. It's the stories we tell about popular sovereignty and the constitutional architecture of the "united" states that give shape to the disorderly array of activities, rules, and laws operating with the force of law. Over our history, as the federal government grew in size and reach, and as the Bill of Rights was extended to cover the individual states and so diminished states' prerogatives to organize social relations based on local custom, that imagined shape congealed into a structure with cleanly delineated lines of hierarchical authority: the federal government at the apex, state and local governments below. Likewise, stories perpetuating the idea that sex is simply "nature" render the disorder, the messiness, the actual indeterminacy of that category neat and clear by putting it spatially "outside" of politics and temporally "before" the creation of political society. "Sex," however, is just as messy and diffuse a concept as "the state." And so, if the only thing we know for sure about sex is what a state actor says it is in any particular instance, and if "the state" is not unitary, coordinated, and hierarchically organized—if, as Foucault suggests, "the state is only a composite reality and a mythicized abstraction whose importance is much less than we think"[35]—then it should come as no surprise that state definitions of sex are also plural.

Indeed, focusing on a generalized idea of *the state* can obscure what is actually happening in the local, micro, particular sites where public authority is being exercised. In her work on the federal regulation of homosexuality in the twentieth century, Margot Canaday starts with the premise that "we can see the state through its practices; the state is 'what officials do.'"[36] Accordingly, rather than beginning with the concept of the state and then measuring what state actors do in light of that concept, we might follow Gilles Deleuze and ask: "In what situations, where and when does a particular thing happen, how does it happen, and so on? A concept, as we see it, should express an event rather than an essence."[37] The events examined in the project at hand are decisions on sex definition. My method centers on those events, rather than on the institutions from which they issue: I do not look at courts, but at decisions. Not at departments of motor vehicles, but at application of their policies to individuals. Not at legislatures, but at their enactments of sex. Not at prisons and jails, but at their practices of sex segregation.

Just as the concept of the state can get in the way of seeing what state actors do, distinguishing between an institution and its actions can also be misleading. (This is the problem with the political science-y term "state *actor*.") The habit of making that distinction is so common that most of us don't realize we do it. But the distinction often structures our analysis, because a certain chain of logic proceeds from it: identifying the institution as an already-existing object, attributing to that object a certain rationality and agency based on its stated function, and understanding its actions in light of that function.[38] Without a determined effort to resist this tendency, a sort of prescriptive functionalism takes over. We come back full circle to the idea of the state, where analyses of what the state (or one of the institutions that constitute it) is doing are shaped by views of what the state (or the institution) should do. Perhaps more in political science than in any other discipline, institutions become the independent variables that explain everything else. From that starting point, the research agenda is to account for differences between institutions in light of their particular settings, histories, and other contingencies. Matters that fall outside the institution's mission or that are merely incidental to it, such as sex definition, don't intrude into that sort of analysis.

But sometimes the most political of decisions—those that deprive, exclude, or distribute—are the ones deemed most insignificant, or are not even recognized as decisions in the first place. It's certainly not the stated purpose of departments of motor vehicles to decide what sex is. In New York State, the DMV's mission is to "provide quality customer service, promote traffic safety, protect consumers, verify identities, issue secure documents, provide information services, protect the privacy of personal information, and collect revenues, all for the benefit of the people of this state."[39] From the slightly more distanced perch of the political scientist, one might say a DMV functions as part of the state's traditional police force, its purpose being to safeguard the health and safety of the population. DMVs carry out that work by regulating motorized vehicles and licensing their drivers. But across the United States, these agencies—as well as many other state actors—do define sex. DMVs create policies, list the evaluative criteria, and use those metrics to judge individuals applying to change their sex on their licenses. Those definitions and decisions appear not as political decisions but as descriptions. To ventriloquize a generic public official: "Male and female exist outside the context of this institution. We've consulted the experts, and now we've developed fair and objective criteria for evaluating whether someone has changed their sex." Sometimes, more often at smaller municipal agencies, these policies are characterized as lowly "housekeeping" or "interpretive" rules; sometimes, they are thought to be so trivial that they're not promulgated as any type of rule but are simply distributed in written memos or even by word of mouth to the agency's employees.

"The state," then, is a poor excuse for an independent variable, since it doesn't come with any absolute preset values. States are not limned in advance by any foundational text, whether it be the US Constitution or the mission statement cited in the New York State DMV's annual report. States are brought into being through their actions. One of these actions is saying what sex is. Decisions about sex, then, play a role—along with many other sorts of decisions—in bringing states into being. Actually, the state is rather like sex. As ideas, both "the state" and "sex" are comfortably fixed, springing forth from a foundational document or from nature, clearly bounded by an authorizing document or by the body. But in practice, there is no singular entity that is "the state," just a plurality of states. States are not defined in advance of the processes that bring them into being. What state actors actually do vastly exceeds their stated functions, just as sex definition does much more than simply describe people.

Instead of an independent and a dependent variable, I've got two dependent variables. All we know about sex is what a particular state actor says it is. All we know about states is that their decisions are backed by the force of law (violence threatened or exercised in the service of legitimate authority). Moreover, as thinkers from Walter Benjamin to Agamben have told us, that notion is at best a tautology: the legitimate authority of the law is installed only through the force that underwrites the law's legitimacy. At worst, the real claim is more brutal: violence begets the law. On the question of sex classification, it is even messier: many of the rules governing sex classification are informal rules. Informal "housekeeping" rules—on putatively obvious or unimportant matters—are not backed by the force of law, according to the Supreme Court.[40] Yet those simple "housekeeping" rules still produce important legal effects, and challenging them requires deploying the same resources (attorneys, arguments, experts) that must be deployed when challenging formal rules.

So, to summarize, we have groups and individuals contesting the rules on sex reclassification. We have state actors using different sets of rules to determine who is M and who is F. We have by now a longish history in feminist and gender studies differentiating sex from gender, the sexed body from gendered social formations. We have a theoretical revolution that transposes the relation between sex and gender such that the former is now understood (in academia at least) as an effect of the latter. The material qualities that fall under the category of sex certainly do exist; they don't, however, provide an incontrovertible basis for the binary distinction between male and female in all cases. As state actors render this unworkable yet naturalized notion of sex binary into regulatory rules, it's not surprising that they make different decisions about the definitive criteria, whether those criteria be birth sex, genital surgery or body modification of some sort, gender identity, or some combination of these. When these different rules are applied to individuals who perceive that they've been misclassified, the rules produce inconsistent results: the same individual might be classified as male by one government agency and female by another, or as male according to the case law in one state and female according to that of another. Someone might have managed to change the sex classification on her birth certificate to female, but a department of corrections determines she is male for the purposes of incarceration. Yet even though, collectively, the regulatory apparatuses for sex classification are awash in contradictions, they haven't collapsed. Agencies still print Ms or Fs on documents and add those documents to records, still evaluate reclassification requests from individuals like myself, still amend those records when the request has met the criteria it requires for change of sex, and still deny other requests that fail to meet the criteria.

It certainly makes sense that those in gender studies and trans rights circles understand the rules on sex classification as contradictory. But what do we do with these contradictions? How should they be approached analytically, or politically? Analytically, the best work in gender and more recently transgender studies has denaturalized gender, untethered it from the body, shown it to be an effect of particular arrangements rather than of biological sex, and challenged the perception that sex itself is epistemologically transparent. Yet in this critical work, what might be the first step in this sort of analysis—pointing out that sex is unstable and that classification systems attempt to stabilize it, but that there is no foundation for it—often becomes its concluding point. Perhaps that self-imposed limit results from the fact that, outside of the intellectual spaces in which the understanding of gender and sex as social artifacts is axiomatic, it's still very much an uphill battle to shift the thinking of students, readers, friends, families, policymakers, and colleagues with regard to sex and gender, nature and culture. In that context, arriving at the contradiction as the culmination of the project is laudatory. Or perhaps contradictions are presented as conclusions rather than jumping-off points because of what Stuart Hall describes as the progressive critical agenda's habit of limiting itself to the task of simply *identifying* ideological inconsistencies. In an essay on the contradictory politics of conservatism in Britain, Hall argues, "In our intellectual way, we think that the world will collapse as a result of a logical contradiction: this is the illusion of the intellectual—that ideology must be coherent, every bit of it fitting together, like a philosophical investigation."[41] Pointing out the impossibility of the project of securing gender to sex to the body in a perfect universal binary will not necessarily conjure away deeply rooted commonsense notions of sex and gender, however. Merely highlighting contradictions does not inevitably destroy the regulatory work of installing and arranging difference, nor will it lead to understanding what work sex does for states.

Most people, including transgender advocates, feel that there is an injustice in the contradiction, in treating two "alike" individuals differently. Even people not interested in transgender recognition claims find it absurd that two "alike" individuals—both assigned male at birth, with female gender identities and identical histories of body modification— end up with opposite sex classifications from different agencies, or when the *same* individual has F on some state-issued documents and M on others. When a contradiction is thought to inhere in the sex classification assigned to two distinct individuals, it depends on the assumption that two things share the same essential "whatness"—a sex assigned at birth, a genital configuration, a social gender that is consistently and publicly presented, a gender identity. If two people both have what is taken to be the ideal characteristic for the legal definition of a male (for some this might be a penis, for others a male gender identity), but one is walking around with an M on his identity document and the other with an F, it appears paradoxical.

But what if we, conversely, located the *whatness* of legal sex not in any ideal attribute or empirically normed combination of attributes, but in the M or F stamped on the state-issued document or kept in a state agency's records? Sex, then, is—indeed "means"—nothing more than the printed mark of M or F, or the electrical pulses that generate the specific binary code of zeroes and ones (01001101 for M and 01000110 for F) that turn into an M or an F on a computer screen. Pretty much everyone— from SSA bureaucrats to legislators to policymakers to transportation security agents to court clerks—imagines that the M or F refers to something beyond itself (that is the whole point of language, after all!). But if we let go of the idea that there is any "there there," any *whatness*, to sex apart from what the state says it is, the contradiction evaporates. State decisions about one's sex—or, more precisely, the M or the F or the X (for non-binary) stamped on documents or coded in records—becomes the only true thing we know. Everything else is in motion. The point of this line of thought is not (ultimately) to forgo arguments about justice and gender, but to see how our assumptions about what sex really is or how it ought to be defined (not the least of which is the notion that sex is a thing that exists, something that we can know and argue about and attempt to codify) might get in the way of understanding better what the state is doing. Instead of organizing this discussion around the idea that what we know about sex is an effect of gender, I want to crop the picture radically and suggest that sex is nothing but a state effect.

Stepping away from the notion of a contradiction also moves us away from arguments about what the state *ought to do* for the sake of consistency and fairness in sex designation. In fact, in not holding sex steady in our grasp (whether that grasp be "essentialist" or "postmodern"), we also loosen our grip on our image of the state as an edifice or personage, perhaps even a benevolent if slumbering night watch-man who will make things right when prodded awake. Letting go of our grasp of what sex "really is" means letting go of our grasp of the state. We don't know what "the state" *is*, but we can figure out what it does. Entering into the analysis by thinking we know what sex is, or what the state is, having them fixed in our mind's eye—as a priori facts, as edifices—makes it much more difficult to understand the pro-cesses through which they come into being. Instead of seeing the ap-parent contradictions produced as a result of these different rules not making sense, let's presume that *the contradiction exists only because of our assumptions about sex and the state*: that they are unitary, inten-tional, ever-rational, ever-centralized, clearly circumscribed, identifi-able. Nietzsche's critical intervention—that "there is no 'being' behind doing, acting, becoming; 'the doer' is merely a fiction imposed on the doing"[42]—applies equally as well to the construction of state effects as it does to constructions of sex. Moreover, this "doing"—in this case, the doing consists of assigning people to one sex or the other—is not a "once-and-for-all" deed through which a system of sex classification produces itself, but is endlessly recurring.[43] Writing about the larger formations of legal, cultural institutions and discourses that organize gender, Wendy Brown points out that "gender does not exist prior to its regulation," nor does the apparatus that regulates gender exist prior to the act of regulating: "There is no sharp distinction between what is produced and what is regulating—we are not simply targets but vehicles of power. Thus . . . we must be able . . . to understand regulation as only and always materializing in its effects, and to understand these effects as specific to that which is being regulated."[44] In this way, it is not only useful but imperative to think of the sex definition (that which is regu-lated) and the state actors/decisions (that which regulate) in relation to each other. Decisions on sex classification turn processes of sex and states into things—intelligible identities and rules, backed by the force of law, congealing into institutions.

For any particular state apparatus at a given moment, the apparently minor issue of the criteria for sex classification might be supporting more weight than we imagine; calling for its reform might involve more changes than we anticipate, and consequently engender more resistance than initially seems reasonable. So it's important to understand in each particular context, no matter how apparently mundane, what sex is doing and how that doing is imbricated with other systems of social stratification. We don't know what a politics of resistance will look like until we understand what it is we're resisting.

Ultimately, the arguments of this book should not just better our understanding of states' decisions about sex, but also inform a politics that challenges these injustices. Certainly, there is a real harm here—many transgender people are *mis*classified by states and do not wish to be— that should be resolved. But the conviction that sex misclassification is unjust is not grounded in the findings of science or medical authority. Nor is it based on any utopian ideal of a state that does not classify and does not (mal)distribute. Of course, state decisions on sex classification have real effects on individuals and those effects can be unjust. Having the "wrong" sex designation creates obstacles to full and equal participation in social and civic life. As an advocate for transgender equality, I have relied on the traditional rights-based approach to recognition and have crafted policy proposals for agencies to reform their standards for determining sex. I have sat on agency advisory committees and worked with officials to change standards for sex reclassification, relying heavily on the "medical model" in the process. As a political theorist, I have also critiqued attempts to fit into systems of sex classification and argued for the "disestablishment" of sex.[45] I have suggested that the goal of recognition leaves intact the power of the state to decide who gets what, and that ending its ability to use sex to distribute resources, rights, and privileges—marriage, and the benefits that derive from it, is the most obvious example—should be a priority for the movement. Like many in and around movements for transgender rights, transgender equality, and gender justice, I hold both positions simultaneously. They are not necessarily incompatible. One might see them, instead, as inhabiting different time frames, or moving at different speeds: one is a short-term objective of recognition to alleviate the material problems of misclassified individuals in the here and now, and the other is a long-term vision of a government that does not tell anyone what sex they are. Despite my earlier breakdown of the various camps and their arguments, these different viewpoints are not necessarily held by distinct sets of people. The appearance of one or the other might depend, instead, on what position is most intelligible and useful in a particular context.

Transgender people have often become inhabitants of residual categories, that which was unaccounted for during the construction of the category. The answer, though, is not to denaturalize the sex of only transgender people and leave the a priori and apolitical sex classification of everyone else intact and unquestioned. The approach here is to see all sex classification as falling, firmly and decisively, within the realm of politics. Indeed, to undertake an investigation into the former without the latter—to show how sex classification policies for those who change their sex are the stuff of politics and to neglect how all sex classifications further state ends—would buttress the very binary that positions transgender people outside of it: as the anomaly, the joke, the unanticipated remainder.

By allowing the individual to fade into the background and by looking at the differences among state actors on the question of sex, it becomes easier to see the phenomenon of sex classification as a matter of and for politics. If we temporarily let go of the idea that there is a transparent and objective reality to sex and that we know what it is but that most state actors don't, and if for a little while we drop the claim that it's unjust for governments to put people in the "wrong" box or in any box at all, we can develop a deeper understanding of what sex classifications *do*. And they do different things, for different reasons. There is not one state ("the state"), but many state actors, and they do different things. "Discrepancies" (birth, genitalia, secondary sex characteristics, or gender identity) in how sex is verified can be a measure of those differences. We can see that states *do* something—in this case, they make sex classifications—and it is in the doing that they are brought into being; they are not a priori. (That is the contemporary iteration of the sovereignty narrative.) Similarly, when it comes to classification, the Ms or Fs don't refer to properties or to traits (things), but to actions, and they are always in motion. No doubt, the very idea of an M or an F on a record *doing* something seems to be a bit much. Despite the revolution in thinking about sex and gender that moved us into the third wave of feminism, in the realm of sex classification, of M or F, it's hard to think of sex as anything but a property (one that purports to signify something real), an effect. But as I'll show in the following chapters, sex *does do* things, make things happen; it's not only an effect. In its work of setting out distinctions—and in the indeterminacy of those distinctions—it generates peoples, families, nations; it recognizes, it surveils, it distributes, it charts out lines of inheritance, it provides the authority to freeze the transition of incarcerated people, it denies or secures the relationship of parents to children, it naturalizes citizenship, and it turns the metaphor of blood into a legal/political fact.

4

Till Birth Do Us Part

Marriage, ID Documents, and the Nation-State

For those critical of identity politics, the transgender rights movement often stands as its reductio ad absurdum, fixated as it seems to be on pronouns and bathrooms. Imagined this way, the movement appears to have a narrow political agenda, one that does not resonate with the problems that concern most voters.[1] While the bathroom issue is relatively new to the cisgender public—though transgender people were individually and collectively negotiating access to bathrooms long before the matter became the subject of plebiscites and state house bills—the transgender rights movement and the wider LGBT movement have been critiqued by the left (including the queer left) as representative of all that's wrong with identity politics. From this perspective, LGBT rights movements seek nothing more than inclusion and representation in the liberal (now neoliberal) order. At the other end of the political spectrum, the right wing has been dragging LGB rights claims into the culture wars since the 1980s, using the specter of same-sex marriage and the erosion of traditional gender norms—now taken to the extreme by a movement that seeks to allow men in dresses into women's bathrooms!—to unify its base. Indeed, the Trump administration's attack on LGBT people particularly targeted transgender people. From both perspectives, battles for LGBT rights divert attention from questions of economic justice. (For the right, of course, that's a good thing.)

The purported antagonism between identity politics and economic justice is a contemporary iteration of a long tradition in orthodox left thinking that distinguishes economy from culture. Those who emphasize economy believe it is the appropriate object of political mobilization; any other divisions only serve capital by obscuring the material source of inequality. According to this view, differences based on race, nationality, gender, and religion—and the unequal treatment that results from those differences—are ultimately epiphenomenal. Reformist quests for equal treatment based on these surface distinctions shouldn't be confused with the real struggle for human emancipation. This opposition has often been fashioned as a battle between movements seeking recognition of differences and those seeking redistribution of wealth and an end to class-based exploitation. In a highly influential essay reframing this opposition, philosopher Nancy Fraser argued that "the struggle for recognition" had become "the paradigmatic form of political conflict in the late twentieth century." In the essay's opening salvo, Fraser announced that "demands for 'recognition of difference' fuel struggles for groups mobilized under the banners of nationality, ethnicity, 'race,' gender, and sexuality. In these 'postsocialist' conflicts, group identity supplants class interest as the chief medium of political mobilization. Cultural domination supplants exploitation as the fundamental injustice. And cultural recognition displaces socioeconomic redistribution as the remedy for injustice and the goal of political struggle."[2]

For Fraser, some forms of identity politics, such as the demands articulated by people of color and women, can redress both injustices of misrecognition and those of maldistribution. For example, the racialization of poverty and the unpaid reproductive and domestic labor of women are matters of economic injustice rather than just status-based inequality. Indeed, even as Fraser used the recognition-redistribution framework to theorize the displacement of class politics by identity politics, she also saw culture and economy as deeply imbricated, going so far as to describe the tension between the two terms as a "false antithesis."[3] In Fraser's view, the antagonism does hold, however, when it comes to homosexuality: injustices based on sexuality, she writes, are "quintessentially a matter of recognition."[4] Indeed, it seems as if the coherence of the entire framework depends on positioning queer demands as the ideal case of the politics of recognition. By putting sexuality on only the cultural side of the dichotomy, Fraser rehearses old-school reductionist Marxist thought, in which homosexuality was seen as merely epiphenomenal. In response, Judith Butler returned to Marx and Engels's texts on the family and reproduction to show how capitalist social formations organize sexuality, including non-normative sexualities, in systems of production and reproduction, and thus distribution.[5]

Given the assumptions of the antagonists outlined above, it's difficult to imagine a struggle for justice more squarely focused on cementing the link between identity and recognition than that of transgender rights. Rules for deciding whether one will be labeled male or female might be the very best exemplar of a politics of recognition. What could exemplify the desire for recognition better than a group demanding that governments acknowledge their gender identity? Indeed, while Fraser's original analysis did not touch on the misrecognition of transgender people, she later identified transgender issues as the epitome of neoliberalism. "Rejecting 'economism' and politicising 'the personal,'" she wrote in 2013, "feminists broadened the political agenda to challenge status hierarchies premised on cultural constructions of gender difference. The result should have been to expand the struggle for justice to encompass both culture and economics. But the actual result was a one-sided focus on 'gender identity' at the expense of bread-and-butter issues."[6] For Fraser, what could have been a more robust feminist approach to economic injustice was displaced by the fetishizing of cultural struggles over "gender identity," a term that is almost always deployed to signal transgender people.

The politics of recognition propelling the mainstream transgender rights movement has also been subjected to thoroughgoing critiques from leftist and antiracist scholars *within* transgender studies, including Aren Aizura, Che Gossett, Jin Haritaworn, Dan Irving, Viviane Namaste, C. Riley Snorton, and Dean Spade, among others.[7] Some of the most trenchant appraisals show how white supremacy and class inequality are reproduced by a movement that assents to current political arrangements by seeking inclusion within them. Indeed, much of this work is modeled on critiques of assimilationist GLB politics that emerged at the beginning of this century. In 2004, Lisa Duggan raised the specter of a "new homonormativity" in gay politics, one "that does not challenge heterosexist institutions and values, but rather upholds, sustains, and seeks inclusion within them."[8] Similarly, an emerging "queer liberalism" was identified in 2005 by queer theorists David Eng, Jack Halberstam, and José Muñoz, who worried that the "contemporary liberal demands of a nationalist gay and lesbian U.S. citizen-subject petitioning for rights and recognition before the law" reflects "a type of reactionary (identity) politics of national and global consequence." Instead of working to dismantle the institutions that structure inequality—marriage, the military, the family, the capitalist workplace—the gay and lesbian political imaginary had shrunk to seeking "a place at the table," mere formal equality and recognition.[9] Post-9/11, homonormativity transformed into homonormative nationalism, or "homonationalism." Jasbir Puar, writing in 2008, examined "collusions between homosexuality and U.S. nationalism" that lead to the incorporation of the "good" gay subject "into the body of the normalized nation."[10] These insights into the trajectory of queer and trans politics are important and necessary: the question of present-day transnormativity and its role in the reproduction of economic inequality, anti-Black social policies, and misogyny is taken up in the discussions of incarceration in chapter 5 and of gender pluralism in the conclusion. There is no doubt that trans people's appeals to be classified according to gender identity align with classical liberal constructions of the rights-bearing subject. The project of this book, however, is not to rehash these powerful critiques of reformist politics and the subjectification and interpellation of "transgender people" through discourses of belonging, citizenship, and nationalism; it is to understand why state apparatuses *respond* to petitions to have one's gender identity recognized as they do.

This chapter, then, troubles the relegation of sex reclassification to the noneconomic. It shows how the status-based wrongs experienced by people whose gender identity doesn't conform to social expectations have been deeply imbricated in matters of distributive injustice. To do so, it is set in a moment in recent US history when transgender demands for sex reclassification collided with the institution of heterosexual marriage. The analysis centers on the period between 1999 and 2004 and examines appellate state court decisions that invalidated marriages involving a transgender person. (Until *Obergefell v. Hodges*, the 2015 Supreme Court decision finding bans on same-sex marriage unconstitutional, states could and indeed did ban same-sex marriage. In 2004, Massachusetts became the first state to allow same-sex marriage.) For the transgender person in these marriages, the union was an opposite-sex union. These courts decided, however, that the sex assigned at birth remained one's sex for the purposes of marriage; that meant that these marriages were, in the eyes of the court, same-sex marriages, invalid under state law. What's especially significant, for the purposes of the "sex is as sex does" argument of this book, is that those decisions conflicted with sex reclassification policies on identity documents, which had been liberalizing over the previous three decades. For the purposes of identity documents (from passports to birth certificates to driver's licenses), sex was generally not fixed at birth.

What accounts for this bifurcation in sex reclassification policy? How could courts decide that sex was set for life at birth even as identity document policies were being revised to accommodate the needs of transgender people? How is it that state actors would reclassify the sex on an individual's identity document but, for the purposes of marriage, declare that sex was fixed at birth? This inconsistency makes sense only if we understand that these very dissimilar constructions of sex furthered different government projects. The purpose of an identity document is to establish a relationship between it and the person who carries it. Sex markers on the document that do not reflect the gender presentation of the person who carries it weaken that connection. An F on the driver's license of a balding, bearded man (me) hinders the public and private protectors of the security state. The relatively more liberal policies on sex reclassification with regard to identity documents reflect spatial logics, specifically the state's function of watching over individuals and tracking their movements across its territory. Marriage, on the other hand, furthers a very different kind of project, a distributive one, and is enunciated in the language of property and temporality.

Marriage

Since at least the late 1960s, activists across the United States have pushed to make it possible for people to change the sex designation on their identity documents. Before this time, individuals had requested changes in their sex classification and some, on a case-by-case basis, got the result they wanted. But it wasn't until the 1960s that advocates for what we now call transgender people turned to reforming policies. Over time, these efforts were successful: most states changed their policies on birth certificates and driver's licenses.[11] By 2004, all the states but Idaho, Ohio, and Tennessee would issue new or amend existing birth certificates to reflect the new sex—and "sex" was by far the most commonly used word.[12] The particular contours of those policies were far from ideal by today's standards, and many remain onerous. These policies required proof of surgery and often a legal name change. For example, the state of Arkansas then required, and still requires, "a certified copy of a court of competent jurisdiction indicating that the sex of an individual born in this state has been changed by surgical procedure and that such individual's name has been changed."[13] Since 2005, jurisdictions in bluer states have reformed these policies by dropping the requirement for proof of body modification—surgery and/or hormone therapy.[14] This is not to suggest that all policies and decisions on sex classification—at all levels of government, in all branches, in all jurisdictions, over the entire timespan of the modern administrative state—fall neatly on the side of the equation that fits the argument here. As with the study of any empirical phenomenon in the social sciences, there's a lot of messiness around the edges. But the differences in these years between the policies on sex classification for identity documents and those for the purposes of marriage are quite stark and bring the different governing logics into sharp relief.

Before I move further into the analysis of trans marriage cases, I offer a brief word on how those cases fell under the scrutiny of state courts. While they may be relatively rare in proportion to the general population, marriages involving one or more transgender parties were not necessarily exceptional. That is, the people getting married did not construe their legal union as an intentional act of gender subversion. Instead, these marriages happened like everyone else's: the weddings were rushed or planned; the result of a long-term engagement or a short one; and held at a courthouse, a reception hall, or a house of worship. The bureaucratic part of this ritual was also no different. Couples applied for a marriage license, paid a fee, presented identification to an official, and made arrangements for an officiant. In the cases discussed below, it's unlikely that the clerks who processed the applications for a marriage were aware that one of the parties had a transgender history. Had they been, these marriage license applications might possibly have been construed as attempts by people of the same sex to get married, and, because all states banned same-sex marriage at the time, the applications would have been denied. Many of these individuals would have assumed, understandably, that the sex classification on their passport or driver's license or birth certificate established their sex for the purposes of marriage. They would not have realized that their sex classification could change depending on what it was used for.

Of course, the vast majority of these marriages followed the same course as marriages of two cisgender people—ending in divorce or death—and the issue of a spouse's transgender status was never raised. But because of the sex classification issue, these marriages were vulnerable to challenges. In the case of divorce, sometimes the non-transgender party wanted to have the marriage declared invalid rather than obtain a divorce. This strategy, if successful, meant that any legal battles over child custody, alimony, or the disposition of property would be moot. In instances involving the death of the cisgender person in the marriage, cases were sometimes brought by a third party with an interest in the estate.[15]

Legal scholar Ruthann Robson has examined the decisions and advocacy in cases concerning transgender people and marriage and found that it "too often serves to recapitulate and reinscribe the most traditional visions of marriage and heterosexuality."[16] That's certainly true of both the earliest set of cases in the United States as well as the spate of later appellate cases on the question that I discuss below. Significantly, one of the first published cases on this question had a positive outcome for the transgender party. The 1976 case *M. T. v. J. T.* involved the dissolution of a marriage. "M. T." and her husband, "J. T.," had lived together for years before she had surgeries that removed her male sex organs, constructed a vagina, and added breast implants. She applied to New York State to change her birth certificate; soon after, the couple married. J. T. left the marriage, and argued in divorce proceedings that he should not have to pay alimony because M. T. was actually male and their marriage had never been valid. This argument failed to convince the two courts that considered it. According to the appellate court's reasoning, "if such sex reassignment surgery is successful and the postoperative transsexual is, by virtue of medical treatment, thereby possessed of the full capacity to function sexually as a male or female, as the case may be, we perceive no legal barrier, cognizable social taboo, or reason grounded in public policy to prevent that person's identification at least for the purposes of marriage to the sex finally indicated."[17] Because M. T. had the capacity for penis-vagina intercourse—and the record apparently established that they had intercourse—for the purposes of marriage M. T.

was a woman. Two years earlier, the same logic had produced a different judicial outcome in a New York State district court. This case concerned a man, "Mark B.," who had had a hysterectomy and top surgery and who took masculinizing hormones. Unfortunately, according to the judge in the case, he had not "successfully escaped" the female body. And what is the test of successfully escaping the bounds of one's birth sex? Again, it's the ability to engage in heterosexual intercourse. Without a penis, the judge said, he could not "perform male functions in marriage."[18]

But on a more granular level, the cases examined below, taking place between 1999 and 2004, can be distinguished from the earlier ones: the metric for heterosexuality undergoes a subtle shift.[19] M. T. and other lower-court cases make the action of "sex" essential to determining whether or not a marriage is an opposite-sex marriage. Is penis-vagina intercourse possible? If so, then the marriage is valid. But the later cases define sex as a status, focusing not on the activity of sex but on sex as a status assigned at birth. That difference provided a rationale that the courts used to rule, for example, that "fully post-operative" transgender women should be classified as male for the purposes of marriage. What had been sufficient for M. T. to be classified as a woman in 1976—"the full capacity to function sexually" as a woman—would no longer suffice. The outcome no longer depended on whether or not an individual could perform heterosexual intercourse, but instead became the question of whether sex could change. What altered between 1976 and these later cases? When M. T v. J. T. was decided in 1976, the issue of same-sex marriage was not yet a matter of widespread public debate; it had not yet been enrolled in the culture wars.[20] By the late 1990s, however, same-sex marriage had become one of the most divisive social issues of the day.

Christie Lee Littleton, née Cavazos and born in Texas, married a man named Jonathan Mark Littleton in Kentucky in 1989. When he died in 1996, Christie Littleton filed a medical malpractice suit against his physician, Mark Prange. Someone working for Prange's insurance company came up with a brilliant idea: if they could convince the court that Christie Littleton, classified as male at birth, was still legally male, her marriage would be invalid. If she wasn't the surviving spouse, she would lack standing to sue. In another case, J'Noel Gardiner, born in Wisconsin, had married Marshall Gardiner in Kansas in 1998; Marshall died intestate one year later. J'Noel, also assigned male at birth, had had her Wisconsin birth certificate changed to reflect her gender identity. Marshall Gardiner's son, Joe, argued that he was the sole heir to the estate, since J'Noel had been born male. J'Noel countered that she was legally female at the time of the marriage, and that, under the full faith and credit clause, the sex classification on her Wisconsin birth certificate should be recognized in Kansas. A third case involved the dissolution of the marriage between a transgender man, Michael Kantaras, and his wife, Linda Kantaras. Soon after they were married in 1989 in Florida, Michael adopted his wife's first child. During their marriage, Linda gave birth to a second child (with sperm from Michael's brother). When Michael filed for divorce and began proceedings to get custody of the children, Linda counterpetitioned. She argued that because Michael was transsexual, the marriage should be annulled and he should have no parental rights. She threw in, for good measure, that his adoption of her first child was nullified by Florida's ban on homosexual adoption.

The question of time sat at the crux of the analysis in these appellate marriage decisions. At what *time* does sex get fixed and begin to function as a guarantor of a subject's future gender identity? At birth? After particular surgeries? In interpreting the marriage statutes that banned same-sex marriage, the question became, as the *Littleton* decision put it in its second sentence, "*When* is a man a man, and *when* is a woman a woman?"[21] The *Gardiner* decision constructs the question before it as pinning "down the time when the two parties [must be] . . . of the opposite sex"—at birth, or at the moment of marriage?[22] The *Kantaras* decision asked whether or not "Michael was male at the time of marriage."[23] The 1999 *Littleton* decision, heavily cited in the *Kantaras* and *Gardiner* decisions, put it thus: "The deeper philosophical (and now legal) question is: can a physician change the gender of a person with a scalpel, drugs, and counseling, or is a person's gender immutably fixed at birth?"[24] In all three cases, the short answer is birth. "Once a man, always a man," the *Littleton* decision declared.[25] Michael Kantaras was female at birth, and female at the time of marriage, according to the Florida appellate court: "Until the Florida legislature recognizes sex-reassignment procedures and amends the marriage statutes to clarify the marital rights of a postoperative transsexual person, we must adhere to the common meaning of the statutory terms and invalidate any marriage that is not between persons of the opposite sex determined by their biological sex at birth."[26] In reviewing the literature on gender assignment at birth, the decisions in *Littleton*, *Gardiner*, and *Kantaras* point out that gender attribution is made on the basis of a *visual* inspection of an infant's genitalia at birth. J'Noel Gardiner, the Kansas court declared, is "a male because she had been identified on the basis of her external genitalia at birth as a male."[27] But Gardiner and Littleton had done everything they needed to do to change their outward physical appearances, as both courts acknowledged. Both litigants had submitted to the courts detailed medical reports and surgical records. According to the Texas court, "Through the intervention of surgery and drugs, Christie appears to be a woman."[28] For J'Noel Gardiner, the Kansas court said, her external sexual characteristics, "though all man-made . . . resemble those of the opposite sex."[29] Still, in these cases, the sex assigned at birth trumped all else.

For the purposes of marriage, then, in this pre-*Obergefell* era one's sex classification was fixed forever at birth—at least in the view of these appellate courts. This was, and remains, the position also adopted by many on the religious right and in the Republican Party.[30] Indeed, over time, as they began to notice the existence of transgender people, conservatives attacking same-sex marriage started to specify that sex referred to the sex assigned at birth. (And some proposals even called for fixing sex at conception!) In the early 2000s, state Republican Party platforms began recognizing a potential connection between sex reclassification policies and the bans on same-sex marriage. For example, the 2010 Idaho Republican Party platform called on government officials and legislators to "use all means possible to prevent expansion of the definition of marriage beyond that of a bond between one *naturally born* man and one *naturally born* woman" (italics added).[31]

Identification Documents

In March 2001, a woman living in Maryland but born in Pennsylvania petitioned a Maryland court to issue an order changing her name from a traditionally male one to Janet Heilig Wright and her sex classification from male to female. Maryland had a policy allowing the sex classification on birth certificates to be changed; to do so, one had to submit a court order indicating that one's sex "has been changed by surgical procedure."[32] While the Maryland Circuit Court granted Wright's petition for a name change, her request for a court order recognizing her as female was denied. After a loss at the first appellate level, Wright appealed to the state's highest court, the Maryland Court of Appeals. Living in Maryland, what was she to do? asked her attorney, the long-time trans rights advocate Alyson Meiselman. Since the state legislature had a statute on the books that made it possible for one to change the M or the F on a birth certificate issued in Maryland, the legislature had certainly recognized that sex can change. Why would the fact of her birth in Pennsylvania be the reason to deny her the opportunity afforded those born in Maryland? As a matter of fairness, the court should have applied that policy to residents of Maryland not born in the state. "Otherwise," the state justices suggested, two "similarly situated post-operative, male-to-female transsexuals—one born in Maryland, and one not born in Maryland—while both citizens of Maryland would be regarded differently by Maryland law: one as male, one as female."[33] In addition, they argued, if a Maryland court can issue orders granting a name change—another situation in which there is no party contesting the change—why can't it issue a similar order granting a change of sex? The court of appeals agreed. Writing for a unanimous panel of seven judges, Judge J. Wilner found that the lower court could rule on the question and directed it to do so.[34] Reviewing the medical facts about the "new" phenomenon of transsexualism, Wilner determined that sex can change.

It was not a groundbreaking decision: at that time, many agencies and legislatures had policies and statutes on the books making it possible to change one's sex classification. What's especially useful about this example of state action, however, is that, unlike most policy changes regarding birth certificates and driver's licenses, as a judicial decision it rehearsed in great detail the thinking behind it. In other policy arenas, the rationales are often less accessible. And the reasoning in *Heilig* provides a good point of comparison to the explanations in decisions about sex classification for the purposes of marriage.

As in the marriage cases, much of the court of appeals opinion focused on the question of sex classification itself.[35] Wilner produced an incredibly thorough review of the current medical literature on the topics of sex, gender, and transsexualism. A section in the opinion titled

"Transsexualism: Medical Aspects" runs over forty-six hundred words and cites thirty sources, from John Money to Milton Diamond to the Harry Benjamin International Gender Dysphoria Association (since renamed the World Professional Association for Transgender Health). The crux of the debate in legal arenas, the opinion observed, is whether gender, defined as a "psychosocial individuality or identity," or sex, which "denotes anatomical or biological" differences, is the "more relevant concept deserving of legal recognition."

To understand "what gender is and whether, or how, it may be changed," Wilner listed seven factors that medical discourses contain under the rubric of gender: (1) internal morphological sex (seminal vesicles/prostrate or vagina/uterus/fallopian tubes); (2) external morphologic sex (genitalia); (3) gonadal sex (testes or ovaries); (4) chromosomal sex (presence or absence of Y chromosome); (5) hormonal sex (predominance of androgens or estrogens); (6) phenotypic sex (secondary sex characteristics; e.g., facial hair, breasts, body type); and (7) personal sexual identity. After a lengthy review of the medical literature, Wilner concluded by enumerating the following "facts": (1) gender itself is a fact that may be established by medical and other evidence; (2) it may be, or possibly may become, other than what is recorded on the person's birth certificate; and (3) a person has a deep personal, social, and economic interest in having the official designation of his or her gender match what, in fact, it always was or possibly has become.[36]

This court had determined that sex can change. But which criteria should courts rely on to verify a change? The court of appeals left this question up to the district court, though it offered guidance in the form of a review of the requirements that other courts and agencies had set. Most policies, the court opined, require transsexuals to show that their "gender has been changed 'by surgical procedure.'"[37] Although one's psychosocial gender identity may be more relevant than genitalia or other biological factors, surgery signifies that the change is "permanent and irreversible."[38] The case was remanded back to the district court, which was instructed to give Wright the opportunity to present evidence of a permanent gender change. At this point, unfortunately, the litigation trail ends; it doesn't indicate if Wright was able to provide the evidence the lower court required to obtain the court order for which she had originally petitioned. But the ruling, and its rationale, remain.

This positive decision, however, ended with one important qualification. If Wright were to get the court order that the court of appeals deemed possible, would she be female once and for all, everywhere, for all purposes? No. In discussing the effect of such a court order, Judge Wilner made this very clear: "[Marriage] is an issue that is not before us in this case and upon which we express no opinion." The M or F on a document or a court order does not establish sex for all purposes. For those whose sex classification differs from the sex assigned to them at birth, the new classification will not necessarily stand when it is deployed in any area of the law or policy that relies on sex classification to do its work. As the decision explained, "What effect a judgment has *depends on the law governing what the judgment holder seeks to do*, and that is true in this regard as well." (italics added)[39] What "sex is" for identity purposes may not be what sex is deemed to be for other purposes—it depends. Indeed, exactly as Judge Wilner suggested, the majority of the published appellate decisions during this period regarding the validity of marriages involving one or more transgender parties came to very different conclusions than *In Re Heilig* about whether or not one's sex assigned at birth can change.

Nation and State

While the courts in the marriage decisions made a show of approaching marriage as a formal question of sex definition, the issue before them concerned an institution that is not simply a publicly sanctioned contract between two individuals. Marriage is and has long been an instrument of governing that turns some individuals into families and families into nations. Defined in temporal terms ("till death do us part"),[40] marriage plays a central role in binding the past to the present and the present to the future in building a nation. It is, as we have heard over and over again, in the rhetoric that justified same-sex marriage bans, in Justice Kennedy's opinion in *Obergefell* overturning those bans, and in the congressional findings prefacing welfare "reform" laws promoting "the foundation of a successful society."[41] Nancy F. Cott explains in her history of marriage in the United States that "the nation originally had few technologies of governance to monitor and control a people strewn unevenly over a huge expanse of land. Monogamous marriages that distinguished citizen-heads of households had enormous instrumental value for governance, because orderly families, able to accumulate and transmit private property and to sustain an American people, descended from them."[42]

Of course, the "people" to be reproduced and sustained does not include everyone in the territory. Historically, the "American people" often signified—and still does, in many precincts—particular sorts of people, most centrally white people. The history of marriage law reveals its work as a distributive mechanism. From miscegenation laws to social welfare programs to immigration laws, marriage and laws of descent have been cornerstones of nation-building efforts. For example, in her research on antimiscegenation law and racial categories, historian Peggy Pascoe shows how marriage linked "white supremacy and the transmission of property." Among the many examples she describes, her account of Oklahoma's antimiscegenation laws stands out. Before statehood, Black people and American Indians had often married. After Oklahoma's constitution was put in place, "colored" and "negro" were defined as including "all persons of African descent," while the "white race" included "all other persons." (Indigenous people still owned significant amounts of property when the territory became a state.) Pascoe explains that the effect of these laws was to "allow White men to marry and inherit property from Indian women while preventing Black men from doing the very same thing."[43] Antimiscegenation laws determined which racial groups could intermarry; rules and case-by-case decisions on an individual's racial classification dictated which group one belonged to.

Marriage channels individuals into a diachronically organized formation for social reproduction and inheritance—otherwise known as the "family." Still, why must sex have been fixed at birth for marriages involving someone whose gender identity does not correspond to that sex? In each of these cases, someone wanted to possess things generally conveyed by and indexed to the family form: children or property. Gardiner's stepson wanted his father's estate, Littleton's husband's physician's insurance company didn't want to pay out on the wrongful death claim, and Kantaras's wife didn't want to share custody of their children. Unlike the *Heilig* case, which concerned identification (who one is), the marriage decisions examined here centered on questions of distribution (what one gets). If the former reflected the imperative to identify and surveil, the latter was crucial in furthering biopolitical projects of national formation and distribution. If we dispense with the one-size-fits-all explanation that sees the presence or absence of transphobia as the cause of the divergent outcomes, it becomes clear that M and F were not immobile essences for these state actors but malleable outputs in the service of different governing projects. These differences were made visible by individuals who moved from one gender to another, but the significance of this analysis is not limited to the situations faced by trans people.

One way to think though these differences is to map them onto two distinct objects of governance—territory and people—and two distinct rationalities of governance—state and nation. Previously in this book, the work of governing in all its forms has been attributed to the now pluralized concept of *states*.[44] The provisional approach below may help connect the divergent outcomes in the sex classification cases to larger historical formations and trajectories. Weber famously defines the state as a successful monopoly over the legitimate use of violence within a given territory.[45] Recognizing inhabitants is as requisite a function of modern statehood as the establishing and policing of territorial borders. The advent of larger centralized European state formations put greater distances between magistrates and citizens, creating the need for standardized systems for identifying and individuating populations.[46] Identity documents constitute an attempt to make an individual uniquely identifiable, recognizable, classifiable. For philosopher J. G. Fichte, ensuring "each citizen shall be at all times and places . . . recognized as this or that particular person" constitutes "the chief principle of a well-regulated police state." Unique aspects of identity—full name, date of birth, location of birth, parentage—are meant to establish a permanent correspondence, as historian Jane Caplan describes it, "between a person and a set of signs."[47]

Sociologist John Torpey has updated Weber's formulation of the relationship between states and territory, suggesting that "modern states . . . have expropriated from individuals and private entities the legitimate 'means of movement,' particularly through though by no means exclusively across international borders." Individuals are now, Torpey writes, "dependent on states for the possession of an 'identity' . . . which may significantly shape their access to various spaces."[48] Controlling the movement of bodies through space, across national borders, or interior jurisdictions, requires state actors to have reliable methods of identification in place. On identity documents, Ms and Fs help verify who someone is. That's why almost all states allowed individuals to change the sex designation on their driver's licenses and birth certificates during the time of the marriage cases. (Non-binary gender identities were not yet an option between 1999 and 2004.) And most states allowed individuals who have not had genital surgery to change the sex classification on driver's licenses.[49] As Mara Keisling, the executive director of the National Center for Transgender Equality, explained in 2006, "It is in the interest of security to have accurate ID" reflecting a person's gender, not their "hidden genitals."[50] Securitizing a territory and its inhabitants is fundamentally organized around space. The only time that matters is the present. The sex assigned at birth is not relevant for these purposes.

In contrast to what Henri Lefebvre refers to as the "spatial logistics of the state," for the nation it is time and narrative that matter.[51] Ernest Renan, in his 1882 essay "What Is a Nation?," points out that the nation is delineated not by borders but by time: a "large-scale solidarity, constituted by the feeling of the sacrifices that one has made in the past and of those that one is prepared to make in the future."[52] Benedict Anderson describes nationalist projects as moving a population together through time, propelling an imagined community into the future.[53] In Doreen Massey's account, expansive nationalist projects, from the formation of the nation to colonialism to globalization, prioritize temporal sequence over spatial heterogeneity, "conven[ing] space into time."[54] The nation provides a form of belonging, of stickiness, and that enmeshment is forged through institutions that bind the past to the future, such as marriage, reproduction, and inheritance. Anchored in myths of the past and moving toward the future, the nation lurches forward by suspending awareness of its fundamental indeterminacy in each present moment, from one day to the next.[55]

But not all the inhabitants of a territorial jurisdiction are national subjects, or at least not fully so. In the United States, settler colonialism and slavery created constitutive exclusions of internally dispossessed peoples. The national project of expansion, economic growth, and imperialism was made possible by genocide, the violent appropriation of the land of Native Americans and the labor of enslaved persons. This violence gets written out of the narrative of the nation, or at least relegated to the past, depicted as an atypical moment that has since been rectified.[56] Indigenous studies scholar Mark Rifkin points out that "Native peoples, histories, and sovereignties appear not simply as irrelevant, but as aberrant, as if they could not exist in time because they do not form part of the trajectory through which the present emerges from the past."[57] In this formulation, then, the national jurisdiction is composed not only of a people but of populations: some relegated to the past, some outside the national narrative, some barely surviving under conditions of what Lauren Berlant has called *slow death*—"the physical wearing out of a population and the deterioration of people in that population."[58] It is the narrative of nation, of belonging in time and over time, that turns a population into a people, and withholds or distributes resources to groups, to particular sorts of families.

Queer theorists have shown how national narratives of belonging also exclude queer subjects: Jack Halberstam has observed how national time reflects a "reproductive temporality" that puts queer people "in opposition to the institutions of family, heterosexuality, and reproduction;"[59] Elizabeth Freeman shows how queer temporalities can operate as points of resistance to the hegemonic temporal order;[60] and Dana Luciano calls "the sexual organization of the time of life" *chronobiopolitics*.[61] Perhaps most famously, Lee Edelman argues that policies justified by the rhetoric of "the Child" depend on a "reproductive futurity" that positions queers as having no future, as being out of time.[62] But not everyone marches to antinormative queer time.[63] Certainly, the transgender parties in the marriage cases discussed in this chapter didn't. After all, they all chose to get married, and Kantaras and his wife had children. Through property or children or both, they all at one point in their lives planned to participate in the myth of intergenerational continuity that the institution of marriage makes possible. The litigation trail reveals nothing especially queer or antinormative about their intentions. In that sense, they all partook of the assimilation politics of fitting in, what Fraser calls the politics of recognition, which for trans people has been called *transnormativity*.

The apparent absurdity of the situation faced by Gardiner, Kantaras, Littleton, and many others—individuals classified as both male and female by state actors in the same place at the same time—may well have been an expression of a dissonance between the different registers of state and nation, of sovereign power and biopower.[64] In this reading, sex figures as both a place—with its own particular topographies, clearly bounded and static—and a narrative, articulated in the language of temporality (as linear, a trajectory). States count, classify, recognize; nations distribute. The term "nation-state," despite its ubiquity, conceals an antagonism between peoples and territories. For Hannah Arendt, the eighteenth-century substitution of "natural rights" for "historical rights" paradoxically establishes a link between nation and state that produces new exclusions: internally displaced national minorities, stateless people.[65] Nira Yuval-Davis suggests that the idea of the nation-state, premised on "a complete correspondence between the boundaries of the nation and the boundaries of those who live in a specific state," is "virtually everywhere a fiction."[66] Similarly, for Giorgio Agamben, the coupling of nation with state is expressed in birthright citizenship, which depends for its coherence on the "fiction . . . that *birth* immediately becomes *nation* such that there can be no interval of separation."[67] Even after the passage of the Fourteenth Amendment and its guarantee of birthright citizenship, much of the work of government in the United States has involved creating and policing distinctions between populations on the basis of race and ethnicity, either formally through the law or less explicitly through the design of social policy. Regardless of whether the distinctions are de jure or de facto, the effects are to ensure that white people accrue more wealth and longevity than other segments of the population. Indeed, Ruth Wilson Gilmore defines racism as "the state—sanctioned or extra-legal production or exploitation of group-differentiated vulnerability to premature death."[68] The tension between state and nation outlined above is described by legal scholar Devon Carbado as a distinction between citizenship and identity: "American citizenship here means formal citizenship, or citizenship as legal status. American identity means the capacity, as a racial subject, to be a representative body—figuratively and materially—for the nation."[69] For Carbado, who is writing about people of African ancestry here, the process of racial naturalization simultaneously accomplishes their exclusion as national subjects deserving of representation and resources *and* their inclusion as citizens governed by law.

Looking at the pluralities of sex classification gives us a glimpse of the processes through which peoples are aligned to territories, nations to states, and the exclusions the coupling between nation and state produce. Gender relations as organized within the institutions of marriage and inheritance have traditionally secured the tie between one generation and the next. As anthropologist Marilyn Strathern explains, families are thought to be "social arrangements not just imitating but based on and literally deploying processes of biological reproduction."[70] Enactments of sex perform a vital role in marrying territory to people, joining state with nation, and connecting the governmental imperatives to identify the individuals inhabiting its territories with national distributive projects organized through the family, private property, and race. This process requires ensuring that no uninvited guests appear to unmask these ongoing processes of naturalization. In these trans marriage cases, the tensions between the logics of state and nation are brought to bear on spouses whose gender identity is not associated with the sex they were assigned at birth. In that sense, contradictory sex classifications express not confusion about sex definition but competing governing rationalities.

In the registers of recognition and judicial doctrine, the ending of the *formal* establishment of gender—and perhaps *Obergefell* was its death knell—resonates with the progress narrative of America, the slow but inevitable expansion of equality before the law. The situations faced by Kantaras, Littleton, and Gardiner can no longer happen; at the very least, marriages such as theirs could be classified as same-sex marriages. In the registers of distribution and political economy, however, the expansion of marriage to same-sex couples followed a fundamental shift in the family's role. Though still occupying a privileged position as the symbolic center for the reproduction of hetero/homonormative values, it is no longer the conduit of social support through policies such as those that made the breadwinner wage feasible. Instead, as Melinda Cooper has shown, the family has taken on a greater burden as the provider of care in the wake of the neoliberal shredding of the social safety net.[71] The structural privileges accorded to particular types of people—male, heterosexual, cisgender: aka "heads" of households—are beginning to matter less as market logics favor fungibility over status. And states have generally decommissioned gender as a sorting hat for the distribution of resources.

Returning to the debate described at the beginning of this chapter: are the legal demands of trans people symptomatic of all that's wrong with identity politics? Are trans rights representative only of a limited politics of recognition? Or should we refuse the dichotomy, as Fraser herself does for categories of race and gender (as in male and female cisgender people), though not for GLB people and those with non-normative gender identities? Certainly, the dichotomy reduces the complexity and messiness of the relation between formal and substantive equality. Indeed, the governing projects of recognition and redistribution are not always in conflict, nor is the distinction static. Instruments of identification are certainly put in the service of distribution.[72] Birth certificates, for example, were central components of states' efforts not only to surveil but to channel inheritance.[73] But there is a more fundamental problem: Rahul Rao argues, rightly, that the debate has been phrased as if it's a matter of choosing the correct side. If we accept Duggan's admonitions, he writes, "we are tempted to fantasize that if the LGBT movements had refused the recognition/distribution distinction, they might not have succumbed to homonormativity in the way that they did."[74] This voluntaristic approach ascribes an excess of agency to queer people—and, I would add, to trans people. In doing so, it recapitulates not only an individualist ethos but the vision of "the state" that accompanies it. To eschew recognition and liberal inclusion is to position oneself as some sort of antinormative outlaw—and what could be more American than that, with the nation's mythos of the frontier, the rebel battling (or escaping) the law?[75] *Of course* the quest for gender recognition partakes of identity politics. But the markers of difference that propel identity politics have not been incidental to the distributional matrix: they help make it work.

Incarceration, Identity Politics, and the Trans-Cis Divide

In January 2006, the Inmate Sex Change Prevention Act became law in Wisconsin. According to a press release trumpeting the bill's passage, taxpayers would no longer pay for what the two legislators who introduced the legislation described as "extreme prison makeovers." The legislation prohibited the use of federal or state funds to "facilitate the provision of" hormone therapy or gender-affirming surgery for any prisoner in Wisconsin. The law was passed after a Wisconsin prisoner had filed a lawsuit arguing that her inability to undergo gender-affirming surgery in prison violated the US Constitution. It was a violation of the Eighth Amendment, prisoner Donna Konitzer's counsel had argued, to be denied treatment for her serious medical condition, gender identity disorder. "It's the most absurd thing I've ever heard of," said one of the bill's sponsors.[1] Referring to the Eighth Amendment, Representative Mark Gundrum elaborated, "I think the founders of our country—when they wrote that clause—they were envisioning preventing people from being burned in oil or burned at the stake, not simply refusing to use taxpayer dollars to allow inmates to get a sex change or breast implants or whatever else."[2]

The figure of the convict who demands a "sex change" might not have been anticipated in the popular imaginary, but once it was conjured by the press, public outrage erupted. Commenting on a news story about a doctor's recommendation that Ophelia De'Lonta, a transgender woman serving a seventy-year sentence in Virginia for robbery, weapons offenses, and drug offenses, be provided with gender-affirming surgery, one individual wrote, "If he/she wants to cut off his/her dick and balls that's his/her choice [but] the state should not pay for the sex change operation." Another chimed in, "Why do ALL trans people want to be victims and claim that they need surgery, want the government and everyone else to pay for it, and use the 'But I'll kill myself if I don't get it!' mantra?" A third wrote, "Ugh, trannies are the worst. Now they actually expect me to pay for their dick-chopping surgery with *my* tax dollars? Just tuck that thing like any other drag queen."[3] And those comments appeared on a website that aggregates news for the *gay* community, a group that generally tends to be more receptive to appeals for equal treatment from transgender people. In a case involving Michelle Kosilek, sentenced in Massachusetts in 1993 and serving a life sentence, a federal judge ruled that she be provided with appropriate counseling, possibly hormone therapy, and potentially even gender-affirming surgery. In response, CBS's Crime Insider headline read, "Tax Dollars at Work: Will State Pay for Wife-Killer's Sex Change?"[4] When Wisconsin's Inmate Sex Change Prevention Act became law in 2006, advocates for trans prisoners knew of no incarcerated people in the United States who had had gender-affirming surgery. Yet the very idea that a prisoner had filed suit for a "taxpayer-funded sex change" generated such social hysteria that similar legislation was introduced in a handful of other state legislatures between 2006 and 2020. Some bills would allow for the provision of hormone therapy to prisoners diagnosed with gender dysphoria, but would explicitly prohibit gender-affirming surgeries. Others would make prisoners pay all the costs of transition-related care.[5]

One could say that trans prisoners find themselves on the wrong side of two sets of exclusions. First, as prisoners, they have fallen into the maw of the criminal justice system in a nation that has the world's highest incarceration rate.[6] Second, as people whose gender identity confounds social expectations, trans prisoners are punished by the gender policies that govern incarcerated populations.[7] In prison, transgender people of all genders suffer the consequences of their gender nonnormativity through three mechanisms: the rules of sex classification in a system in which placement is governed by the gender binary, the violence perpetrated by guards and other prisoners, and the lack of access to transition-related medical care. On the question of sex classification, most municipal jails and state and federal prisons assign prisoners to men's and women's prisons based on their genital sex. The Obama-era rules for the Prison Rape Elimination Act, which sets standards for federal and state prisons, had insisted that individuals be evaluated on a case-by-case basis when making decisions about gender placement.[8] The Trump administration reversed even that weak gesture in 2018 with rules specifying that "biological sex" would be the "initial" metric for determining whether a prisoner will go to a men's or women's prison—indeed, the rules advised that "the designation to a facility of the inmate's identified gender would be appropriate only in rare cases."[9] Three years later, the Biden administration reversed course once again, arguing that "categorically refusing" to place transgender prisoners in a facility that corresponds to their gender identity violates the Constitution.[10] Regardless of the political football that trans people seem to have become in regulatory apparatuses driven by partisanship, even under Democratic administrations these rules had little effect. While many trans prisoners prefer to be housed according to the sex they were assigned at birth, many do not. Yet almost all trans inmates remain housed according to the sex they were assigned at birth.[11] Many are denied the personal items—including binders, bras, prostheses—they request.

On the issue of violence, transgender and gender non-conforming prisoners experience high levels of harassment, violence, and humiliation at the hands of fellow prisoners and corrections officials. Transgender women incarcerated in men's institutions are much more likely to be sexually assaulted: one highly regarded study found "59% of transgender women reported having been sexually assaulted in contrast to 4.4%" of a random sample of inmates.[12] In another study, trans prisoners reported being sexually victimized at ten times the rate of other prisoners.[13] In some cases, transgender prisoners—once described as "victim-prone" by a New York State corrections official[14]—are placed in administrative segregation, putatively for their own protection.[15] While that may make transgender and gender non-conforming prisoners less vulnerable to violence at the hands of fellow prisoners, some advocates report that administrative segregation increases the violence and humiliation inflicted by corrections officers. Additionally, prisoners in administrative segregation are isolated, cut off from recreational, social, and educational opportunities.[16] It is a punishment, not a perk.

Between the disciplinary violence of rules for sex classification and the brute violence of physical and sexual assault lie corrections policies on the provision of medical treatment related to gender transition, which is the subject of this chapter. The very title of the Inmate Sex Change Prevention Act, along with the copycat bills from other states, suggests that transgender prisoners across all these United States are receiving all the counseling, hormones, and surgeries they need. That is far from the case. In fact, the first known gender-affirming surgery for an incarcerated person anywhere in the United States did not happen until 2017.[17] One 2017 review of state policies on transition-related health care found that only thirteen states would allow a prisoner to begin hormone therapy while incarcerated; twenty-seven would not, and ten more states had no public policies on that question and would not respond to the investigators' queries. On the question of gender-affirming surgery, thirty-two states had, at the time the study was conducted, policies explicitly banning these procedures.[18]

Although a number of state corrections departments have created or amended policies to provide transition-related care to prisoners diagnosed with gender dysphoria in the last decade, at the level of policy *implementation* many trans prisoners are still denied the care they need.[19] For example, in 2015, California reformed its policy, allowing individuals to obtain gender-affirming surgery while incarcerated. While this policy was remarkable in that it was the first of its kind in the United States, it did contain a caveat—the committee must be satisfied that there would be no "penological contraindications" for inmates who, after having gender-affirming surgery, would be housed with "inmates of his/her postoperative gender." And prison administrators, not doctors, would have the final say.[20] Unsurprisingly, over the next four years, of the requests made by trans women, only 5 percent were granted.[21] In another example, the Georgia Department of Corrections violated its own policy of providing hormones to individuals who had been receiving them before incarceration when it denied prisoner Ashley Diamond such care, even though she had been on hormones seventeen years and living as a woman since she was a teenager. Despite having a diagnosis of gender identity disorder (now gender dysphoria), Diamond was incarcerated with men and suffered repeated harassment, physical assault, and sexual assault, even being punished with solitary confinement for "pretending to be a woman." It took the spotlight of national news story to get the state of Georgia to adhere its own policy regarding medical care.[22]

Prisoners have challenged these policies in court, with mixed results. With thousands of county, city, state, and federal corrections and detentions systems, and with litigation occurring in different jurisdictions, the issue is far from settled. Michelle Kosilek's win in federal district court was eventually reversed at the appellate level in 2014.[23] Similarly, in 2019, another federal appellate court found that a "state does not inflict cruel and unusual punishment by declining to provide sex reassignment surgery to a transgender inmate."[24] But trans prisoners in the Midwest were dealt a victory when a third appellate court found that Wisconsin's Inmate Sex Change Prevention Act ran afoul of the Eighth Amendment's ban on cruel and unusual punishment.[25] And in 2019 another appellate court ordered the Idaho Department of Corrections to provide prisoner Aidree Edmo with gender-affirming surgery as a medically necessary treatment for her gender dysphoria—because not doing so would violate the Eighth Amendment.[26] In addition, none of the state bills intended to affirm formal or informal corrections policies that deny transition-related health care to prisoners had actually passed by 2021. But the underlying motivation of champions of this sort of legislation—to prevent transition-related health care in prisons—remains reflected in many policies and even more so in actual practices still in place.

It's easy to pin the blame for these bad policies and practices on transphobia—or, more broadly, on systems bent on maintaining a rigid, pretty much uncrossable gender binary. Similarly, one can identify the lessening of transphobia and the growing recognition that gender is a spectrum rather than a binary as the impetus driving policy in the right direction. Those explanations are obviously useful to some degree. But here I set aside, at least provisionally, the typical strategy for understanding the injustice. Instead of locating the problem of transgender prisoners as a specifically *transgender* problem, this chapter takes a lateral cut and looks at connections to the larger social logics of incarceration. Certainly, radical and progressive trans advocacy groups and some academics have done exactly that—they have situated the plight of incarcerated trans people firmly within an analysis of capitalism and racism's role in maintaining the world's largest prison population.[27] They have argued, rightly, that the solution to the problems they face is not to reform prison policies seemingly specific to trans people but to abolish prisons.[28] While in alignment with this goal, here I want to stay focused on the present and recent past to figure out how a policy that seems limited to the question of gender transition in prison and that seems to be a result of transphobia might reflect the more general relationship between prisons and civil society; even a policy seemingly particular to trans people might spring from the same ways of thinking that govern incarceration in general. This approach challenges the presumption in mainstream advocacy that transphobic policies in prisons are merely a more severe extension of transphobic policies on the outside. It calls into question the distinction between transgender and cisgender that governs most policy analysis and that has been imported, without question, into research on and advocacy for prisoners who need transition-related medical care. That this argument will be counterintuitive to many (including myself in earlier times) reveals the seductive draw of trans identity politics, which elevates one relatively abstract characteristic (incongruence with the sex assigned at birth) over more historically grounded forms of difference (such as socioeconomic status and race).

The last chapter argued that those occupying and defending their rights as transgender people had been too quickly written off—thrown into the dustbin of bourgeois history—as the reductio ad absurdum of identity politics. The analysis centered on the erasure of sex misclassification in left analyses of distributional justice. Even though those identity document policies and marriage decisions involved only a minuscule percentage of people, their outcomes reflected the different ways state enactments of sex are deployed—in some cases to inventory and track, in others to secure segments of the population to the nation through marriage. In this chapter, identity politics—at least in its transgender instantiation—plays a different role. The collective effect of state constructions of sex is to do away with the idea that there is just one definition of M or F. Instead, backed by the force of law, sex is dispersed across a range of possibilities, depending on the governing logic in a particular context. The momentum of "transgender" identity politics, on the other hand, builds by gathering: all those whose gender identity or gender expression is not traditionally associated with the M or F assigned at birth become part of the congregation, all issues somehow related to an incongruence between gender identity and assigned birth sex become aspects of a single problem. In this chapter, then, the focus is not on state actions but on mainstream trans rights advocacy. The analysis centers not on what sex classifications do but on what "transgender" does in advocacy organized around this category, including constructing the overincarceration of transgender people as merely a problem of discrimination—of transphobia—in society.

In the rest of the chapter, I describe how mainstream advocates frame the problem of incarcerated transgender people and contrast that approach with scholarship that understands incarceration as central to constructions of citizenship and that challenges axiomatic truths about the "free" market's relation to incarceration. Then I read an early and formative policy—the "freeze-frame" policy that dictated that the transition of "transsexual inmates" be "frozen" at the moment of incarceration and that still governs much thinking about transition in prison—with Solzhenitsyn's and Foucault's notions of the "carceral archipelago." The chapter ends with observations on the growing divide between free and incarcerated trans people on the issue of transition-related medical care and the work of trans identity politics in obscuring those divisions.

Arguing That Transphobia Is the Cause of Overincarceration

While the absolute number of prisoners who are transgender is very small, since trans people in general make up a tiny slice of the general population,[29] their rate of incarceration appears to be significantly higher than that of non-trans people. Indeed, according to Lambda Legal, a GLBTQ litigation nonprofit, "nearly one in six transgender Americans—and one in two black transgender people—has been to prison."[30] ("Americans" seems to be a rhetorical gesture here; it's unlikely their survey asked about citizenship status.) Another survey, conducted in 2015, of 27,715 (not randomly selected) self-identified trans people in the United States found that 2 percent of its respondents had spent time in jail or prison or juvenile detention *in the last year*.[31] By way of contrast, a report from the Bureau of Justice Statistics found that 2.7 percent of all people living in the United States *had ever* served time in a state or federal prison.[32] Because the latter percentage doesn't include people who spent time in jail but did not go to prison—jails are run by municipalities and hold people awaiting trial or sentencing as well as those with sentences of less than a year, and prisons are state and federal facilities— these numbers don't allow for a perfectly neat comparison. But the notable difference has led many to conclude that it is very likely that transgender people are incarcerated at much higher rates than cisgender people. The analysis of the same seventy-question survey identified many correlations between experiences of gender-based discrimination and violence and being incarcerated. For example, respondents who had experienced family rejection, domestic violence, or physical or sexual assault in school were more likely to have been incarcerated at some point in their lives than respondents who had not. Those who were currently homeless or unemployed or who had lost a job because of bias against transgender or gender non-conforming people were 85 percent more likely to have been incarcerated than those who had not. Of the survey respondents, 48 percent of those who had engaged in sex work had been incarcerated compared to the overall incarceration rate of 16 percent among all survey respondents.[33] These correlations suggest that disparate rates of incarceration are among the cascading effects of transphobia. Because violating social rules of gender can cause trans people to be cut off from access to family support, education, stable housing, and legal employment and thus to engage more frequently in survival strategies that are criminalized, the chance of a trans person finding themselves on the wrong side of the law is magnified.

The transphobia explanation doesn't capture the whole story, however. Black respondents in the 2009 and 2015 trans surveys were about four times more likely to have been incarcerated than white respondents; in the US population as a whole, the rate of incarceration for Black people has been about five times that of white people (based on the 2010 US census), although the racial gap has narrowed since 2010.[34] Michelle Alexander, Jackie Wang, and others have argued that mass incarceration is an essential element of the apparatus of the nation's ongoing project of white supremacy.[35] Moreover, the rate of incarceration of sex workers in general is also extremely high. For example, one study found that 70 percent of "female" sex workers in Baltimore had been incarcerated at least once—and the mean amount of times was fifteen.[36] As for class, the correlation between unemployment and incarceration is strong. Writing about California, Ruth Wilson Gilmore connects the growing disparity between the number of jobs available and the number of people seeking work to increases in the state's prison population. The "surplus population"—useful to capital by depressing wages—is controlled by shifting large segments of it to prison.[37] Loïc Wacquant describes the "penalization of poverty" as a consequence of the state's retreat from welfare and redistributive economic policy: "*the poverty of the social state against the backdrop of deregulation elicits and necessitates the grandeur of the penal state.*"[38] Jackie Wang ties the growth of incarceration to the needs of capital and anti-Black racism—twinned together in a formation Cedric Robinson had examined under the name "racial capitalism"—explaining that the "evolution in the social function of the state from *provider of social services* to *provider of security* also represented an evolution in how racialized populations in the United States would be managed."[39] Finally, gender also matters here, though there is much less data on this question when it comes to trans populations. Contrary to the cisgender population, where men's incarceration rates far exceed that of women,[40] the 2009 survey found trans women were about twice as likely to have been incarcerated as trans men (the report refers to "MTF" and "FTM").[41] Non-binary individuals were less likely to have been incarcerated than binary trans individuals.[42] Given these statistics, it comes as no surprise that one study concluded that "transgender women of color, particularly Black, Native American/Alaskan Native, and mixed race/ethnicity women, disproportionately experienced corrections system engagement relative to white transgender women."[43]

These advocacy reports do not fail to underscore discrepancies around race, class, and gender that the research has found. Yet even as they draw attention to what one report calls the "compounding effects of other forms of discrimination" found in their own and others' studies,[44] activists, allies, and sympathetic media stick to a narrative centered on transphobia and the category of transgender.[45] Elías Cosenza Krell aptly ventriloquizes it thus: "'We need to care about trans lives, especially trans women's lives, especially trans women of color's lives.'"[46] As Nira Yuval-Davis has pointed out in another context, such an "additive" approach to intersectionality conflates different levels of analysis (experiential, structural, representational) and reduces ontologically distinct social divisions to "identities," which are then "often required to 'perform' analytical tasks beyond their abilities."[47] That certainly may be the case here. For example, it's not just that Black trans feminine individuals are much more likely to spend time in jail or prison than white trans feminine individuals. It's that in the United States there is a close relationship between white supremacy and mass incarceration, and, more recently, between the economic dislocations of recent decades and prison. Given the historical circumstances surrounding the construction of the categories of transsexual and transgender, as C. Riley Snorton, Julian Gill-Peterson, and others have suggested, the terms themselves may be constitutively white—or, at the very least, largely fabricated through the elision of anything other than the autonomous liberal employable subject and normative whiteness.[48] Trans, then, might occupy a different position vis-à-vis incarceration than what is suggested by its inclusion in a "triply oppressed" analytic. It's possible that one of the identity categories held out as an axis of oppression may be complicit in the problem it has been charged with dismantling.

Still. For many trans advocates, it is axiomatic that the disproportionate presence of trans people in prison and the mistreatment they face once incarcerated reflect the effects of transphobia on the outside. With regard to this view, the solution requires changing the social and legal landscape in civil society to lessen the possibility that one will enter the downward spiral leading to incarceration. That means working to increase the likelihood that trans children and teens will be accepted at home and at school, and passing laws that prohibit discrimination in housing, employment, and public accommodations. Indeed, the transgender rights apparatus in the United States has largely consolidated around this agenda, which was also reflected in the policy priorities identified by NGLTF's survey respondents in 2011: passing employment nondiscrimination laws, getting insurers to pay for transition-related health care, and improving policies for sex reclassification on identity documents and government records.[49] It's telling that passing hate crime laws was ranked third in the survey's list of priorities while working on transgender and gender non-conforming prisoners' rights was ranked ninth, even though supporting enhanced penalties for particular crimes feeds the carceral leviathan that disproportionately imprisons people of color and trans and gender non-conforming people, especially those who are Black. Working on issues specific to incarcerated trans people is not prioritized, however, because, according to this view, incarceration represents a failure of the system, not a problem in itself. Because gender policing in prison is understood as a mere amplification of gender policing on the outside, for those who do end up incarcerated the fix for particular policy problems (violence, sex classification, medical care) is to recite to corrections officials and courts the arguments that have had some success in improving the situation for trans people on the outside. The recommendations are infused with the rhetoric of corporate diversity. For example, one report recommends that jails and prisons establish a "culture of respect for diversity, including of transgender and gender non-conforming people" and that "corrections staff should be given comprehensive training on how to treat transgender and gender non-conforming inmates with respect, including allowing people to express their gender identity through clothing and grooming."[50] Treating prisoners with respect is without doubt a good thing. But the recommendation implies that that gesture would raise the treatment of these prisoners to the level of non-trans prisoners. In an institution organized around the distribution of pain—bodies relatively immobilized in space for years or decades, lack of adequate health care (for everyone), isolation and threats of isolation, generalized vulnerability to violence and harassment—calling for more respect brings deck chairs to mind. Reforms like these assume the fundamental soundness of the ship that is incarceration.

The downward spiral narrative and these policy priorities suggest that the relation between civil society and carceral institutions is essentially continuous. While the distinction between being free and being imprisoned is not discounted, those different social locations are imagined as operating on the same plane: free individuals who run afoul of the law are trafficked into and out of prisons according to the reigning arithmetic of punishment, debt, and repayment. Outlawing discrimination and promoting policies that would lead to changes in social norms would gradually decrease this traffic because it would remove obstacles for trans people seeking employment. Under the heading "Economic Opportunity," a National Center for Transgender Equality publication pointed out that "extreme levels of unemployment and poverty lead many to become involved in underground economies—such as sex and drug work—in order to survive."[51] In a very similar vein, the Human Rights Campaign draws a direct line from the lack of employment nondiscrimination laws to poverty to homelessness to engagement in "underground economies like drug sales or survival sex work" to arrest.[52] The solution? In arguments directed at both policymakers and the public, trans people and their advocates should work to dispel the irrational animus toward people whose gender identity and/or expression does not comport with the social expectations based on their assigned sex at birth. This is to be accomplished by invoking the commonsense mantras of transgender rights advocacy, which typically rely on medical accounts of the immutability of gender identity; advancing the liberalism of an embodied possessive individualism ("everyone has a gender identity"); describing forms of gender non-normativity as benign variations in a social field increasingly perceived as composed of group instantiations of difference; and narrating nontraditional gender presentations and embodiments as forms of free expression—and deploying any or all combinations of these rationales.[53] For mainstream trans advocates, then, the essential storyline is inevitably one of inclusion within the reigning liberal paradigm. As Aren Aizura points out, inclusion in normative citizenship depends on adhering to "the imperative to be 'proper' in the eyes of the state: to reproduce, to find proper employment; to reorient one's 'different' body into the flow of the nationalized aspiration for possessions, property, [and] wealth."[54] While citizenship is usually thought to be a formal category, political theorist Judith Shklar makes clear that, along with voting, earning—that is, the ability to make a living in the official economy and to be independent—has long been an essential attribute of hegemonic conceptions of what is it to be an American.[55]

There's no doubt that, with the exception of passing hate crime laws (which give prosecutors even more power to force plea bargains on members of groups already singled out by the criminal justice system), achieving these policy priorities would certainly go some way toward improving the lives of individuals on the outside who are disadvantaged because they violate social gender norms and reducing the likelihood that they might be imprisoned as a result. But there are other ways of thinking about the question of incarceration. The above account is produced by a conceptual apparatus dependent on a particular set of assumptions, some general to individualism and some specific to the dominant analytics of mainstream movements for transgender justice:

that incarceration is an effect of an *individual's* lack of employability; that the declared function of punishment is largely coextensive with its effects; that criminal laws target individuals; that the social and legal regulation of gender and sex on the inside, while more intense than what occurs on the outside, is not qualitatively different from it; and that comparing the treatment of trans prisoners to that of cisgender prisoners will generate the clearest picture of the injustice. But the approach taken in this chapter (the last row in Table 5.1) is to imagine trans *prisoners* as the constitutive other of trans *non-prisoners*, rather than of cisgender prisoners. That framework makes visible the growing differences between trans people who are incarcerated and those who have never been. Instead of focusing on differential rates of discrimination between trans and cisgender people in civil society, or comparing the treatment of trans prisoners to that of cisgender prisoners, incarceration itself becomes the starting point.

Incarceration is central to constructions of liberal freedom and the principal of state noninterference in free markets. As Dylan Rodriguez puts it, the intelligibility of "civil freedom relies on carceral and punitive unfreedom," which requires rendering the prison as "an alien cultural and geographic figuring, a place that is somewhere else altogether, territorially distant and experientially incomprehensible to the ideal-typical 'free' person."[56] In addition to serving as the ideological antipode of the negative freedom that the nonincarcerated are meant to enjoy, Bernard Harcourt argues that prisons function as the "other" in neoliberal notions of limited government—the only arena where state intervention, increasingly draconian and costly, has been not only sanctioned but welcomed.[57] Imprisonment in the United States—from the rate of incarceration to the severity of solitary confinement to felon disenfranchisement—is not just an empirical problem of excess, of too much punishment. It's also not just an afterthought to what gets cast as the normal activities of civil life—earning and studying, reproducing and consuming, traveling and nest-making. Incarceration is a load-bearing pillar in the architecture of society, economy, and politics: the racial and structural inequalities not visible in liberal and neoliberal abstractions of the market and the contract, the citizen and their doppelgänger, the earner, are laid bare in the concrete injustices of the criminal justice system.[58]

TABLE 5.1. Perspectives and comparisons

Perspective	Domain of the comparison	What is compared	What this comparison makes visible
Transgender rights approach in general	Civil society	Trans non-prisoners to cisgender non-prisoners	Higher rates of discrimination leading to higher rates of incarceration Discrimination as the root cause of incarceration
Advocates for trans prisoners	Prisons	Trans prisoners to cisgender prisoners	Gender rules in prisons: sex classification, treatment of gender dysphoria Institutional and informal punishment for violating gender norms Differential vulnerability to sexual assault
Approach taken here	Prisons and civil society (market)	Trans prisoners to trans nonincarcerated	Constitutive role of white supremacy Prisons as part of the economy, not separate from it Widening policy gap (availability of transition-related health care, identity documents, and sex classification) between incarcerated and nonincarcerated

The Carceral Archipelago and the Freeze-Frame Policy

The first and still formative corrections policy regarding gender transition in prison was the "freeze-frame" policy. The concept of "freeze-framing," in both its formal and informal implementation, rests on two criteria. First, was the prisoner on hormones *before* incarceration, or was hormone therapy sought only *after* they were incarcerated? Second, if the prisoner was receiving hormones prior to incarceration, was the medical treatment provided by medical practitioners, or was it secured through other means—on the streets? In most cases, prisoners who meet the first criterion must have been treated for gender identity disorder (or gender dysphoria) under the supervision of a physician. Maintenance policies expressly preclude the possibility of surgery. The rationale for maintaining prisoners at precisely the level of gender transition they had attained at the moment of incarceration was outlined in guidelines written in 1990 by Robert Dickey, who was on the faculty of the Clarke Institute of Psychiatry in Toronto. (From the 1970s to the aughts, the faculty at the Clarke Institute played an outsized role in policy matters regarding trans people in the Canada, the United States, and internationally. At one time, the Clarke was the only institution in Canada with the power to authorize gender-affirming surgery. They were notorious for treating trans people "with contempt" and for their extreme gatekeeping practices.[59] As Andrea James explains, it was "nicknamed 'Jurassic Clarke' in the trans community for its regressive policies."[60] Indeed, googling "Clarke Institute," "transsexual," and "notorious" generated 1,730 results.) If there is an architect of the freeze-frame policy, it's Dickey. While some prisons already had formal or informal maintenance policies in place, Dickey's interventions cloaked them with the mantle of medical authority. In a 1990 article, "Gender Dysphoria and Antisocial Behavior," he wrote that a "reasonable general policy is to 'freeze' incarcerated gender dysphorics at whatever stage of hormonal or surgical feminization or masculinization they have attained by the time they enter the correctional system."[61] There should be no further surgery while incarcerated, and hormones should be provided in prison, Dickey argued, only if they had been prescribed by a "recognized expert in treating gender disorders" before the individual was incarcerated.[62] He also recommended housing transsexuals—most of his analysis concerns people assigned male at birth, whom Dickey referred to as "transsexual males" or, if they had had genital surgery, as "castrated" males—according to the sex assigned at birth if they had not had genital surgery.[63] As an expert in gender dysphoria among incarcerated populations, Dickey served as a consultant to correctional systems across the United States and Canada.

A few years later, Maxine Peterson, Dickey, and other colleagues from the Clarke Institute conducted a survey of correctional systems in a number of jurisdictions in Australia, Europe, and North America. According to the sixty-three surveys returned (about a 60 percent response rate), just under half the corrections systems indicated they would continue hormone therapy for incarcerated individuals "provided this had been prescribed prior to admission to prison." The rest of the institutions simply discontinued hormone therapy. In some senses, then, Dickey's freeze-frame policy was a progressive one for the time. The policy of "freeze-framing" became the rubric that for many years organized not only transition-related medical care but also sex classification in prison.

Since in the majority of corrections systems placement in sex-segregated institutions is based on genitals, the freeze-frame policy meant that one's genitals would not change once one was incarcerated—there would be no surgery. For Dickey, the rationale for maintaining the status quo was based on three factors: "the artificial nature of the prison environment, the inability to assess the intensity of gender dysphoria in such an environment, and the lack of a genuine real-life test in such a controlled setting."[64] As Dickey explains, "The prison environment is not representative of society at large."[65] It's the first and third rationales—the artificiality of the prison environment, and prisoners' inability to engage in the "real-life" test required by the American Psychiatric Association's then-operative treatment protocols—that matter for the purposes of the analysis in this chapter.

The rationale for the policy of preventing prisoners from moving "further along the continuum of transgender changes," then, rests on the distinction between prisons and "real life," a distinction that in turn has been mapped onto the very different registers of space and time between the two. The figure of the archipelago was famously invoked by Aleksandr Solzhenitsyn as a way of imagining the spatial landscapes of incarceration. According to Brady Thomas Heiner, Solzhenitsyn deployed the term both geographically and theoretically. In the first sense, "the archipelago designates a series of . . . scattered carceral 'islands'— sites in which captive bodies were tortured, interrogated, and confined incommunicado." In the latter sense, writes Heiner, "Solzhenitsyn speaks of the archipelago as a grid of 'dead zones,' a 'prison sewage system,' around which the 'seas' of civil society unremittingly flow, and about which civil society remains unaware or inattentive."[66] Foucault, nodding to Solzhenitsyn, speaks of a "carceral archipelago" as "the way in which a form of punitive system is physically dispersed yet at the same time covers the entirety of society."[67] In contrast to real life, prisons, as Solzhenitsyn observed, are islands around which time and civil society flow, but which they do not penetrate. In real life, outside the prison walls, people are apparently at large, free to move; to make decisions; to work; to buy; to sell; to change; to author, edit, and revise their life's story from moment to moment; to reproduce the narratives that fashion the kinship structures of family, community, and race; and to participate in national projects organized around distribution.

Opposed to this notion of real life are the carceral islands, the closed spaces where movement is radically constrained or, in the case of supermax institutions, precluded almost completely, and where contingency is managed and aleatory events are prevented. Foucault's musings on the devaluation of space in favor of temporal epistemes speaks to this opposition: "Space was treated as the dead, the fixed, the undialectical, the immobile. Time, on the contrary, was richness, fecundity, life, dialectic."[68] As Regina Kunzel puts it, "the essence of incarceration was forced spatial confinement, of course, but many prisoners experienced it as temporal rupturing as well."[69] Incarceration, "doing time," means immobilizing bodies in place, while "real life" is imagined as structured around flows and temporalities: nation, family, reproductive time, monumental time, even eschatological time.

Of course, imprisoned bodies are not static. Living, becoming ill, suffering, and dying take place in those spaces. Dickey admits as much when addressing the question of violence directed at "gender dysphorics." Initially, Dickey wrote, there might be some problems with "physical maltreatment" of the transsexual inmates housed in men's prisons. But over time, he argued, prisoners would adjust. In fact, he suggested, prison could even function like a matchmaking service: "The transsexuals themselves often solve this dilemma [the danger of assault] by forming liaisons or 'marriages' with what appear to be otherwise heterosexual and often dominant males. Protection from other inmates is given in return for sexual favors (usually fellatio, sometimes anal intercourse) from the transsexual. Interestingly, these liaisons sometimes continue after both inmates have been released from custody and sometimes even in those rare instances in which the transsexual goes on to complete surgical sex reassignment."[70] That these liaisons begin in prison and "sometimes continue" when these couples are released and returned to the flow of civil society troubles the neat distinction between prison and "real life" that undergirds the rationale for the freeze-frame policy. Dickey is no Jane Austen, but his narrative does recall the heterosexual romance, and all of the work it does for marriage, the family, the transmission of property, the regulation of race, and the production of a national imaginary. These romances begin in prison (which is supposed to be "an environment . . . not representative of society at large"), but the plot of Dickey's particular fairy tale can come to a resolution (gender-affirming surgery, perhaps even marriage) only in civil society. Prison is not the place of becoming.

In her important 2005 book *For Space*, geographer Doreen Massey points to the "association between the spatial and the fixation of meaning" in Western culture and philosophy. She reappraises the subjugation and dismissal of space as "static, closed, immobile, as the opposite of time." For Massey, the construction of space as subsumed under time's projects (e.g., empire, and now globalization) means that "spatial heterogeneity gets translated into temporal sequence."[71] The temporal frame renders what could be spatial multiplicities as homogenous unities that only change over time. Ergo, difference gets narrated as metamorphosis. For example, a place/locality/material object/practice/culture/embodied individual doesn't get described as potentially multiple; instead, it's narrated as "X *was* this, then *became* that."[72] But time's hegemony is not meant to penetrate the "not real life" space of the prison. As spatial projects, prisons "wall up" the incarcerated in islands separate from the flows of community, family, civil society, nation. In prison, X should not become Y, even over time. Hence the ideal policy related to transition, the one most widely adopted by correctional institutions, was "freeze-framing the inmate at the state he or she was in at the time of incarceration."[73] In the carceral logics of gender, at any one moment in time one can only be male *or* female. And neither can one metamorphose into something different in a place that time is meant to bypass.

Massey suggests that we need to reimagine "things as processes," not as fixed, static, material.[74] And the body is always in process. Regardless of the fantasy of freezing bodies in place, in reality there can be no freeze-frame. The bodies of transgender prisoners could not remain frozen at "whatever stage of hormonal or surgical or masculinization they have attained by the time they center the correctional system." Contra Dickey, the bodies of transgender women in prison are not inert, static; these prisoners do not simply "adapt" to the environment by finding boyfriends to protect them on the inside, and later, back on the outside, in "real life," joining the march of time by partaking of the heterosexual narrative and marrying after their surgical transition is complete. The punitive structures of carceral institutions transfer violence onto transgender bodies. For example, secondary sex characteristics atrophy as a result of inadequate levels of or complete denial of hormones; violence and sexual assault mark bodies and psyches; prisoners have been known to cut themselves and self-castrate, often in response to denial of appropriate treatment; and some commit suicide.[75] The situation the freeze-frame policy creates is both critical and chronic. It's both eventful, a crisis, *and* uneventful, "ordinary, chronic and cruddy."[76] Sara Lamble explains, "prison is a site that produces the conditions of living death; it is a place where bodies are subject to regimes of slow death and dying. Not only are deprivation, abuse, and neglect regular features of incarceration but the monotonous regime of caged life—the experience of "doing time"—involves the slow wearing away of human vitality and the reduction of human experience to a bleak existence."[77] Incarceration is not only spatial confinement for a period of time, then, it also has to be understood as a sort of "living death"—an extended dying, a prolonged period of decay, of "bodily and subjective disintegration," that might not end in death.[78]

Instead of seeing the hysteria and hatred directed at the figure of "the convict who demands a sex change" as merely a particularly noxious condensation of a generalized transphobic animus, that reaction might be also understood as a manifestation of the commonsense distinction between being in prison and being free. Prisons are to punish, not reward, criminal behavior. One should not be treated in prison to medical treatments that are not available to most free individuals. In a 1997 decision denying hormone therapy to a transsexual prisoner, Judge Richard Posner, a Chicago School neoliberal and law and economics thinker, explained his logic: "Withholding from a prisoner an esoteric treatment that only the wealthy can afford does not strike us as a form of cruel and unusual punishment. It is not unusual; and we cannot see what is cruel about refusing to benefit a person who could not have obtained the benefit if he had refrained from committing crimes. We do not want transsexuals committing crimes because it is the only route to obtaining a cure."[79] Indeed, the point of incarceration, according to Posner, Gary Becker, and other neoliberal thinkers, is to punish those who have attempted to bypass, in Posner's words, "the system of voluntary, compensated exchange—the 'market.'"[80] As one of the sponsors of Wisconsin's Inmate Sex Change Prevention Act explained, "When most health plans do not cover these types of procedures the state should not have to foot the bill for convicted felons to get it either."[81] The freeze-frame policy—not to mention the complete denial of transition-related care in some correctional systems—ensures that those on the inside do not get services unavailable to those on the outside.[82]

Denaturalizing Gender but Not Markets

The terrain has shifted radically since the Wisconsin Sex Change Prevention Act became law in 2006. Trans people who aren't incarcerated are much more likely to get transition-related medical care now should they want it. In Wisconsin, for example, state policy now bans private insurance companies from discriminating based on gender identity, which means insurance companies can no longer refuse to cover transition-related health care. Moreover, the state's Medicaid plan now also explicitly includes such care. These policy shifts have been widespread in the United States: one advocacy organization suggests that, based on jurisdictions and demographic data, the majority of the LGBTQ population are protected by policies that prohibit trans exclusions in health care coverage.[83] Amid the welter of state and federal policies on private insurance and Medicaid, and state and federal employee health plans, there has been, since at least 2012, an emerging trend line of increasing coverage.[84] The passage of the Affordable Care Act, which went into effect in 2010, has also made a significant difference because it bans sex discrimination in the provision of health care. In 2016, the Obama administration promulgated regulations interpreting sex to include gender identity. As a result, exclusions for transition-related care would run afoul of the law. In 2019 a conservative federal judge in Texas vacated the rule, known as Section 1557 of the Affordable Care Act; that same year the Trump administration, for good measure, also took steps to rescind it. This regulation's prospective future as a political football, changing from one administration to the next, was cut short in 2020 when the Supreme Court ruled, in a 6–3 decision, that "it is impossible to discriminate against a person for being homosexual or transgender without discriminating against that individual based on sex."[85] While the case before it concerned employment discrimination, it's already become clear that the Supreme Court's construction of sex to include transgender individuals will likely apply to nondiscrimination laws in other areas, including health care. Indeed, in 2020 a federal judge in New York granted an injunction against the Trump administration's attempt to change the rules, finding that "the proposed rules are, indeed, contrary to Bostock."[86] Categorical bans on transition-related care will be viewed as a form of sex discrimination—as long as the Affordable Care Act remains undisturbed.[87] Certainly, the ACA's ban on sex discrimination *should* apply to incarcerated people seeking transition-related care. But public officials' deference to prison administrators and their "security" concerns, the relative powerlessness of prison populations, the shocking inadequacy of the health care provided to incarcerated people in need of any medical treatment, and the lack of social support generally for the incarcerated has made it much more difficult for incarcerated trans people to reach the level of access to transition-related care available to those not in prison. In the first section of this chapter, I described some positive developments, but in general the situation on the outside remains considerably better than the situation on the inside. Posner no longer needs to indulge in the fantasy that, were corrections departments to provide transition-related medical care, transgender individuals would commit crimes in order to be incarcerated and receive the treatment denied them by market forces.

Even without the "lure" of free transition-related health care in prison, however, transgender people are still more likely to be incarcerated than cisgender people. According to the downward spiral explanation proffered by mainstream trans rights advocates, it all boils down to discrimination. As the National Center for Transgender Equality explains in a pamphlet promoting federal legislation that would ban employment discrimination based on gender identity, "homelessness, poverty, violence, and working in the street economy are consequences of workplace discrimination. These issues can only be addressed by working to eliminate the root cause. Allowing people to have and keep jobs to support themselves and their families is vital."[88] Furthermore, transphobia (and homophobia) are irrational, even vestigial, accomplishing nothing except interfering with the market's natural efficiency. As President Obama proclaimed when he signed an executive order banning discrimination based on gender identity and sexual orientation in federal employment, this "doesn't make much sense." He continued: "Today in America, millions of our fellow citizens wake up and go to work with the awareness that they could lose their job, not because of anything they do or fail to do, but because of who they are—lesbian, gay, bisexual, transgender. And that's wrong."[89] (Though Obama waited until his second term to issue the executive order righting this wrong.) Paul Krugman and Robin Wells, the authors of an acclaimed economics textbook, explain that "discrimination is *not* a natural consequence of market competition." In fact, they argue, "market forces tend to work against employment discrimination." Otherwise-rational employers are able to treat different types of people differently only because of market interference (e.g., labor unions or minimum-wage laws that cause wages to rise above the market equilibrium rate) or government policy (e.g., segregated schools that result in inferior education).[90] But while nondiscrimination laws and policies also constitute state intrusion in the market, the interventions are benign because they offset outmoded attitudes that "don't make sense," not the market itself. Eliminating transphobia from the workplace would allow for the full participation of responsible, self-governing, and employable transgender individuals. It would then no longer be necessary for trans people to engage in criminalized survival strategies that bypass the market and land them in jail.

The employability narrative, however, leaves out one inconvenient fact—the market cannot provide a job with a living wage to everyone who wants one. From this perspective, prisons do not punish those who bypass the market but instead warehouse some of the populations that the market cannot provide for because, in fact, it depends on their exclusion. Harcourt's account of "neoliberal penality" as "a form of rationality in which the penal sphere is pushed outside political economy and serves the function of a boundary" is helpful here.[91] The idea that there is a "categorical difference between the free market, where intervention is inappropriate, and the penal sphere, where it is necessary and legitimate," has two effects: it justifies massive expansion of the penal sphere (and the concomitant slashing of the social safety net), and it obscures how much regulation and government interference the supposedly natural forces of the market require to distribute inequality.[92] Those at the top of the economic heap are protected by tax policies, regulatory apparatuses, and the structure of government itself (the undemocratic yet constitutional institutions of the courts, the Senate, and the Electoral College), which ensure that workers do not receive a fair share of the wealth they create. At the bottom, according to Wacquant, poverty has been criminalized because it is *"the indispensable complement to the imposition of precarious and underpaid wage labor* as civic obligation from those locked out at the bottom of the class and ethnic structure."[93] Moreover, as Dilts points out, neoliberal rationality, although it apparently eschews social difference, "at least partly (if not totally) rests on and operates through preexisting categories of difference such as class and race."[94] The formal recognition groups receive through the passage of nondiscrimination laws, however, does little to rectify the historical formations that have produced such gross inequality. The commonplace that "discrimination is bad because it interferes with the work of the markets," writes Adolph Reed, "has the salubrious effect of locating a discussion of inequality safely outside the realm of economics."[95]

If purveyors of the transphobia explanation spent as much time denaturalizing the market as they do denaturalizing gender, the mechanisms that distribute vulnerabilities so unevenly would be more apparent. It might also help us see that the transgender-cisgender binary, the grid of intelligibility that dominates so much of trans studies and advocacy, possibly obscures more than it reveals. Indeed, transgender has become a category of increasing cultural currency in the rhetoric of diversity, stitching together people whose only commonality is that, one way or another, their gender didn't turn out as expected, given the sex they were assigned at birth. For example, the chances of a trans person going to jail or prison differ greatly depending on race, class, and gender, among other things. Earlier, I suggested that rather than comparing transgender prisoners to cisgender prisoners, a more useful juxtaposition might be to compare incarcerated and never-incarcerated transgender people. The increasing policy divergence affecting prisoners and the "free" with regard to rules for sex classification and the provision of transgender-related health care is made very visible by that comparison. This approach doesn't set up transgender as a unifying category of sameness, but rather becomes a method for identifying difference. That trans purports to describe people who are so very differently situated in relation to their vulnerability to violence, incarceration, illness, homelessness, and slow death might be one of the more miraculous feats of identity politics. The fact that removing barriers to the employability of trans people gets cast as the solution to the severe situation now facing trans prisoners is an example of neoliberal rationality in action. Indeed, the three policy changes that would make the *most* difference to the *most* trans people are prison abolition, the adoption of universal public-payer health care, and a large-scale assault on income inequality. None of the specific policies purveyed by mainstream trans rights groups—such as adding gender identity to a federal nondiscrimination law, which Justice Gorsuch effectively accomplished in the June 2020 Supreme Court decision in *Bostock v. Clayton County*[96]—would have anywhere near the effect on the lives of trans people that those three policies would.

To complicate matters a little more—in looking at prisons, it's important not to fall into the trap of reproducing the too-neat distinction between the imprisoned and the free. It might be more apt to rethink the geography of the carceral archipelago, to rearrange the map into zones of safety and precariousness. When the assumptions of the freeze-frame policy are unpacked, it becomes clear that of course time penetrates the realm of the living dead inhabiting those carceral islands. But the converse is also true. Civil society—in the form of the market—contains its own dead zones, warehouses for disposable populations. While Dickey tells us that "the prison environment is not representative of society at large," many parts of "society" are also not representative of what in the social imaginary is thought to constitute living. For example, not all unincarcerated people have access to transition-related care. Prisons aren't "real life," but for many, neither is the realm of putative freedom. For many, it's slow death.[97]

Conclusion

In this book, I made three arguments. The first is that the misclassification of trans people was historically a consequence not simply of transphobia, but of the denial to women of the rights and resources available to men. Sex classifications were necessary to the administration of policies that used gender as a technology of government. When people with a gender identity not traditionally associated with the sex assigned to them at birth—members of a residual category that hadn't been anticipated when the system was put in place—attempted to change their sex classification, they were unintentionally challenging the entire apparatus governing sex-based legal subordination. With the gradual decommissioning of gender from its role in distributing rights and resources, barriers to sex reclassification for transgender people also began to crumble. The *Obergefell* marriage decision felled one of the last relics of this state-sponsored discrimination. As sex reclassification become more and more possible, contradictions in sex reclassification policies emerged—one policymaking arm of government determining that sex classification is inalterably determined at birth, another demanding gender-affirming surgery, a third requiring only an avowal of gender identity. The second argument suggested that the existence of conflicting rules for classifying sex does not necessarily reflect muddled thinking on the part of policymakers and judges; rather, it expresses the different work that sex does in different contexts. While advocates presented arguments about what sex and gender really *are*, policymakers were often more concerned with what sex *does* for a particular state project. In that sense, sex was not a fixed property, but operationalized as a mobile technology of governing. Its definition depended on the outcome it was needed to produce. By the second decade of this century, much of the work of governments could be carried on without sex classifications.

Third, I argued that an increasingly popular identity politics organized under the name "transgender" now accounts for positive policy changes that use gender identity as the criterion for sex classification. The "sex is as sex does" framework (situating sex as a technology of government) has now largely been displaced by the push-pull of forces organized around the concept of transgender. A visible transgender identity politics had appeared on the social map in the first years of this century, came into its own during the Obama era, and burgeoned when allies horrified at the Trump's administration's attempt to "define transgender out of existence" took up the cause.[1] In reaction, an organized anti-transgender countermovement, steered by religious organizations battling what they call "gender ideology" and a rump assortment of individuals who insist that the mission of feminism is to oppose trans people instead of sexism and misogyny, push back. Under President Obama, transgender advocates successfully lobbied federal agencies to adopt trans-inclusive policies across a broad range of issues, from schools and homeless shelters to health care and prisons. Under President Trump, these were systematically reversed. Under President Biden, the pendulum likely swings back once again. As a result, good and bad sex reclassification policies, as well as other policies such as nondiscrimination laws, now tend to reflect blue-red politics.[2] Using a restroom, entering a sports competition, accessing the health care one needs to live in one's body—when the person doing them has a gender identity not traditionally associated with the sex they were assigned at birth, these day-to-day activities suddenly become matters of great political significance.

Certainly, these neatly drawn analytical-historical arguments do not account for all the messiness and contingency in policymaking across the United States. Transformative political actors—sometimes a lone transgender person or ally—spring up in unlikely times and places, wresting trans-affirmative changes from seemingly hidebound institutions. Moreover, differences in the structures of political institutions at state and federal levels have their own effects on the speed and likelihood of policy change.[3] Finally, though the arguments are loosely chronological, there are no hard-and-fast borders between the periods. For example, one of the first sightings of a trans identity politics in the United States might be seen in the appearance of the Street Transvestite Action Revolutionaries, founded in 1970 in New York City by Sylvia Rivera, Marsha P. Johnson, and others, though their political agenda was much broader than the assimilationist project typical of the main currents of trans identity politics now.[4]

None of this should be taken to mean that the transgender movement's goals with respect to sex classification—basing sex classification on gender identity in the short term and ending the entire system of classification in the longer term—are not just and worthy. I do not side with the critique of identity politics by those who have always been able to proffer ID that matches their identity (blithely unaware of their privilege in being able to do so). Nor do I side with those who index the value of trans people to our potential to deconstruct gender and smash the binary. My project has been to examine how demands for sex reclassification have been enmeshed with other histories and structures, and to understand the distinct rationales of governance and politics in resisting—or in acquiescing to—requests for reclassification.

For the most part, this book has focused on the relatively narrow question of sex classification. My main concern has been the use of sex classifications to further state projects. Throughout, sex has generally been used to refer to classifications backed by the force of law and gender has referred to norms, narratives, practices, and conventions that arrange bodies, identities, roles, and expressions in hierarchies of difference based on notions of male/female, man/woman, and masculinity/femininity. Many sex classification rules have changed with the decommissioning of sex and, in recent years, in response to demands from those whose gender identity doesn't correspond to the sex they were assigned a birth. That does not mean that huge swaths of the population are not still bound by, or in thrall to, a hierarchical and sometimes deadly vision of gender norms and relations outside of formal legal architectures.

I want to end this book by returning to a point I raised in the introduction—the relationship between women's movements and trans movements. In the last decades, movements for transgender equality appear to have advanced with astonishing speed, while other issues of concern to women's movements have largely stalled, either making little progress (equal pay) or suffering real setbacks (abortion access). From policy reforms to public opinion trends, it seems that the situation has changed faster, and in a more positive direction, for trans people as a constituency than for women—and shorn of particularities, the trans constituency refers to people who in other respects would be privileged "but for" the fact that they are not cisgender.[5] Compare the very positive transgender rights decision in 2020, *Bostock v. Clayton County*, authored by a justice appointed by President Trump, to the restrictions on abortion that are certain to be delivered in the coming years. At the conclusion of the culture wars of the last forty years, the almost inseparable bond between movements for sexual and gender freedom that marked liberationist discourse of the 1970s has been torn asunder,[6] reconstituted through the logic of an identity politics that affirms the demands for recognition of sexual and gender minorities but finds the sexism and misogyny that still structure women's lives less intelligible politically, not fully inside the scope of diversity discourse and the liberal project of inclusion.[7]

For example, when North Carolina passed a law that would mandate individuals use the public bathroom that corresponded to the sex on their birth certificates, the leaders of Apple, Facebook, and eighty other Fortune 500 corporations had no hesitation calling anti-LGBT laws "bad for our employees and bad for business."[8] Indeed, because of boycott threats from the business community, North Carolina's bathroom policy was rescinded, and no other states' bathroom bills have been enacted. But business leaders are largely silent on antiabortion legislation. In fact, one 2015 poll found that 72 percent of the millennial generation in the United States favor laws banning discrimination against transgender people—a proportion very close to the 73 percent who support protections for gay and lesbian people. But only 55 percent of this generation, born between 1980 and 2000, say abortion should be legal in all (22 percent) or some (33 percent) cases.[9] Given this divergence in public opinion on trans rights and abortion access, it's no wonder that businesses are silent on abortion rights, not to mention more redistributionist demands for reproductive justice that include the positive economic rights needed to raise a child.[10]

Earlier in my career, I called for the disestablishment of gender.[11] By that I meant getting the state out of the business of policing the relation between sex as assigned at birth, gender identity (as male or female and now I would add non-binary), and gender expression. I also celebrated the gender pluralism that had become the organizing principle of the transgender umbrella.[12] It allowed for all sorts of ways of being gender different, from old school transsexual people not particularly critical of the medical model of the gender binary that made their transitions possible to people who rejected the gender binary altogether to people who sought to reconstitute it in very new and unexpected ways. I saw this kind of gender pluralism as a move away from an identity-bound rights discourse. Within gender non-normative communities, this ethos could accommodate a critique of the medical model (in which transsexuality is seen as merely reinscribing gender) *and* a critique of the critique (in which transgender as it's been absorbed into queer theoretical projects becomes the new revolutionary class). Gender pluralism should be, I thought and still think, the normative ideal for how states treat trans people.

While state actors should be agnostic on gender, just as movements for trans equality have effectively become,[13] I have realized that it's not a matter of clicking our heels three times to bring a better state into existence. That wishful thinking represents the doctrinal/popular sovereignty approach described in chapter 2, which imagines the state as a sometimes muddled yet potentially benevolent night watchman: just make the correct argument about what sex and gender really are, and eventually legislators, courts, and policymakers will get it right. Instead, while on the surface it seems a matter of simply adjusting the criteria for particular labels, those labels may have been anchored by forces deeply embedded in the machinery of governance—as advocates learned the hard way. Recall that the attorneys defending the city of New York's birth certificate policy (discussed in chapter 1) once argued that the existence of different sex reclassification rules for different city agencies was not arbitrary or capricious but rational: sex definition depended on the remit of the particular agency. Even now, when sex classification has largely been decommissioned as a technology of governance and rules tend to reflect divisions over culture wars and identity politics, in the political jurisdictions most progressive on trans issues that agnosticism is not universally applied. For example, when the city finally assented to the appeals of trans advocates and eliminated all barriers to sex reclassification on birth certificates and added non-binary as an option as well, it did not stop assigning M or F at birth to the vast majority of the newborn population.[14] Parents can opt out on behalf of their child, but for everyone else, inking Ms or Fs on the birth certificate remains the default. Though one's sex classification has never mattered so little to states for most purposes, the strong gravitational pull of traditional gender norms confines demands for the destabilization of gender to the transactional arithmetic of identity politics. A gender pluralist approach rightly sidesteps imperatives to decide on a singular truth of sex, gender, and the connection between them. Yet, counterintuitively, it still allows for the packaging of a diffuse collection of gender non-normative ways of being into a group for the purposes of identity politics. In the move to gender pluralism, one crucial tool risks getting lost: the emphasis on *asymmetry*.[15]

With a gender-pluralistic frame, the struggle no longer centers on those subjugated by the binary challenging those who are privileged by it; rather—and with some exceptions, such as sports—the struggle moves to dismantling the binary altogether. One can see this shift in the evolution of the central terms and their significations in the United States. By the late 1990s, the division between what Jay Prosser called the transsexual person who "literalizes" gender and the transgender subject who "deliteralizes" it has been resolved: transgender emerged as the conceptual victor. At this point, the "transgender umbrella" begins to circulate widely as a device representing the many different ways of being gender non-normative. More recent iterations of the umbrella dispense with most of the pathologizing labels and list less binary identities, such as genderqueer, demiboy, demigirl, neutrois, genderfluid, bigender, agender, and of course non-binary.[16] The plasticity of transgender means it can accommodate specificity of all kinds—including "wrong body" transsexual men and women—under the abstract construction of gender non-normativity. The transgender umbrella makes possible a coherent politics of identity without compressing disparate non-normative genders into a single legible figure. While the umbrella metaphor is beginning to fall out of favor, transgender itself remains the master term, capacious, protean, adding new genders and molting older ones as they lose their interpellatory appeal.

It found an intellectual foundation in what became the dominant tendency in US feminist theory. Just as transgender superseded transsexual, the notion of gender won out over the conceptual frame of sex difference. Rather than seeing gender as a binary structure defined by the symbolic, as in psychoanalysis, or by the somatic, as in radical feminism, what was then called postmodern feminism has, Rita Felski noted in 1996, "sought in different ways to break out of the prisonhouse of gender by reconceptualizing masculinity and femininity as performative, unstable, and multiply determined practices."[17] The fixed binary was replaced by what people took to be gender fluidity and the seemingly endless potential for the proliferation of gender difference. With that approach, in academic and activist realms the binary became a continuum and sex was absorbed by gender.

Much was gained with this move away from the centrality of the binary in gender theory, queer theory, and trans studies. The sexual difference framework established it as universal and ahistorical, and as a consequence, made it difficult to pay more than cursory attention to race, class, and other social locations involving structural disadvantages. Moreover, gender provided a theoretical home for queer and transgender subjects that sexual difference mostly could not. Indeed, the necessity of moving away from a stark sexual difference framework is made evident in conservatives' and revanchist "gender critical feminists'" reliance on it. They dismiss the very idea of gender as distinct from what they imagine to be biological sex when they argue that trans women—they have focused almost exclusively on trans women until very recently—are men.[18] (The rhetoric of gender critical feminists and their right-wing fellow travelers is saturated with transmisogyny.) For both, the exclusion of trans women from the category of womanhood is made possible by a binary defined by sexual difference. This version of binary does a lot of work: not only does it limit the category of women to those assigned female at birth, it also excludes those whose bodies don't comport with hegemonic ideals of femaleness. For example, trans celebrity Caitlyn Jenner is cast out, but so too is Black South African athlete Caster Semenya, along with other women from the Global South who are much more likely to emerge from the "sex testing" inflicted on them with their femaleness in question than white athletes.[19] Because the binary developed against the backdrop of colonialism and the invention of racial difference, because idealized white bodies were the metric of sexual difference, it should come as no surprise that policing the borders of sex is bound up with white supremacist fictions about the body.[20]

A gender pluralist politics makes room for, even celebrates, all the ways in which gender can be revised, remixed, reworked. And that is a good thing. But it's not everything. Sometimes it's assumed that the demise of the binary (and the medical model that undergirds it) for sex classification purposes will have broader political effects. This trans-as-revolutionary scenario has likely been imported from queer studies, which has, Robyn Wiegman observes, a "well-honed insistence that normativity names the problem and antinormativity the solution to the political complexity of our social world."[21] Certainly, conservatives and gender critical feminists cling to the idea of a binary defined by sexual difference; certainly, the binary can't escape its roots in colonialism and white supremacy. But being *against* something that conservatives and gender critical feminists are *for* does not necessarily have far-reaching antiracist or redistributive consequences. In fact, it may be that some gender non-normative identities and expressions harmonize with the individualism of today's entrepreneurial economic culture. Indeed, Jasbir Puar describes the emergence of "a new transnormative citizen predicated not on passing but on 'piecing,' galvanized through mobility, transformation, regeneration, flexibility, and the creative concocting of the body."[22] This sort of gender pluralism and the reconstructed autonomy that attends it can resonate with a neoliberal ethos that has begun to value some trans people as potentially valuable forms of human capital. For the privileged among us, gender non-normativity can be something we cultivate, invest in, and brand. Neoliberal technologies of governance have proven able to accommodate some new articulations of social difference—Goldman Sachs flies the transgender flag!—without having to do much to modify the fundamental algorithms for the distribution of inequality.

It makes sense to see the conscription of transgender people into the culture wars as a reaction to the success of the mainstream trans rights movement. Because classifying people as male or female matters much less in work of the state, it's now possible for an individual to simply declare their sex designation as M, F, or X—in some jurisdictions, during some presidential administrations, at some levels of government, and for some, though not all, purposes. The new common sense of gender has not yet, however, entirely supplanted the older common sense. Indeed, state legislatures dominated by conservatives have doubled down by introducing legislation targeting access to bathrooms, girls' and women's sports, and gender-affirming care for youth.[23] Most of these bills have failed to pass, but those that have shouldn't be seen as the last gasps of a dying conservative gender order. These laws are not merely symbolic politics, they cause real harm, just as advances for trans and non-binary people make material differences in people's lives. It's crucial that we value legal reform and choose the just side of the antagonism between gender revanchism and gender pluralism. But restricting our options to this binary encloses our political imagination and makes it harder to envision the kinds of changes we need to make life livable.

ACKNOWLEDGMENTS

I am deeply indebted to many people for their help and support. When I first embarked on this project (I will not say how long ago that was!), books on transgender topics beyond Trans 101 and outside of the humanities were vanishingly rare. Lucky for me, Ilene Kalish at New York University Press was enthusiastic about this project from the get-go and her support never flagged through its long gestation. Andrea Long Chu read the manuscript and mined crystals of thought I hadn't realized were buried in it. On so many occasions, Shannon Minter generously shared his deep and wide knowledge of all things related to trans people and the law. Corey Robin gave a much-needed haircut to two chapters. He also never stopped prodding me to get the manuscript in. Lisa L. Moore, of the University of Texas at Austin, read and commented on every chapter and announced—forcefully enough for me to believe it— that it had been in the oven long enough. B Stone's research assistance tracking down policy changes and updates was invaluable during the final revisions. I am grateful to Lynne Ferguson, who copyedited an earlier draft of this book (of course, I couldn't stop myself from rewriting chapters), and to Dan Geist, who copyedited the final version. Many others commented on parts of the manuscript or related presentations, gave advice on sources, or provided the intellectual companionship needed to carry out this work: B Lee Aultman, Kyla Bender-Baird, Jesse Bayker, Michelle Billies, C Ray Borck, Laura Brahm, Margot Canaday, Monica J. Casper, Nancy F. Cott, Megan Davidson, Laurie Essig, Joseph Fischel, Emily Grabham, Katrina Karkazis, Ido Katri, Sonya Katyal, Reese Kelley, Drake Logan, Nancy Love, Serena Mayeri, Stephanie McCurry, John McMahon, Tey Meadow, Lisa Jean Moore, Tara Mulqueen, Heidi Andrea Restrepo Rhodes, Lara Rodriguez, Robert O. Self, Noah Alan Smith, TC Tolbert, Tre Wentling, and Angie Wilson. Griffin Hansbury made a real difference. On campus, Barbara Haugstatter and Irva Adams did much to smooth out the bureaucratic wrinkles that invariably come with working at a public university. Kyle Aaron Reese has provided invaluable support for my work in women's and gender studies—and, as a research assistant, provided crucial help in the last stages of preparing the manuscript. I have been fortunate in getting my work supported, in the form of time and money, from a variety of sources, including: a two-year appointment as the Brooklyn College Women's and Gender Studies Program's Endowed Chair, a two-year Tow Professorship, a grant from the LGBT Social Science and Public Policy Center of the Roosevelt House Public Policy Institute at Hunter College, the Williams Institute's Small Research Award, the Wayne F. Placek Award from the American Psychological Foundation, and three PSC-CUNY Research Awards. I was very fortunate to have the opportunity to work with and learn from Susan Stryker in founding and editing *TSQ: Transgender Studies Quarterly*. My perspective as a scholar has been indelibly shaped by my collaboration with thinkers such as Genny Beemyn, Spencer Bergstedt, Kylar Broadus, Carrie Davis, Justus Eisfeld, Phyllis R. Frye, Alexander John Goodrum, Jamison Green, Mauro Cabral Grinspan, Jennifer Levi, Shannon Minter, Liz Seaton, Dean Spade, and Stephen Whittle, among so many others. It's my good fortune to work at a place where, when I share my work with the campus community, the smartest comments come from the college president, Michelle Anderson. My students never cease to disrupt (creatively of course) my thinking, challenging me to be a better teacher and scholar. Thanks also are due to members of my family, both chosen and given: Georgia Moore, Grace Moore, Kel Currah, Kelsang Kunden, Lesley Dingle, and Fraser Currah. And finally, I am grateful to Greta Currah for always asking the hardest questions and for helping me stay in the present.

NOTES

PREFACE

1 Office of the Commissioner, State of New York Department of Motor Vehicles, "Change in Required Documentation for Proof of Sex Change" (Memo), Albany, New York, April 29, 1987.

2 T. Benjamin Singer, "From the Medical Gaze to Sublime Mutations," in *The Transgender Studies Reader*, ed. Susan Stryker and Stephen Whittle (New York: Routledge, 2006), 616.

3 T. Benjamin Singer, presentation at the Center for Lesbian and Gay Studies, 1999.

4 Jamison Green, "Introduction to Transgender Issues," in Paisley Currah and Shannon Minter, *Transgender Equality: A Handbook for Activists and Policymakers* (New York: Policy Institute of the National Gay and Lesbian Task Force, 2000), 3.

5 Susan Stryker, "My Words to Victor Frankenstein above the Village of Chamounix," *GLQ: A Journal of Lesbian and Gay Studies* 1, no. 3 (1994): 251n2.

6 Julia Serano, *Whipping Girl: A Transsexual Woman on Sexism and the Scapegoating of Femininity*, 2nd ed. (Berkeley, CA: Seal Press, 2016), 12, 23.

7 For a thoughtful critique of the deployment of cisgender by allies, see Finn Enke, "The Education of Little Cis: Cisgender and the Disciplining of Opposite Bodies," in *Transfeminist Perspectives*, ed. Finn Enke (Philadelphia: Temple University Press, 2012), 60–77.

8 David Valentine, *Imagining Transgender: An Ethnography of a Category* (Durham, NC: Duke University Press, 2007), 39.

9 Christine Labuski and Colton Keo-Meier argue against using transgender as a "proxy" variable that reduces complexity "into more quantifiable forms of data." Instead, they recommend that "transgender's instability as a research variable" be foregrounded. Christine Labuski and Colton L. Keo-Meier, "The (Mis)Measure of Trans," *TSQ: Transgender Studies Quarterly* 2, no. 1 (2015): 13.

10 For example, transgender rights advocates tend to speak generally about employment discrimination against transgender people, but it may be the case that trans men experience less gender-based discrimination than similarly situated trans women. See, for example, Kristen Schilt, *Just One of the Guys? Transgender Men and the Persistence of Gender Inequality* (Chicago: University of Chicago Press, 2010).

11 Paisley Currah, "The New Transgender Panic: 'Men' in Women's Bathrooms," *PaisleyCurrah.com* (blog), March 31, 2016, https://paisleycurrah.com.

12 Aristotle, *Nicomachean Ethics*, in *The Complete Works of Aristotle*, ed. Jonathan Barnes (Princeton, NJ: Princeton University Press, 1984), Vol. 3, 1131a10–b15.

13 I have generally been guided by Alex Kapitan's recommendations for writing about transgender people. Alex Kapitan, "The Radical Copyeditor's Style Guide for Writing about Transgender People," 2017, www.radicalcopyeditor.com.

14 Paisley Currah and Shannon Minter, *Transgender Equality: A Handbook for Activists and Policymakers* (New York: Policy Institute of the National Gay and Lesbian Task Force and National Center for Lesbian Rights, 2000).

15 Julie A. Greenberg, *Intersexuality and the Law* (New York: New York University Press, 2012).

INTRODUCTION

1 John Marzulli, "900G Toys 'R' Us Bias Suit," *New York Daily News*, June 19, 2002.

2 Complaint, *Magrath v. Toys 'R' Us*, No. CV-01-3071 (United States District Court, Eastern District of New York May 15, 2001).

3 Associated Press, "Trans Customers Accuse Toys 'R' Us of Harassment," *New York Blade*, June 28, 2002.

4 Email message from plaintiff's attorney, Tom Shanahan, to author, October 10, 2002.

5 Currah and Minter, *Transgender Equality*.

6 Robert P. Jones and Daniel Cox, "How Race and Religion Shape Millennial Attitudes on Sexuality and Reproductive Health" (Public Religion Research Institute, 2015), www.publicreligion.org.

7 Daniel Trotta, "Women, Young More Open on Transgender Issue in U.S.–Reuters/Ipsos Poll," Reuters, April 21, 2016, www.reuters.com; Halley P. Crissman et al., "Youth Perspectives Regarding the Regulating of Bathroom Use by Transgender Individuals," *Journal of Homosexuality* 67, no. 14 (December 5, 2020): 2034–49.

8 Katy Steinmetz, "The Transgender Tipping Point," *Time*, June 9, 2014.

9 Bill Walsh, "The Post Drops the 'Mike'—and the Hyphen in 'E-Mail,'" *Washington Post*, December 4, 2015, www.washingtonpost.com. Indeed, "they" as a singular pronoun was chosen as the word of the year by members of the American Dialect Society: according to one language columnist, "a win for singular *they* would also symbolize how mainstream culture has come to recognize and accept transgender and gender fluid people, some of whom reject traditional pronouns." Jeff Guo, "Sorry, Grammar Nerds. The Singular 'They' Has Been Declared Word of the Year," *Wonkblog* (blog), January 8, 2016, www.washingtonpost.com. In 2019, a *New York Times* columnist suggested that everyone, binary people included, use they/them. Farhod Manjoo, "It's Time for 'They,'" *New York Times*, July 10, 2019, www.nytimes.com.

10 Goldman Sachs (@GoldmanSachs), "PHOTO: $GS is proudly flying the transgender flag at our 200 West headquarters today #Pride2016 #Stonewall," June 28, 2016, 9:51 a.m., https://twitter.com/GoldmanSachs/status/747834825831292928. (I am indebted to Doug Henwood for drawing my attention to this tweet).

11 Maggie Astor, "Danica Roem Wins Virginia Race, Breaking a Barrier for Trans-gender People," *New York Times*, November 7, 2017, www.nytimes.com. Roem was reelected in 2019. With the 2019 election, the total number of transgender elected officials at any level of government in the United States increased to twenty-one. W. Matt Baume, "Transgender Candidates Won Big in Elections Last Night," *Out Magazine*, November 6, 2019, www.out.com.

12 Piper McDaniel and David Garcia, "Trans and Nonbinary Candidates Set Record Wins in Red and Blue States," *National Public Radio*, November 9, 2020, www.npr.org.

13 For an account of the successes of the transgender rights movement, especially as it has been organized as an identity politics movement, see Jami K. Taylor, Daniel C. Lewis, and Donald P. Haider-Markel, *The Remarkable Rise of Transgender Rights* (Ann Arbor: University of Michigan Press, 2018).

14 T. Benjamin Singer, "Umbrella," *TSQ: Transgender Studies Quarterly* 1, no. 1–2 (2014): 259–61. See also Megan Davidson, "Seeking Refuge under the Umbrella: Inclusion, Exclusion, and Organizing within the Category Transgender," *Sexuality Research & Social Policy: Journal of NSRC* 4, no. 4 (2007): 60–80.

15 Susan Stryker, *Transgender History: The Roots of Today's Revolution*, 2nd ed. (New York: Seal Press, 2017), 1.

16 Regarding the uneasiness of locating non-binary underneath the proverbial "transgender umbrella," and the ambivalence that some non-binary people feel about identifying as transgender, see, e.g., Helana Darwin, "Challenging the Cisgender/Transgender Binary: Nonbinary People and the Transgender Label," *Gender & Society* 20, no. 10 (2020): 1–24.

17 Andrew R. Flores et al., "How Many Adults Identify as Transgender in the United States?" (Los Angeles: Williams Institute, June 2016), www.williamsinstitute.law.ucla.edu.

18 Jan Hoffman, "Estimate of U.S. Transgender Population Doubles to 1.4 Million Adults," *New York Times*, June 30, 2016, www.nytimes.com.

19 In 1991, Sandy Stone used the phrase "myriad of alterities" to describe the "mul-tiple dissonances" produced by the transsexual body. Sandy Stone, "The Empire Strikes Back: A Posttranssexual Manifesto," in *Body Guards: The Cultural Politics of Gender Ambiguity*, ed. Julia Epstein and Kristina Kraus (New York: Routledge, 1991), 299.

20 Wendy McKenna and Suzanne J. Kessler, "Transgendering: Blurring the Bound-aries of Gender," in *Handbook of Gender and Women's Studies*, ed. Kathy Davis, Mary Evans, and Judith Lorber (London: Sage Publications, 2006), 4.

21 *Obergefell v. Hodges*, 76 US 644 (2015).

22 Arrest warrant. Photocopy in possession of the author. (An alias has been used to respect the privacy of the individual.)

23 "False personation" originates in English common law: "The offence of falsely personating another for the purpose of fraud." George Sharswood, Henry Roscoe, and Thomas Colpitts Granger, *A Digest of the Law of Evidence in Criminal Cases* (Philadelphia: T. & J. Johnson, 1840), 414–15.

24 Suzanne Kessler and Wendy McKenna, *Gender: An Ethnomethodological Approach* (Hoboken, NJ: John Wiley and Sons, 1978).

25 B Lee Aultman, "Cisgender," *TSQ: Transgender Studies Quarterly* 1, no. 1–2 (May 2014): 61–62.

26 Office of the Mayor, "Mayor de Blasio Announces Department of Correction Will House Incarcerated Individuals According to Gender Identity, Working with City Human Rights Commission to Maintain Transgender Housing Unit," April 16, 2018, www1.nyc.gov.

27 Keri Blakinger, "A Look at How New York Houses Trans Inmates—and Where Sophia Burset of 'Orange Is the New Black' Would Be Jailed in Real Life," *New York Daily News*, February 11, 2016, www.nydailynews.com.

28 Counsel's Office, Republican National Committee, "Resolution Condemning Governmental Overreach Regarding Title IX Politics in Public Schools," February 25, 2016, at https://prod-static-ngop-pbl.s3.amazonaws.com.

29 In 1994, at the time of Jane's arrest, the state refused to change sex designations on birth certificates, according to the Idaho administrative code. Through litigation, the Idaho Department of Health and Welfare has since been forced to allow individuals to change the sex designation on their birth certificate. *F. V. v. Jeppesen*, No. 1:17-CV-00170-CWD (US District Court for the District of Idaho, August 7, 2020).

30 Paisley Currah and Lisa Jean Moore, "'We Won't Know Who You Are': Contesting Sex Designations in New York City Birth Certificates," *Hypatia* 24, no. 3 (2009): 113–35. This policy has since been reformed, and is discussed at length in chapter 1.

31 Talia Mae Bettcher, "Evil Deceivers and Make-Believers: On Transphobic Violence and the Politics of Illusion," *Hypatia* 22, no. 3 (2007): 43–65.

32 Robbie Brown, "Transgender Candidate Who Ran as Woman Did Not Mislead Voters, Court Says," *New York Times*, October 6, 2008, www.nytimes.com.

33 Paisley Currah and Susan Stryker, "Introduction: Making Trans Count," *TSQ: Transgender Studies Quarterly* 2, no. 1 (2015): 1–12.

34 Eve Kosofsky Sedgwick, *Epistemology of the Closet* (Berkeley: University of California Press, 1990), 1.

35 Florence Ashley divides the gradual inclusion of trans people under the law in Quebec into two chronological models: first, the medical model, which positions a "transitional and liminal moment between two states of being binary," and second, a "minority model, which sees transness as an exceptional reality defined by its opposition to the dominant social framework." Ashley concludes that "more remains to be done in order to truly include trans people as usual subjects of law." Florence Ashley, "L'In/visibilité constitutive du sujet Trans: l'exemple du droit québécois," *Canadian Journal of Law and Society* 35, no. 2 (2020): 317–18. An English language version of this article is forthcoming in the *UCLA Women's Law Journal*.

36 Certainly, within transgender scholarship there is an important and still developing body of work that demonstrates the necessity of understanding the

mutual imbrication of misogyny and transphobia or transmisogyny. See, e.g., Emi Koyama, "The Transfeminist Manifesto," in *Catching a Wave: Reclaiming Feminism for the 21st Century*, ed. Rory Dicker and Alison Piepmeier (Boston: Northeastern University Press, 2003), 244–59; Serano, *Whipping Girl*; Finn Enke, "Collective Memory and the Transfeminist 1970s: Toward a Less Plausible History," *Transgender Studies Quarterly* 5, no. 1 (February 1, 2018): 9–29; Elías Cosenza Krell, "Is Transmisogyny Killing Trans Women of Color? Black Trans Feminisms and the Exigencies of White Femininity," *TSQ: Transgender Studies Quarterly* 4, no. 2 (2017): 226–42; Moya Bailey, "Misogynoir in Medical Media: On Caster Semenya and R. Kelly," *Catalyst: Feminism, Theory, Technoscience* 2, no. 2 (2016): 1–31. Claudia Sophía Garriga-López argues that the most exciting transfeminist or "transfeminismo" political projects originated in Spain in the 1980s and soon after circulated to Latin America. As she points out, transfeminismo is "part of a broader subculture that encompasses resistance to capitalism and austerity measures; anti-racist, postcolonial, and pro-migrant critiques of state policies; antiinstitutional and leaderless social movements; and a posporno (i.e., post-pornographic or 'post-porn') performance art scene that appropriates and subverts the medium of pornography." Claudia Sophía Garriga-López, "Transfeminism," in *Global Encyclopedia of Lesbian, Gay, Bisexual, Transgender, and Queer History*, ed. Howard Chiang (New York: Gale, 2019), 1619–23. See also Susan Stryker and Talia Mae Bettcher, "Introduction: Trans/Feminisms," *TSQ: Transgender Studies Quarterly* 3, no. 1–2 (2016): 5–14.

37 Longtime trans activists Phyllis Frye and Alyson Meiselman certainly saw that matters of recognition for trans people and feminist projects were more deeply linked, though their arguments about the importance of transgender quests for recognition to the same-sex marriage debate were pretty much ignored by the gay rights impact litigators who did not want the stigma attached to transsexuals to contaminate the marriage equality movement. Phyllis Randolph Frye and Alyson Dodi Meiselman, "Same-Sex Marriages Have Existed Legally in the United States for a Long Time Now," *Albany Law Review* 64, no. 3 (2001): 1031–71. Julie Greenberg's important 2000 article explained that the transsexual marriage cases could matter in litigation around same-sex marriage. Julie A. Greenberg, "When Is a Man a Man, and When Is a Woman a Woman," *Florida Law Review* 52, no. 4 (2000): 745–68.

38 Catherine A MacKinnon, *Toward a Feminist Theory of the State* (Cambridge, MA: Harvard University Press, 1991); Linda Gordon, ed., *Women, The State, and Welfare* (Madison: University of Wisconsin Press, 1990); Gwendolyn M. Mink, "The Lady and the Tramp: Gender, Race, and the Origins of the American Welfare State," in *Women, the State, and Welfare*, ed. Linda Gordon (Madison: University of Wisconsin Press, 1990); Mike Savage and Anne Witz, eds., *Gender and Bureaucracy* (Cambridge: Blackwell, 1992); Suzanne Mettler, *Dividing Citizens: Gender and Federalism in New Deal Public Policy* (Ithaca, NY: Cornell University Press, 1998); Wendy Brown, "Finding the Man in the State," *Feminist Studies* 18,

no. 1 (Spring 1992): 7–34; Jacqueline Stevens, *Reproducing the State* (Princeton, NJ: Princeton University Press, 1999); Cathy Marie Johnson, Georgia Duerst-Lahti, and Noelle H. Norton, *Creating Gender: The Sexual Politics of Welfare Policy* (Boulder, CO: Lynne Rienner Publishers, 2007); Carole Pateman and Charles Mills, *The Contract and Domination* (New York: Polity Press, 2007). In addition to scholarship on gender and state political development, Margot Canaday's work demonstrates how sexual orientation advanced particular state projects. Margot Canaday, *The Straight State: Sexuality and Citizenship in Twentieth Century America* (Princeton, NJ: Princeton University Press, 2011).

39 Janice Raymond, *The Transsexual Empire: The Making of a She-Male* (New York: Teachers College Press, 1994).

40 C. Riley Snorton, *Black on Both Sides: A Racial History of Trans Identity* (Minneapolis: University of Minnesota Press, 2017), 7–8.

41 Shannon Minter, email message to author, July 8, 2016.

42 There are some exceptions: scholarship on the question of transgender social formations and capitalism includes Dan Irving, "Normalized Transgressions: Legitimizing the Transsexual Body as Productive," *Radical History Review*, no. 100 (Winter 2008): 38–59; Aren Aizura, "Transnational Transgender Rights and Immigration Law," in *Transfeminist Perspectives in and beyond Transgender and Gender Studies*, ed. Finn Enke (Philadelphia: Temple University Press, 2011), 133–50; Dean Spade, *Normal Life: Administrative Violence, Critical Trans Politics, and the Limits of Law*, 2nd ed. (Durham, NC: Duke University Press, 2015); Dan Irving and Vek Lewis, eds., "Special Issue on Trans Political Economy," *TSQ: Transgender Studies Quarterly* 4, no. 1 (February 2017); Jules Gleeson and Elle O'Rourke, eds., Transgender Marxism (London: Pluto Books, 2021).

43 Harold Garfinkel, "Passing and the Managed Achievement of Sex Status in an 'Intersexed' Person," in *The Transgender Studies Reader*, ed. Susan Stryker and Stephen Whittle, vol. 1 (New York: Routledge, 2006), 58–93.

44 Andrew Hartman, *A War for the Soul of America: A History of the Culture Wars* (Chicago: University of Chicago Press, 2015).

45 Adolph Reed Jr., *Class Notes: Posing as Politics and Other Thoughts on the American Scene* (New York: New Press, 2000), xxvii.

46 As Geoffrey Bowker and Susan Leigh Star put it, a "category is a desiccated form of a complex narrative." Susan Leigh Star and Geoffrey C. Bowker, "Enacting Silence: Residual Categories as a Challenge for Ethics, Information Systems, and Communication," *Ethics and Information Technology* 9 (2007): 273.

47 María Lugones, "Heterosexism and the Colonial/Modern Gender System," *Hypatia* 22, no. 1 (2007): 187–209.

48 Kyla Schuller, *The Biopolitics of Feeling: Race, Sex, and the Science of the Nineteenth Century* (Durham, NC: Duke University Press, 2018), 17. Xhercis Méndez writes that "chattel slavery by definition reduced Africans to the legal status of objects that could be bought and sold as opposed to beings that could be understood as either 'Men' or 'Women.'" Xhercis Méndez, "Notes toward a Decolonial Femi-

nist Methodology: Revisiting the Race/Gender Matrix," *Trans-Scripts* 5 (2015): 43. See also Krell, "Is Transmisogyny Killing Trans Women of Color?," 233–34.

49 Janet Shibley Hyde et al., "The Future of Sex and Gender in Psychology: Five Challenges to the Gender Binary," *American Psychologist* 74, no. 2 (March 2019): 171–93.

50 Madeline Pape et al., "Resisting and Remaking Sex in the Petri Dish, the Clinic, and on the Track," *Catalyst: Feminism, Theory, Technoscience* 6, no. 2 (2020): 1–17; Katrina Karkazis, *Fixing Sex: Intersex, Medical Authority and Lived Experience* (Durham, NC: Duke University Press, 2008); Rebecca Jordan-Young, *Brain Storm: The Flaws in the Science of Sex Differences* (Cambridge, MA: Harvard University Press, 2011); Julie A. Greenberg, "Defining Male and Female: Intersexuality and the Collision between Law and Biology," *Arizona Law Review* 41 (1999): 266–328; Donna Haraway, "Monkeys, Aliens, and Women: Love, Science, and Politics at the Intersection of Feminist Theory and Colonial Discourse," *Women's Studies International Forum* 12, no. 3 (1989): 295–312; Candace West and Don H. Zimmerman, "Doing Gender," *Gender & Society* 1, no. 2 (1987): 125–51.

51 Greenberg, *Intersexuality and the Law*, 48.

52 Joanne Meyerowitz, *How Sex Changed: A History of Transsexuality in the United States* (Cambridge, MA: Harvard University Press, 2002).

53 George James, Commissioner of Health, to Harry Krause, Executive Secretary, Committee on Public Health, New York Academy of Medicine, April 2, 1965, in Archives of the New York Academy of Medicine. As one author pointed out in a 1973 article on the issue of transsexuals and birth certificates, "legally, a definition of male or female does not exist. The presumption that gender is so well understood as not to need defining does not survive examination." L. O. Schroeder, "Renaissance for the Transsexual: A New Birth Certificate," *Journal of Forensic Sciences* 18, no. 3 (July 1973): 237–45.

54 Star and Bowker, "Enacting Silence," 274; Geoffrey C. Bowker and Susan Leigh Star, *Sorting Things Out: Classification and Its Consequences* (Cambridge, MA: MIT Press, 1999), 300–301.

55 Indeed, the state in its earliest modern European formations was essentially coterminous with patriarchy. See, e.g., Carole Pateman, *The Sexual Contract* (Stanford, CA: Stanford University Press, 1988); Sarah Hanley, "Engendering the State: Family Formation and State Building in Early Modern France," *French Historical Studies* 16, no. 1 (1989): 4–27; Maria Mies, *Patriarchy and Accumulation on a World Scale: Women in the International Division of Labor* (London: Zed Books, 1986); Pavla Miller, *Transformations of Patriarchy in the West, 1500–1900* (Indianapolis: Indiana University Press, 1998).

56 See, e.g., Hortense J. Spillers, "Mama's Baby, Papa's Maybe: An American Grammar Book," *Diacritics* 17, no. 2 (1987): 65–81; Cheryl Harris, "Whiteness as Property," *Harvard Law Review* 106, no. 8 (1993): 1707–91; Jennifer L. Morgan, *Laboring Women: Reproduction and Gender in New World Slavery* (Philadelphia: University of Pennsylvania Press, 2004); Ariel J Gross, *What Blood Won't Tell: A History*

of Race on Trial in America (Cambridge, MA: Harvard University Press, 2008); Peggy Pascoe, *What Comes Naturally: Miscegenation Law and the Making of Race in America* (New York: Oxford University Press, 2009); Jeffory Clymer, *Family Money: Property, Race, and Literature in the Nineteenth Century* (New York: Oxford University Press, 2012); Tera W. Hunter, *Bound in Wedlock: Slave and Free Black Marriage in the Nineteenth Century* (Cambridge, MA: Harvard University Press, 2017); Snorton, *Black on Both Sides.*

57 See, e.g., Mink, "The Lady and the Tramp"; Ira Katznelson, *When Affirmative Action Was White* (New York: W. W. Norton, 2005); Michelle Alexander, *The New Jim Crow: Mass Incarceration in the Age of Colorblindness* (New York: New Press, 2010); Richard Rothstein, *The Color of Law: A Forgotten History of How Our Government Segregated America* (New York: Liveright, 2018).

58 Same-sex marriages were so inconceivable when most state marriage statutes were passed that in some cases the statute neglected to specify that this legal relation was available only to one man marrying one woman. As the battle over same-sex marriages intensified in the 1990s, however, state laws and even constitutional amendments were written to make this exclusion clear. Outside of trans advocacy circles, however, little attention was paid to criteria for sex classification in the marriage cases.

59 Matthew Rosenberg and Dave Phillips, "All Combat Roles Now Open to Women, Defense Secretary Says," *New York Times,* December 4, 2015, www.nytimes.com.

60 Chris Johnson, "RNC Endorses Anti-Trans Bathroom Bills," *Washington Blade,* February 25, 2016, www.washingtonblade.com; Emily Wax-Thibodeaux and Samantha Schmidt, "Republican State Lawmakers Push Bills to Restrict Medical Treatments for Transgender Youths," *Washington Post,* January 22, 2020, www.washingtonpost.com.

61 Donald J. Trump (@realDonaldTrump), ". . . [T]he United States Government will not accept or allow / Transgender individuals to serve in any capacity in the U.S. Military. Our military must be focused on decisive and overwhelming / victory . . ." Twitter, July 6, 2017, 6:04 a.m., https://twitter.com/realDonaldTrump/status/890196164313833472?ref_src=twsrc%5Etfw.

62 Corey Robin, *The Reactionary Mind* (New York: Oxford University Press, 2011), 15.

63 Recent scholarship has focused on the connection between traditional values and neoliberalism. While some forms of neoliberalism celebrate gender parity and inclusion and eschew social conservatism, a number of scholars have pointed out connections between certain other strains of neoliberalism, including ordoliberalism and patriarchal family values. The political moment inaugurated by the election of Donald Trump and, for my purposes, the recent politicization of transgender issues has made this work even more crucial. See, for example, Melinda Cooper, *Family Values: Between Neoliberalism and the New Social Conservatism* (Brooklyn, NY: Zone Books, 2017); Quinn Slobodian, *Globalists: The End of Empire and the Birth of Neoliberalism* (Cambridge, MA: Harvard University Press, 2018); Jessica Whyte, *The Morals of the Market: Human Rights and the*

Rise of Neoliberalism (Brooklyn, NY: Verso, 2019); Wendy Brown, *In the Ruins of Neoliberalism: The Rise of Antidemocratic Politics in the West* (New York: Columbia University Press, 2019).

64 Michel Foucault, *Discipline and Punish: The Birth of the Prison*, trans. Alan Sheridan (New York: Vintage, 1979), 31.

65 "Police powers" refers to the laws enacted for the protection of the health, safety, welfare, and morals of the population. See, e.g., Mariana Valverde, "Genealogies of European States: Foucauldian Reflections," *Economy and Society* 36, no. 1 (2007): 159–78.

66 See, e.g., Jacques Derrida, "Declarations of Independence," *New Political Science* 7, no. 1 (1986): 7–15.

CHAPTER 1. "IF SEX IS NOT A BIOLOGIC PHENOMENON"

1 *Anonymous v. Weiner*, 50 Misc.2d 380 (1966).

2 This number does not include cases involving intersexed people. For the birth certificates of "pseudo hermaphrodites," officials would declare that an error had been made in the original birth certificate and make the requested change. The Board of Health had maintained a distinction between intersexed individuals and individuals whose gender identity later turned out not to match the sex assigned at birth. The policy for change of sex classification for intersexed individuals was not under debate.

3 George James, Commissioner of NYC Board of Health, letter to Dr. Harry Krause, Executive Secretary, Committee on Public Health, New York Academy of Medicine, April 2, 1965.

4 New York Academy of Medicine Committee on Public Health, "Change of Sex on Birth Certificates for Transsexuals," *Bulletin of the New York Academy of Medicine* 42, no. 8 (1966): 723.

5 Ibid., 724.

6 *Anonymous v. Weiner*, 50 Misc.2d 380 (1966).

7 While an individual's sex appears in the second box of information on the vast majority of birth certificates, the 1971 policy simply eliminated the box on the reissued birth certificates of those who had changed their sex.

8 Minutes of the City of New York Board of Health meeting, December 16, 1971, 5.

9 Letter from Sol Blumenthal Director, Office of Biostatistics, New York City Department of Health to (addressee's name removed), June 3, 1980.

10 There are fifty-seven birth registration jurisdictions in the United States. New York City is a birth registration jurisdiction distinct from New York State.

11 New York City Department of Mental Health and Hygiene, "Notes from the Meetings of the Advisory Committee on Amending Birth Certificates for Transgender Persons," February 7, March 7, April 28, 2005.

12 This policy debate is detailed extensively in Currah and Moore, "'We Won't Know Who You Are.'"

13 *Berkley et al. v. Farley*, Petitioners Opening Brief, Supreme Court of the State of New York, County of New York (March 17, 2011), 2–5, 17.

14 Erin Durkin, "More than 700 New Yorkers Have Officially Changed Gender since City Adopted New Rules in 2015," *New York Daily News*, March 9, 2017, www. nydailynews.com.

15 New York City Health, "Correct a Birth Certificate," www1.nyc.gov, accessed December 22, 2020.

16 Letter from Charles R. Council, Chief, Registrations Methods Branch, Division of Vital Statistics, Department of Health, Education and Welfare, to Carl. L. Erhardt, Director, Bureau of Records and Statistics, City of New York Health Department, New York City, June 11, 1965.

17 In addition to resistance from city agencies, the Board of Health also identified the federal Real ID Act as one of the reasons the city couldn't proceed with a classification policy based on gender identity: because of "anticipated federal regulations [on the verification of birth certificate data] and the importance of sex as a key verifier of identity, it is important to wait for their promulgation." Memo from Lorna P. Thorpe, Deputy Commissioner, Division of Epidemiology and Stephen Schwartz, Registrar and Assistant Commissioner, Bureau of Vital Statistics, to Thomas Friedan, Chairperson, Board of Health, "Response to Public Comments and Additional Recommendations regarding Proposal to Amend Section 207.05 of the New York City Health Code," December 5, 2006, 2.

18 *Berkley et al. v. Farley*, Respondents' Memorandum of Law, Supreme Court of the State of New York, County of New York (July 15, 2011), 22.

19 New York Academy of Medicine Subcommittee on Birth Certificates, Minutes, June 14, 1965.

20 Carrie Davis, one of the members of the 2005 New York City Task Force, recalled at least one official referring to the same-sex marriage issue, but this is not reflected in the official minutes. Interview with Carrie Davis, March 2007.

21 New York City Department of Health and Mental Hygiene, "Health Department Announces New Law Offering Third Gender Category on Birth Certificates," press release no. #104–18, December 31, 2018, www1.nyc.gov.

22 On "transgender ideology," see, e.g., Colin M. Wright and Emma N. Hilton, "The Dangerous Denial of Sex," *Wall Street Journal*, February 13, 2020, www.wsj.com.

23 The New York City Department of Health and Mental Hygiene's description of the changes to the health code makes it clear that X is not an option among the categories assigned at birth. Parents can elect to change the sex designation to X after the original birth certificate has been issued. Interestingly, the department names the designation options at birth as sex categories and the categories that can be opted into later as gender categories: "The Board is now (1) eliminating the requirement that a person requesting a change to the sex designation on a birth certificate present proof from a health professional and instead allow applicants to self-attest as to their gender, and (2) approving 'X' as an additional sex designation gender option that is not exclusively female or male for birth certificate sex change requests. The sex designation on the US Standard Certificate of Live Birth is completed by the hospital or attendant at the time of birth. The four choices

are male, female, unknown, and undetermined. These are 'sex' categories and not gender categories. The original public health data reported by the hospital is not changed under this amendment. 'Gender' categories are only applied on the birth certificate during an amendment process. When the gender on a birth certificate is amended the original record is placed under seal and a new record is created. There is no indication on the record of the amendment history. A sex designation of 'X' will be allowed for those applicants who want a designation other than female or male on their birth certificate." New York City Department of Health and Mental Hygiene, "Notice of Adoption of Amendment to Article 207 of the New York City Health Code," 2019, www1.nyc.gov.

24 Flores et al., "How Many Adults?"

25 For a different but fascinating and generative account of the legal distinction between sex and gender, see Sonia K. Katyal, "The Numerus Clausus of Sex," *Chicago Law Review* 84 (2017): 389–494.

26 Indeed, in suggesting that sex isn't a thing in itself to some audiences, one risks the prospect of immediately losing one's audience or at least prompting a posture of resistance to all the other arguments that follow. For example, when I suggested that sex might be more usefully understood as a state effect at the annual meeting of the American Political Science Association some years ago, the response of one member of the audience can only be described as apoplectic. Getting to his feet, waving his hands in the air, and actually shouting, he repeatedly yelled out, "Do you not know what XX and XY mean?" He apparently meant that chromosomes should be the single rule for classification. For him, as perhaps for some of his more polite colleagues, the very idea that sex classification was a matter of politics was simply outrageous.

27 Judith Butler, *Gender Trouble* (New York: Routledge, 1990), 8.

28 Mariana Valverde, *Law's Dream of a Common Knowledge* (Princeton, NJ: Princeton University Press, 2003), 153–54.

29 Garfinkel, "Passing."

30 "Change of Sex on Birth Certificates for Transsexuals," Report by the Committee on Public Health, New York Academy of Medicine, *Bulletin of the New York Academy of Medicine* 42, no. 8 (August 1966): 721–24.

31 Curtis M. Wong, "50 Percent of Millennials Believe Gender Is a Spectrum, Fusion's Massive Millennial Poll Finds," *Huffington Post*, February 5, 2015, www.huffpost.com; Sidney Bauer, "The New Anti-Trans Culture War Hiding in Plain Sight," *New Republic*, February 11, 2020, www.newrepublic.com.

32 See, e.g., Shannon Price Minter, "'Déjà vu All Over Again': The Recourse to Biology by Opponents of Transgender Equality," *North Carolina Law Review* 95, no. 4 (2017): 1161–204.

33 Gregory Korte, "Judge in Texas Blocks Obama Transgender Bathroom Rules," *USA Today*, August 22, 2016, www.usatoday.com.

34 *Bostock v. Clayton County*, 140 S. Ct. 1731 (2020). See also Paisley Currah, "How a Conservative Legal Perspective Just Saved LGBT Rights," *Boston Review*, June 19, 2020, www.bostonreview.net.

35 Suzanne Kessler, *Lessons from the Intersexed* (New Brunswick, NJ: Rutgers University Press, 1998), 113.

36 Currah and Moore, "'We Won't Know Who You Are,'" 129.

37 Mubarak Dahir, "Whose Movement Is It?," *Advocate*, May 26, 1999.

38 For example, for trans people assigned female at birth, "top surgery" is the most common surgery. Kailas M. Lu and E. F. Rothman, "Kailas M, Lu HMS, Rothman EF, Safer JD. Prevalence and Types of Gender-Affirming Surgery among a Sample of Transgender Endocrinology Patients Prior to State Expansion of Insurance Coverage," *Endocrine Practice* 23 (2017): 780–86.

39 International Conference on Transgender Law and Employment Policy, "The International Bill of Gender Rights," in *Transgender Rights*, ed. Paisley Currah, Richard M. Juang, and Shannon Price Minter (Minneapolis: Minnesota University Press, 2006), 327–31. While this document did not address the question of legal sex classification directly, it did address injustices of sex misclassification when it demanded that no one "be denied access to a space or denied participation in an activity by virtue of a self-defined gender identity."

40 Jo Wuest, "The Scientific Gaze in American Transgender Politics: Contesting the Meanings of Sex, Gender, and Gender Identity in the Bathroom Rights Cases," *Politics & Gender* 15, no. 2 (2019): 336–60.

41 Meyerowitz, *How Sex Changed*, 99.

42 Jennifer Germon, *Gender: A Genealogy of an Idea* (New York: Palgrave MacMillan, 2009), 81–82.

43 Plaintiff's Post-Trial Brief at 12, *Schroer vs. Billington*, U.S. District Court for the District of Columbia (2008) (No. 05-cv-1090).

44 Brief Amicus Curiae of Public Advocate of the United States, Citizens United Foundation, Lincoln Institute for Research and Education, Concerned Women for America, and Conservative Legal Defense and Education Fund in Support of Appellant at 4, *Hyman. v. The City of Louisville*, United States Court of Appeals for the Sixth Circuit (2001) (No. 01–5531). Available online at www.citizensunited-foundation.com.

45 Jemima Repo, *The Biopolitics of Gender* (New York: Oxford University Press, 2016).

46 Germon, *Gender*, 120.

47 See, e.g., Enke, "Collective Memory"; John Stoltenberg, "#GenderWeek: Andrea Was Not Transphobic," *Feminist Times*, 2014, https://web.archive.org/web/20160317032310/http://www.feministtimes.com/%e2%80%aa%e2%80%8e genderweek-andrea-was-not-transphobic; Andrea Long Chu, "On Liking Women," *n+1* 30 (August 2018), www.nplusonemag.com.

48 Thomas Laqueur, *Making Sex: Body and Gender from the Greeks to Freud* (Cambridge, MA: Harvard University Press, 1990), 109. Other highly cited texts on this question include Anne Fausto-Sterling, *Sexing the Body: Politics and the Construction of Sexuality* (New York: Basic Books, 2000); Kessler and McKenna, *Gender*.

49 Butler, *Gender Trouble*, 7. Emphasis in original.

50 Butler explains, "There is no ontology of gender on which we might construct a politics, for gender ontologies always operate within established political contexts as normative injunctions, determining what qualifies as intelligible sex." Ibid., 148.

51 Nancy Hartsock's oft-quoted question put it thus: "Why is it that just at the moment when so many of us who have been silenced begin to demand the right to name ourselves, to act as subjects rather than objects of history, that just then the concept of subjecthood becomes problematic?" Nancy Hartsock, "Foucault on Power: A Theory for Women?," in *Feminism/Postmodernism*, ed. Linda Nicholson (New York: Routledge, 1990), 163–64.

52 Dylan Vade, "Expanding Gender and Expanding the Law: Toward a Social and Legal Conceptualization of Gender That Is More Inclusive of Transgender People," *Michigan Journal of Gender and Law* 11, no. 2 (2005): 291.

53 Heath Fogg Davis, "Sex-Classification Policies as Transgender Discrimination: An Intersectional Critique," *Perspectives on Politics* 12 (2014): 46. Davis's important intervention has been to show that the sex categories are no longer necessary. In showing how sex classifications *used to* matter, my project supplements his. Heath Fogg Davis, *Beyond Trans: Does Gender Matter?* (New York: New York University Press, 2017).

54 Aizura, "Transnational Transgender Rights," 135.

55 Irving, "Normalized Transgressions," 39.

56 Dean Spade, "What's Wrong with Trans Rights?," in *Trans Feminist Perspectives in and beyond Transgender Studies*, ed. Finn Enke (Philadelphia: Temple University Press, 2011), 193; see also Ido Katri, "Trans Bodies, Gay Sexuality, and the Disphoric State between Them," in *Enticements: Queer Legal Studies*, ed. Brenda Cossman and Joseph C. Fischel (New York: New York University Press, forthcoming).

57 Karl Marx, "On the Jewish Question," in *The Marx-Engels Reader*, ed. Robert Tucker (New York: Norton, 1978), 26–46.

58 For a discussion of how the antinormative imperative has been central to queer theory—and, I would add, has been imported into trans theory—see Robyn Wiegman and Elizabeth A. Wilson, "Queer Theory without Antinormativity," *Differences* 26, no. 1 (2015): 1–25.

59 Wendy Brown, *Edgework: Critical Essays on Knowledge and Politics* (Princeton, NJ: Princeton University Press, 2005), 123–24; see also Nira Yuval-Davis, "Intersectionality and Feminist Politics," *European Journal of Women's Studies* 13, no. 3 (2006): 200–1.

60 Robert M. Cover, "Violence and the Word," *Yale Law Journal* 95, no. 8 (1986): 1601–29.

61 For example, writing about "sexual states," Jyoti Puri argues that regulations on "sexuality in its various dimensions, such as behavior, marriage, sexual health and disease, fertility, sexual labor, media representations, and the sex industry, are crucial mechanisms through which states are generated and the expansions and modifications in governance are justified." Jyoti Puri, *Sexual States: Governance*

and the Struggle over the Antisodomy Law in India (Durham, NC: Duke University Press, 2016), 6. See also Michel Foucault, *Security, Territory, Population: Lectures at the Collège de France, 1977–1978*, trans. Graham Burchell (New York: Palgrave MacMillan, 2007); Timothy Mitchell, "Society, Economy, and the State Effect," in *State/Culture: State-Formation after the Cultural Turn*, ed. George Steinmetz (Ithaca, NY: Cornell University Press, 1999), 76–97.

62 *Berkley et al. v. Farley*, Respondents' Memorandum of Law, Supreme Court of the State of New York, County of New York (July 15, 2011), 64.

63 Transcript of the Minutes of the Committee on General Welfare, City Council of New York, May 4, 2001, at 195.

64 US Department of State, "Gender Change," 2018. 8 Fam 4303.3, https://fam.state. gov, accessed January 14, 2021.

65 Discrepancies in policies and decisions on sex classification between state agencies at various levels of government are not limited to the question of whether or not a state actor will reclassify sex, though the starkness of that yes/no binary brings the issue of inconsistency into sharpest relief. Among the many state entities that do allow sex reclassification, one finds significant differences in the criteria that must be met. For example, the Model State Vital Statistics Act recommends that state departments of vital statistics amend the sex on the birth certificate after the individual presents a court order "indicating that the sex of an individual born in this state has been changed by surgical procedure." Model State Vital Statistics Act and Regulations § 21(d) (Ctr. for Disease Control & Prevention 1992), cited in Lisa Mottet, "Modernizing State Vital Statistics Statutes and Policies to Ensure Accurate Gender Markers on Birth Certificates: A Good Government Approach to Recognizing the Lives of Transgender People," *Michigan Journal of Gender and Law* 19, no. 2 (2013): 400. But which surgical procedure? In most sex reclassification policies, "surgical procedure" or "sex change surgery" was thought to be so obvious that the requirement needed no further description in the regulation. But, in fact, transgender people can avail themselves of a wide range of surgical body modifications related to sex, including orchidectomy, oophorectomy, hysterectomy, tracheal shaves, metoidioplasty, breast augmentation, mastectomies, and facial feminization surgery, to name a few. There is also room for a linguistic slippage between what body modifications the policy purports to require and the evidence actually presented. Policies that require a "sex change" without explicitly mentioning surgery could also be interpreted to require only masculinizing or feminizing hormone therapy, which can bring about changes to secondary sex characteristics and make it possible for the appearance of transgender people to match their gender identity. Or those policies could be interpreted to mean that one's gender identity has changed. Then there are significant differences in the evidence that must be proffered to government actors to back up one's request. Surgery reports? Affidavits from physicians? Which professionals are authorized to make the determination—physicians, psychiatrists, licensed social workers? While this may seem like a minor point, it is not.

CHAPTER 2. SEX AND POPULAR SOVEREIGNTY

1 The other municipalities at the time were Orlando, Florida; Sacramento County, California; Phoenix, Arizona; Las Vegas, Nevada; and the Greater Twin Cities area, Minnesota. Social Security Administration, "Social Security Card Center Information," www.socialsecurity.gov, accessed June 7, 2010.

2 Charles R. Council, Registration Methods Branch, Division of Vital Statistics, Department of Health, Education, and Welfare, letter to Carl L. Erhardt, Director of the Bureau of Records and Statistics, City of New York Health Department, June 11, 1965.

3 POMS Section RM 00203.215, "Changing Numident Data—Other than Name Change," May 6, 2008, at http://policy.ssa.gov, accessed November 21, 2008.

4 The idea that a document or file can provide a "verifiable" link to a person rests on some untenable assumptions, from the practical to the epistemological to the ontological. For a review of this literature, and a discussion of the problem in relation to gender screening at US airports, see Paisley Currah and Tara Mulqueen, "Securitizing Gender: Identity, Biometrics, and Gender Non-conforming Bodies at the Airport," *Social Research* 78, no. 2 (2011): 557–82.

5 US Department of Homeland Security, US Citizenship and Immigration Services, Office of Citizenship, "Learn about the United States: Quick Civics Lessons for the Naturalization Test" (Washington, DC, 2019), 2, 4, www.uscis.gov, accessed August 12, 2019.

6 Ibid., 14.

7 Rogers Smith, "Beyond Tocqueville, Myrdal and Hartz: The Multiple Traditions in America," *American Political Science Review* 87, no. 3 (1993): 549.

8 Bonnie Honig refers to this understanding of inexorable progress as "chrono-logic" and suggests, "There may well come what we later call progress, and new identities may be allowed or ushered onto the threshold of justice, but progress does not come with its own guarantee, nor is it a meaningful criterion to guide us. In the moment we do not know in what progress might consist, and new claims may seem laughable." Honig points out that this chrono-logic, on display in the citizenship guide, also erases the agency of the dispossessed: "Looking backward, we can say with satisfaction that the chrono-logic of rights required and therefore delivered the eventual inclusion of women, Africans, and native peoples into the schedule of formal rights. But what actually did the work? The impulsion of rights, their chrono-logic, or the political actors who won the battles they were variously motivated to fight and whose contingent victories were later credited not to the actors but to the independent trajectories of rights as such." Bonnie Honig, *Emergency Politics: Paradox, Law, Democracy* (Princeton, NJ: Princeton University Press, 2009), 47.

9 See, for example, Clarence Henderson, "I Fought for Civil Rights. It Is Offensive to Compare It with the Transgender Fight," *Charlotte Observer*, May 19, 2016, www.charlotteobserver.com.

10 *United States v. Virginia*, 518 U.S. 116, 566–67 (1996) (Scalia, A, dissenting).
11 "Attorney General Loretta E. Lynch Delivers Remarks at Press Conference Announcing Complaint against the State of North Carolina to Stop Discrimination against Transgender Individuals," www.justice.gov, May 9, 2016.
12 Rebecca Ruiz, "The Line in Loretta Lynch's Defense of Transgender Rights That Made Everyone Cry," Mashable, accessed June 10, 2016, http://mashable.com.
13 In *Bolling v. Sharpe*, 347 U.S. 497 (1954), the Supreme Court interpreted the Fifth Amendment's due process clause to include the Fourteenth Amendment's promise of equal protection.
14 *Vacco v. Quill* (1997), 521 U.S. 793, 799, citing *Plyer v. Doe*, 457 US 202, 216 (1982).
15 *U.S. v. Carolene Products Co.*, 304 U.S. 144 (1938).
16 *Clerburne v. Clerburne Living Center, Inc.*, 473 U.S. 432 (1985).
17 *Frontiero v. Richardson*, 411 U.S. 677, 686, 687 (1973) (plurality opinion).
18 *Craig v. Boren*, 429 U.S. 190, 197 (1976).
19 *Michael M. v. Superior Court, Sonoma City.*, 450 U. S. 464, 471 (1981) (plurality opinion).
20 The forms of knowledge the courts relied on to make racial classifications changed from those based on science to those based on "common sense," when scientists could no longer make "race" do the work the courts required it to do in excluding certain types of immigrants. Ian Haney López, *White by Law: The Legal Construction of Race*, revised ed. (New York: New York University Press, 2006).
21 Pascoe, *What Comes Naturally*.
22 Otto H. Olsen, ed., "Brief for Homer A. Plessy, Plessy v. Ferguson," in *The Thin Disguise: Turning Point in Negro History. Plessy v. Ferguson: A Documentary Presentation (1864–1896)* (New York: Humanities Press, 1967), 98. Emphasis in original. For the use of Critical Race Theory in thinking about transgender rights, see Paisley Currah, "The Transgender Rights Imaginary," *Georgetown Journal of Gender and the Law* 4 (2003): 705–20; Ido Katri, "Transgender Intrasectionality: Rethinking Anti-Discrimination Law and Litigation," *University of Pennsylvania Journal of Law and Social Change* 20, no. 1 (2017): 51–79; Ezra Young, "Demarginalizing Trans Rights," in *Deploying Intersectionality: Legal, Intellectual, and Activist Interventions*, ed. Kimberlé Crenshaw (New York: New Press, 2021).
23 Jennifer Hochschild and Vesla Weaver, "Policies of Racial Classification and the Politics of Inequality," in *Remaking America: Democracy and Public Policy in an Age of Inequality*, ed. Joe Soss, Jacob Hacker, and Suzanne Mettler (New York: Russell Sage Foundation, 2007), 160.
24 Reginald Oh, "On Account of Race or Color: Race as Corporation and the Original Understanding of Race," *Albany Law Review* 72, no. 4 (Winter 2009): 1029; Tseming Yang, "Choice and Fraud in Racial Identification: The Dilemma of Policing Race in Affirmative Action, the Census, and a Color-Blind Society," *Michigan Journal of Race and Law* 11, no. 2 (2006): 367–471; Neil Gotanda, "A Critique of 'Our Constitution Is Color-Blind,'" *Stanford Law Review* 44, no. 1 (November 1991): 1–68; David R. Roediger and Elizabeth D. Esch, *The Production of*

Difference: Race and the Management of Labor in U.S. History (New York: Oxford University Press, 2012).

25 In a preface to a later edition of *White by Law*, Ian Haney López writes that, were he writing the book now, he would put more emphasis on "the instrumental function of race and its material consequences." Haney López, *White by Law*, xvi.

26 Pascoe cites a 1924 decision setting out standards of proof for verifying the status of parties to a marriage, in which the Alabama Court of Appeals permitted "a witness, if he knows such to be a fact, to testify that a person is a negro, or is a white person, or that he is a man, or that he is a woman." Pascoe points out, "In order to make an interracial marriage, a couple had to cross both racial dividing lines (to be interracial) and sexual dividing lines (to be a legal marriage), so criminal trials for miscegenation might well have required proving both the race and sex of the partners on trial." Pascoe, *What Comes Naturally*, 130.

27 W. E. B. Du Bois, *Dusk of Dawn: An Essay toward an Autobiography of Race as a Concept* (New York: Routledge, 2017), 133.

28 Indeed, the relation between the two is not only constitutive, it is also contingent, depending on the processes and interests at play in a given historical moment. At the onset of European colonialism, constructions of the gender binary began to shift with the emergence of white supremacism. For example, Kyla Schuller argues that "the rhetoric of distinct sexes of male and female consolidated as a function of race." Kyla Schuller, *The Biopolitics of Feeling: Race, Sex, and the Science of the Nineteenth Century* (Durham, NC: Duke University Press, 2018), 17. C. Riley Snorton demonstrates how "chattel persons gave rise to an understanding of gender as an amendable and mutable form of being." Snorton, *Black on Both Sides*, 57. Sylvia Wynter describes how the category of "Man" represented the European as the prototypical human, in contrast with the lesser-ranked "modes of being human" (those to be colonized or enslaved). Sylvia Wynter, "Unsettling the Coloniality of Being/Power/Truth/Freedom: Towards the Human, after Man, Its Overrepresentation—an Argument," *CR: The New Centennial Review* 3, no. 3 (2003): 298, https://doi.org/10.1353/ncr.2004.0015; see also Denise Ferreria da Silva, *Toward a Global Idea of Race* (Minneapolis: University of Minnesota Press, 2007). Others have shown how representation of the male-female opposition, one of "Man's" constituent elements, also depended on an opposition between Europeans and those from regions to be colonized. María Lugones, "Heterosexism and the Colonial/Modern Gender System," *Hypatia* 22, no. 1 (2007): 187–209.

29 This is not to suggest that individuals did not socially transition before the latter half of the twentieth century; it is only to suggest that the phenomenon did not enter into the public imagination until the 1950s, with Christine Jorgensen's very public transition. See Meyerowitz, *How Sex Changed*; Peter G. Boag, *Re-Dressing America's Frontier Past* (Berkeley: University of California Press, 2011); Clare Sears, *Arresting Dress: Cross-Dressing, Law, and Fascination in Nineteenth-Century San Francisco* (Durham, NC: Duke University Press, 2014); Emily Skidmore, *True Sex: The Lives of Trans Men at the Turn of the Twentieth Century* (New York: New

York University Press, 2017); Jesse Bayker, "Before Transsexuality: Transgender Lives and Practices in Nineteenth-Century America" (PhD diss., Rutgers University, 2019); Jen Manion, *Female Husbands: A Trans History* (New York: Cambridge University Press, 2021).

30 Eric Plemons's research shows that surgeries that change one's visible appearance— such as facial feminization surgery—are increasingly popular among transgender women, though typically not covered by insurance. Eric Plemons, *The Look of a Woman: Facial Feminization Surgery and the Aims of Trans- Medicine* (Durham, NC: Duke University Press, 2017).

31 *Grey v. Arnold*, 9.

32 See, e.g., William V. Padula and Kellan Baker, "Making Health Insurance Work for Transgender Americans," *LGBT Health* 4, no. 4 (August 2017): 244–47. According to the National Center for Transgender Equality, 25 percent of respondents had undergone some type of gender-affirming surgery. S. E. James et al., "The Report of the 2015 U.S. Transgender Survey" (Washington, DC: National Center for Transgender Equality, 2016), https://transequality.org.

33 By 2021, twenty states and the District of Columbia have added a non-binary option to their driver's licenses. For a thoughtful account of the consequences of recognizing non-binary identities in law and policy, see Jessica A. Clarke, "They, Them, and Theirs," *Harvard Law Review* 132 (2019): 894–991.

34 Bureau of Consular Affairs, US Department of State, "Change of Sex Marker," https://travel.state.gov, accessed January 14, 2021.

35 A US Department of State press release announcing reformed policy explains that "the new policy and procedures are based on standards and recommendations of the World Professional Association for Transgender Health (WPATH)." These policies effectively use gender identity as the metric for sex reclassification, although that gender identity cannot simply be avowed by the individual for the reclassification to take effect: it has to be validated by a medical authority in a letter or affidavit. "Change of Sex Marker," Office of the Spokesperson, US Department of State, "New Policy on Gender Change in Passports Announced," June 9, 2010, https://2009-2017.state.gov.

36 Program Operations Manual System, Social Security Administration, "Changing Numident Data for Reasons Other than Name Change," RM 10212.200 (September 2013), https://secure.ssa.gov, accessed October 7, 2019.

37 Jillian Todd Weiss made the case for gender autonomy as a fundamental right in 2001. Jillian Todd Weiss, "The Gender Caste System: Identity, Privacy, and Heteronormativity," *Law and Sexuality* 10, no. 1 (2001): 123–86.

38 Francis Hutcheson, *A System of Moral Philosophy*, Vol. 1 (London: Thoemmes Press, April 2006), 261.

39 International Conference on Transgender Law and Employment Policy, "The International Bill of Gender Rights."

40 Amendment of Records, 68 Tennessee Code, § 68-3-203 (2010), https://law.justia.com.

41 AN ACT to amend Tennessee Code Annotated, Section 68-3-203, relative to vital records: Hearing on HB0187 before the House Subcommittee of Health and Human Resources Committee, 2011, 107th Tennessee General Assembly (March 13, 2012). Statement of Jeanne Richardson, Member, House Subcommittee of Health and Human Resources Committee, wapp.capitol.tn.gov.

42 Gore v. Lee, No. 3:19-cv-00328 (M.D. Tenn., filed April 2019).

43 National Center for Transgender Equality, "Identity Documents and Privacy," https://transequality.org.

CHAPTER 3. SEX CLASSIFICATION AS A TECHNOLOGY OF GOVERNANCE

1 Jan Freeman, "Bootstraps and Baron Munchausen," *Word Blog*, January 27, 2009, www.boston.com.

2 Hannah Arendt, *On Revolution* (New York: Penguin Books, 1963), 183–84.

3 Derrida, "Declarations of Independence," 10.

4 Judith Butler explains further: "If gender is the social construction of sex, and if there is no access to this 'sex' except by means of its construction, then it appears not only that sex is absorbed by gender, but that 'sex' becomes something like a fiction, perhaps a fantasy, retroactively installed at a prelinguistic site to which there is no direct access." Judith Butler, *Bodies That Matter* (New York: Routledge, 1993), xvi.

5 Claudine Dardy, *Identits de papiers* (Paris: L'Harmattan, 1998), 13. Cited in "Introduction," in *Documenting Individual Identity: The Development of State Practices in the Modern World*, ed. Jane Caplan and John Torpey (Princeton, NJ: Princeton University Press, 2001), 6.

6 Gayle Salamon, *Assuming a Body: Transgender and Rhetorics of Materiality* (New York: Columbia University Press, 2010), 183.

7 Patricia J. Williams, *The Alchemy of Race and Rights* (Cambridge, MA: Harvard University Press, 1992), 12.

8 Cover, "Violence and the Word," 1601.

9 Giorgio Agamben, *Homo Sacer: Sovereign Power and Bare Life* (Stanford, CA: Stanford University Press, 1998); Gayatri Chakravorty Spivak and Judith Butler, *Who Sings the Nation-State?* (New York: Seagull, 2007), 42, 40.

10 Paul de Man's reading of Rousseau, cited in Jonathan Culler, *The Literary in Theory* (Stanford, CA: Stanford University Press, 2007), 113–16. On the original exclusion, in addition to Mills, see Iris Marion Young, *Justice and the Politics of Difference* (Princeton, NJ: Princeton University Press, 1990); Pateman, *Sexual Contract*.

11 Carl Schmitt, *Political Theology*, trans. George Schwab (Chicago: University of Chicago Press, 2005), 13.

12 As Charles Mills argues, in fact the "social contract is preceded by the racial contract, an agreement between whites to exclude non-whites." Charles W. Mills, *The Racial Contract* (New York: New York University Press, 1997), 11–12.

13 Anomalies are the "internal condition" of doing something. Jonathan Culler, *On Deconstruction* (Ithaca, NY: Cornell University Press, 2007), 156.

14 Bonnie Honig, "Declarations of Independence: Arendt and Derrida on the Problem of Founding a Republic," *American Political Science Review* 85, no. 1 (n.d.): 106.

15 Karl N. Llewellyn, "Remarks on the Theory of Appellate Decision and the Rules or Canons about How Statutes Are to Be Construed," *Vanderbilt Law Review* 3, no. 3 (1950): 399.

16 Jacques Derrida, *Limited, Inc.*, trans. Samuel Weber and Jeffrey Mehlman (Chicago: Northwestern University Press, 1988), 126–27.

17 J. L. Austin, *How to Do Things with Words* (Cambridge, MA: Harvard University Press, 1962), 12.

18 My reading here draws on that of Culler, *The Literary in Theory*, 112.

19 Austin, *How to Do Things with Words*, 6–7.

20 Culler, *The Literary in Theory*, 142–43.

21 Austin, *How to Do Things with Words*, 14–15.

22 Stryker, "My Words to Victor Frankenstein," 249–50.

23 Austin, *How to Do Things with Words*, 9.

24 Cited in Culler, *On Deconstruction*, 117.

25 Austin, *How to Do Things with Words*, 22, 104.

26 Culler, *On Deconstruction*, 121.

27 Derrida, *Limited, Inc.*, 127.

28 Ibid., 15.

29 Star and Bowker, "Enacting Silence," 276; Bowker and Star, *Sorting Things Out*, 300–1.

30 POMS Section RM 00203.215, "Changing Numident Data—Other than Name Change," May 6, 2008, formerly available at http://policy.ssa.gov.poms.nsf. Accessed November 21, 2008.

31 "I have not studied and I do not want to study the development of real governmental practice by determining the particular institutions it deals with, the problems raised, the tactics chosen, the instruments employed, forged, or remodeled, and so forth." Michel Foucault, *The Birth of Biopolitics: Lectures at the Collège de France, 1978–1979*, trans. Graham Burchell (New York: Palgrave MacMillan, 2008), 2.

32 Paisley Currah and Dean Spade, "Introduction to Special Issue, The State We're In: Locations of Coercion and Resistance in Trans Policy, Part I," *Sexuality Research & Social Policy* 4, no. 4 (December 2007): 3.

33 Mitchell, "Society, Economy," 76.

34 Brown, "Finding the Man in the State," 12; Similarly, legal historian William Novak writes, "The idea that there is some kind of essence or structure . . . to this thing called 'the state' . . . is a source of constant confusion and misdirected, scholarly energy." William J. Novak, "The Concept of the State in American History," in *Boundaries of the State in US History*, ed. James T. Sparrow, William J. Novak, and Stephen W. Sawyer (Chicago: University of Chicago Press, 2015), 337.

35 Foucault, *Security, Territory, Population*, 109.

36 Canaday (quoting John R. Commons), *The Straight State*, 5. Similarly, social theorist and criminologist Mariana Valverde reminds us that it's important to heed Foucault's "warnings against taking these abstract concepts as more real than the practices that constitute them." Valverde, "Genealogies of European States," 60. Scholars who work in the field of American political development have long understood "the state" as fragmented. For an analysis of how the fragmented state affects LGBT individuals, see Stephen M. Engel, "Developmental Perspectives on Lesbian and Gay Politics: Fragmented Citizenship in a Fragmented State," *Perspectives on Politics* 13, no. 2 (2015): 287–311.

37 Gilles Deleuze, *Negotiations 1972–1990*, trans. Martin Joughin (New York: Columbia University Press, 1995), 14.

38 Foucault, *Security, Territory, Population*, 118.

39 New York State Department of Motor Vehicles, 2009 Annual Report, 11.

40 Thomas W. Merrill and Kathryn Tongue Watts, "Agency Rules and the Force of Law: The Original Convention," *Harvard Law Review* 116, no. 2 (2002): 467–592.

41 Hall Stuart, *The Hard Road to Renewal: Thatcherism and the Crisis of the Left* (London: Verso, 1988), 166.

42 Fredrich Nietzsche, *On the Genealogy of Morals*, trans. Douglas Smith (New York: Oxford University Press, 2009), 29.

43 Judith Butler, *Excitable Speech* (New York: Routledge, 1997), 45–46.

44 Brown, *Edgework*, 124.

45 Paisley Currah, "Gender Pluralisms under the Transgender Umbrella," in *Transgender Rights*, ed. Paisley Currah, Richard M. Juang, and Shannon Price Minter (Minneapolis: Minnesota University Press, 2006), 3–31.

CHAPTER 4. TILL BIRTH DO US PART

1 According to some postmortems of the 2016 election, Donald Trump would not have been elected president had Hillary Clinton paid more attention to economic issues and less to identity politics, especially those of the transgender sort. "People in the heartland thought the Democratic Party cared more about where someone else went to the restroom than whether they had a good-paying job," a local Democratic Party chairman pronounced. James Hohmann, "The Daily 202: Rust Belt Dems Broke for Trump Because They Thought Clinton Cared More about Bathrooms than Jobs," *Washington Post*, November 22, 2016, www.washingtonpost.com. Angela Nagle, a leftist cultural critic, positioned gender non-normativity and gender fluidity as symptomatic of the excesses of online cancel culture. She argues that it "has had a huge and unexpected level of influence" in disseminating liberal identity politics' "cult of suffering, weakness, and vulnerability," hence destroying a robust, universalistic left politics. Angela Nagle, *Kill All Normies* (Alresford: Zero Books, 2017), 68–86. Democratic centrists Mark Penn and Andrew Stein accused the Democratic Party of "being mired too often in political correctness," and offered up "transgender bathroom issues" as one of

the symptoms of that political correctness. Mark Penn and Andrew Stein, "Back to the Center, Democrats," *New York Times*, July 6, 2017. In a widely circulated op-ed after the election, historian Mark Lilla proclaimed, "America is sick and tired of hearing about liberals' damn bathrooms." Mark Lilla, "The End of Identity Liberalism," *New York Times*, November 20, 2016.

2 Nancy Fraser, *Justice Interruptus: Critical Reflections on the "Postsocialist" Condition* (New York: Routledge, 1996), 11.

3 Nancy Fraser, "Social Justice in the Age of Identity Politics: Redistribution, Recognition, and Participation" (Tanner Lectures on Human Values, Stanford University, 1996), www.ssoar.info.

4 Fraser, *Justice Interruptus*, 17–18.

5 Judith Butler writes, "Is it only a matter of 'cultural' recognition when nonnormative sexualities are marginalized and debased, or does the possibility of a livelihood come into play? And is it possible to distinguish, even analytically, between a lack of cultural recognition and material oppression, when the very definition of legal 'personhood' is rigorously circumscribed by cultural norms that are indissociable from their material effects?" Judith Butler, "Merely Cultural," *Social Text*, no. 52/53 (1997): 273.

6 Nancy Fraser, "How Feminism Became Capitalism's Handmaiden—and How to Reclaim It," *Guardian*, October 14, 2013, www.theguardian.com.

7 Che Gossett, "We Will Not Rest in Peace: AIDS Activism, Black Radicalism, Queer and/or Trans Resistance," in *Queer Necropolitics*, ed. Jin Haritaworn, Adi Kuntsman, and Silvia Posocco (New York: Routledge, 2014), 31–50; C. Riley Snorton and Jin Haritaworn, "Trans Necropolitics: A Transnational Reflection on Violence, Death, and the Trans of Color Afterlife," in *The Transgender Studies Reader 2*, ed. Susan Stryker and Aren Z. Aizura (New York: Routledge, 2013), 66–76; Spade, "What's Wrong with Trans Rights?"; Viviane Namaste, *Sex Change, Social Change: Reflections on Identity, Institutions, and Imperialism*, 2nd ed. (Toronto: Women's Press, 2011); Irving, "Normalized Transgressions"; Aren Aizura, "Of Borders and Homes: The Imaginary Community of (Trans)Sexual Citizenship," *Inter-Asia Culture Studies* 7, no. 2 (2006): 289–309.

8 Lisa Duggan, *The Twilight of Equality: Neoliberalism, Cultural Politics, and the Attack on Democracy* (Boston: Beacon Press, 2003), 50.

9 David J. Eng, J. Halberstam, and José Esteban Muñoz, "What's Queer about Queer Studies Now," *Social Text* 23, no. 3–4 (2005): 10.

10 Jasbir K. Puar, *Terrorist Assemblages* (Durham, NC: Duke University Press, 2007), 46–47.

11 Driver's license policies tended to have less stringent requirements for sex reclassification than did birth certificates. For example, in the 1970s, New York State's Department of Motor Vehicles required a letter from the physician who had "performed the operation," but by 1987 the policy required only a letter from a physician attesting to the "true gender" of the individual based on "medical, psychological or psychiatric evaluations, with a medical determination that one gender

predominates over the other." Patricia B. Adduci, Commissioner, Department of Motor Vehicles, State of New York, "Memo, Change in Required Documentation for Proof of Sex Change," April 29, 1987. That procedure was later revised again: now those applying to correct information on their New York State driver's license or nondriver's ID document must provide a statement from a health professional certifying "that one gender is your main gender and that you identify as male or female." New York State Department of Motor Vehicles, "How to Change Information on DMV Documents," https://dmv.ny.gov. But until 2011, for both New York State and the city—separate jurisdictions for the purposes of birth certificates—one had to provide proof of surgery to get a birth certificate that did not reveal the sex assigned at birth. There are at least two possible explanations for why driver's license sex reclassification policies across the United States were generally quicker to drop the surgery requirement than birth certificate policies. First, most driver's license policies for sex reclassification were changed by administrative rules rather than by statute; birth certificates, on the other hand, are more likely to be explicitly governed by statutes detailing vital registration categories and processes. Getting a legislature to vote affirmatively on this change is a much more onerous process than convincing officials to make such changes via an administrative rule. (And indeed, in the tradition of "street-level bureaucrats," some of the policies on driver's licenses were unwritten and informal for a long time. In some places, transgender people were advised to go to particular DMV offices, even particular clerks. Michael Lipskey, *Street Level Bureaucracy: Dilemmas of the Individual in Public Service*, 2nd ed. (New York: Russell Sage Foundation, 2010). Second, birth certificates are "breeder documents"—in the argot of bureaucrats, identity documents that can provide proof of identity to get other documents. Driver's licenses have historically not had the same status. Currah and Moore, "'We Won't Know Who You Are,'" 127. The difference between birth certificates and driver's licenses on this issue is a fascinating question worthy of further research, but for the purpose of the analysis in this chapter, what matters is not the difference between these identity document standards but the difference between decisions and policies that held that sex can change and those that held that it can't.

12 For example, see the January 24, 2004, version of Lambda Legal, "Amending Birth Certificates to Reflect Your Correct Sex," https://web.archive.org/web/20041129125038/http://www.lambdalegal.com.

13 Arkansas Code Annotated § 20-18-307(d) (2005).

14 See, generally, Lambda Legal, "Changing Birth Certificate Sex Designations: State-by-State Guidelines," September 2018, www.lambdalegal.org. In the jurisdictions that have dropped requirements for body modification, applicants for new birth certificates generally must submit an affidavit or letter from a health professional that states something along the lines of "the applicant has undergone appropriate clinical treatment for a person diagnosed with gender dysphoria or transsexualism." This particular example is from New York City, "Adopted Rules," http://rules.

cityofnewyork.us. It's important to note that, for transgender health providers, "appropriate clinical treatment" could mean *no* medical interventions.

15 The Social Security Administration could also be an interested party. Surviving spouses in marriages where one of the parties identified as a gender not associated with the sex assigned at birth could be denied survivor's benefits, although this was not a common occurrence. The field officers' manual for the Social Security Administration pointed out, "The laws of States that recognize gender changes differ concerning the criteria which must be met to establish a gender change." As a result, some opposite-sex marriages might actually be viewed as same-sex marriages, depending on the reigning legal authority. Bans on same-sex marriage meant that surviving partners could not receive survivor benefits. The validity of such marriages might have depended on: the state the marriage was performed in; the state the surviving spouse lived in at the time of death; whether the individual in question "transitioned" before or after the marriage; case law on intestate succession in the state the couple lived in, was married in, or where the spouse currently resided; or any number of particular combinations of those individual facts. In fact, the manual uses the phrase "not clear" several times in its section on the validity of "transgender marriages." Field officers were advised to submit the claim to a "Regional Chief Council" for a legal opinion. POMS General GN 00305.005, "Determining Marital Status," July 7, 2010. As Shannon Minter, the legal director of the National Center for Lesbian Rights, wrote in 2002, "In the vast majority of U.S. states—47 out of 50, to be precise—a transsexual person has little or no guidance as to whether he is legally entitled to marry a man or a woman." Shannon Price Minter, "The United States of Chaos: The Uncertain Status of Transsexual Marriages under Current U.S. Law & a Proposed Standard for Future Cases" (National Center for Lesbian Rights, 2002). These discrepancies in the application of federal benefits to similarly situated residents of different states illustrate the point made in the conclusion of chapter 3: that it's vital to examine the many different sovereign exclusions and the work they do in different contexts rather than simply deconstructing the naturalization of sex difference, over and over again.

16 Ruthann Robson, "Reinscribing Normality? The Law and Politics of Transgender Marriage," in *Transgender Rights* (Minneapolis: Minnesota University Press, 2006), 300.

17 *M. T. v. J. T.* 355 A.2d 204 (N.J. Super. Ct. App. Div. 1976).

18 *Frances B. v. Mark B.*, 78 Misc. 2d 112 (Supreme Court of New York, Special Term, Kings County, 1974). The same justification could have been at work in the unpublished district court case *Vecchione v. Vecchione*, CA Civ. No. 95D003769 (Orange County, filed April 23, 1996). In that case, Joshua Vecchione, assigned female at birth, was deemed male for the purposes of marriage by the court. Unlike Mark B., he had had a phalloplasty. See Taylor Flynn, "The Ties That (Don't) Bind," in *Transgender Rights*, ed. Paisley Currah, Richard M. Juang, and Shannon Price Minter (Minneapolis: University of Minnesota Press, 2006), 39.

19 Major published appellate decisions on marriages or applications for marriage licenses involving a transgender person in the US, 1976–2005. Only the first case finds in favor of the transgender spouse. *M. T. v. J. T.* (1976), 140 N.J. Super. 77, 355 A. 2d 204; *In Re Ladrach*, 32 Ohio Misc. 2d 6, 513 N.E.2d 828 (Ohio Probate 1987); *Littleton v. Prange*, 9 S.W. 3d 223 (Tex. App. 1999); *In the Matter of the Estate of Marshall G. Gardiner*, 42 P3d 120 (Kan. 2002); *In Re Application for Marriage License for Nash*, 2003 Ohio 7221 (Court of Appeals of Ohio, Eleventh Appellate District, Trumbull County, 2003); *Kantaras v. Kantaras*, 884 So. 2d 155 (Court of Appeal of Florida, Second District, 2004); *In Re Marriage of Sterling Simmons*, 355 Ill. App. 3d 942 (Appellate Court of Illinois, First District, Third Division, 2005).

20 In 1972, the US Supreme Court upheld a Minnesota Supreme Court ruling that found no fundamental right for same-sex marriage with this thirteen-word sentence: "Appeal from Sup. Ct. Minn. dismissed for want of a substantial federal question." *Baker v. Nelson*, October 10, 1972, docket 71–1027.

21 *Littleton v. Prange*, 9 S.W.3d 223, 226 (Court of Appeals of Texas, 1999).

22 *In Re Gardiner*, 42 P.3d at 126.

23 *Kantaras*, 4 So. 2d at 157.

24 *Littleton*, 9 S.W.3d at 224.

25 *Littleton*, 9 S.W.3d at 226.

26 *Kantaras*, 4 So. 2d at 161.

27 *In Re Gardiner*, 42 P.3d at 133.

28 *Littleton*, 9 S.W.3d at 226.

29 *In Re Gardiner*, 42 P.3d at 123. It's intriguing that even as these courts refuse to recognize gender or gender identity as dispositive in determining legal sex, they do take some time in the decisions telling these individuals' stories of gender development. (For example, the Texas court referred to Gardiner's "long and difficult road.") Also, they usually use the pronoun that reflects the individual's gender identity, not their birth sex.

30 The Republican Party would have sex set not at birth but at conception, and would base it on a visible inspection of the genitals at birth *and* on chromosomes: "A person's sex is defined as the physical condition of being male or female, which is determined at conception, identified at birth by a person's anatomy, recorded on their official birth certificate, and can be confirmed by DNA testing." As is typical, such constructions of the F/M binary do not consider non-binary and intersex people. And one's access to sex-segregated facilities in schools would be based on this construction of sex. Counsel's Office, Republican National Committee, "Resolution Condemning Governmental Overreach regarding Title IX Politics in Public Schools," February 25, 2016, https://prod-static-ngop-pbl.s3.amazonaws.com.

31 2010 Idaho Republican Party Platform, adopted June 26, 2010, Idaho Falls, Idaho, https://web.archive.org/web/20110725104642/http://www.idgop.org/pdf/2010%20 IDAHO%20GOP%20PLATFORM.PDF. Indeed, as early as 1996, it was beginning to dawn on right-wing activists that there was something not quite right about marriages involving transgender people. For example, in 1996—upon

hearing about a planned marriage between a transgender woman and a cisgender woman—Lon Mabon, then the leader of the conservative Oregon Citizens Alliance, announced a voter referendum that would define marriage as a strictly heterosexual institution and sex as determined at conception. "It stops this playing around with Mother Nature," Mabon said. Associated Press, "Oregon Couple Adds Twist to Love Story," December 14, 1996. Of course, if such a resolution were to pass (it did not), it would actually have allowed a marriage between a trans woman and a cis woman in Oregon when bans on same-sex marriage were still constitutional—exactly the kind of ban Mabon wanted to protect.

32 Md. Code Ann, § 4–214(b)(5) (2006).

33 *In the Matter of Robert Wright Heilig*, Brief of Appellant Janet Wright Heilig, Court of Appeals of Maryland, September term, 2002.

34 In the marriage cases discussed, criteria for sex designation are described as a matter of law. The courts in *Gardiner*, *Kantaras*, and *Littleton* all explicitly make this point—that the question before them is one of law, not of fact. This distinction is crucial to determining the legal procedure and, importantly, the outcome of the case. Were the issue of the individual's sex classification deemed a matter of fact, the appellate courts would have to remand the cases back to the lower courts. Under the Seventh Amendment and federal rules of civil procedure and corresponding state rules, lower courts make factual findings; appellate courts are required to treat facts determined by original triers of facts—juries or judges in the lower court—with great deference, unless the findings are clearly erroneous. The lowest court's findings of law, however, can be reviewed de novo, from the beginning, by higher courts. There need be no deference to a lower court's interpretation and application of legal rules and principles. Thus, if an appellate court decided sex was a factual issue, it would be unable to make the final determination in the case. But if an appellate court found sex to be a matter of law, then its disposition on the principle at issue would be final, unless the case were to be heard by an even higher court. However, as Ronald Allen and Michael Pardo document, the distinction between facts and laws has been described by various Supreme Court justices as "elusive," "slippery," and "vexing." Ronald J. Allen and Michael S. Pardo, "The Myth of the Law-Fact Distinction," *Northwestern University Law Review* 97 (2003): 1769–807. In the words of Justice White, often cited in other Supreme Court and appellate decisions on this question, the Court has not found a way to articulate "a rule or principle that will unerringly distinguish a factual finding from a legal conclusion." *Pullman-Standard v. Swint*, 456 U.S. 273, 288 (1982). Indeed, there is some suspicion that a decision as to whether a question before a court is a matter of law or of fact is simply reverse-engineered based on the desired outcome of the judge or the majority of the panel. As Justice Frankfurter noted, "facts do not assess themselves"—rather, someone endowed with authority gets to decide whether something is a factual or a legal question. *Baumgartner v. United States*, 322 U.S. 665, 667 (1944). The reasoning can be convoluted, to say the least. For example, the appellate court in *Heilig* found that,

as a matter of equity law, in matters of identity documents and records "the law depends upon, and to a large extent, must follow medical facts," and directed the lower court to apply the legal principle that sex is a factual issue—outlining the facts that the lower court might consider—to the evidence as presented by the individual petitioning the court. *Heilig*, 372 Md. 692, 722 (2003).

35 In doing so, the judge was practicing the equity jurisdiction tradition that, in the words of an 1894 legal treatise quoted approvingly in the opinion, "recognizes new adjustments to new situations, not upon a dogmatic basis, but upon principles which address themselves to the conscience and intelligence, and therefore admit of a rational and progressive development." C. Phelps, 1894 monograph, cited in *Heilig*, 713.

36 *Heilig*, 710.

37 *Heilig*, 721.

38 In contrast, courts and policymakers were reluctant to use hormonal therapy as a metric of sex reassignment. As the court in *Heilig* explains, "Hormonal therapy alone, which usually can be terminated or perhaps even reversed, has not, to our knowledge, been recognized as effecting either a sufficient change or a permanent one." *Heilig*, 722.

39 *Heilig*, 722.

40 As Tera Hunter points out, the marriage vows of enslaved people are better described as "Until Distance Do You Part." Hunter, *Bound in Wedlock*, 6.

41 Justice Kennedy writes, "It demeans gays and lesbians for the State to lock them out of a central institution of the Nation's society." 576 U. S. ___, 17 (2015); Welfare Reform Act of 1996; see also Gwendolyn Mink, "Ending Single Motherhood," in *The Promise of Welfare Reform*, ed. Keith M. Kilty and Elizabeth A. Segal (New York: Haworth Press, 2006), 155–168.

42 Nancy F. Cott, *Public Vows: A History of Marriage and Nation* (Cambridge, MA: Harvard University Press, 2000), 157.

43 Pascoe, *What Comes Naturally*, 121. Adjacent to marriage, laws on descent have also been malleable in the service of white supremacy. For example, legislators in colonial Virginia reversed British common law that held children inherited the status of their father. Instead, children born to African women would now inherit their mother's status. In one stroke, this made the rape of enslaved women less visible and increased slaveholders' wealth by enlarging their holdings in enslaved persons. Hunter, *Bound in Wedlock*; Eva Saks, "Representing Miscegenation Law," *Raritan* 8, no. 2 (1988): 39–69; Clymer, *Family Money*.

44 Certainly, especially after the neoliberal turn in the United States in the 1990s, states no longer enjoy a monopoly over governance, which Wendy Brown defines as "the meshing of political and business lexicons through which neoliberal reason is disseminated." Wendy Brown, *Undoing the Demos: Neoliberalism's Stealth Revolution* (Brooklyn, NY: Zone Books, 2015), 7. Similarly, Laura S. Jensen distinguishes government from governance, describing the latter as embracing "all actors, organizations, and institutions, public and non-public, involving in struc-

turing polities and their relationships, whether within nation-states or without." Laura Jensen, "Government, the State, and Governance," *Polity* 40, no. 3 (2008): 379–85. See also David Singh Grewal and Jedediah Purdy, "Law and Neoliberalism," *Law and Contemporary Problems* 77 (2015): 1–23. In this chapter, however, I am mostly not examining nonpublic forms of governance over transgender subjects, though the privatization of support for social reproduction, discussed in the conclusion, is an example of nonstate governance.

45 Max Weber, *Charisma and Disenchantment: The Vocation Lectures*, ed. Paul Reitter and Chad Wellmon, trans. Damion Searls (New York: New York Book Review Classics, 2020), 53.

46 James C. Scott, *Seeing Like a State* (New Haven, CT: Yale University Press, 1998).

47 Jane Caplan, "'This or That Particular Person': Protocols of Identification in Nineteenth-Century Europe," in *Documenting Individual Identity: The Development of State Practices in the Modern World*, ed. Jane Caplan and John Torpey (Princeton, NJ: Princeton University Press, 2001), 49, 50. See also James B. Rule et al., "Documentary Identification and Mass Surveillance in the United States," *Social Problems* 31, no. 2 (December 1983): 222–34.

48 John Torpey, *The Invention of the Passport: Surveillance, Citizenship, and the State* (Cambridge: Cambridge University Press, 2000), 4. In *Going Stealth: Transgender Politics and U.S. Surveillance Practices* (Durham, NC: Duke University Press, 2019), Toby Beauchamp shows how state security apparatuses regulate gender conformity.

49 Even today, however, Alabama continues to require surgery. At the time of writing, the ACLU was in the midst of a lawsuit against the state of Alabama for requiring that individuals who request a change of sex marker on their driver's license provide proof of surgery. "Corbett v. Taylor" (American Civil Liberties Union, April 1, 2019), www.aclu.org.

50 Mara Keisling, interview with author, 2006.

51 Hayden White uses the term "emplotment" to describe historical work that situates discrete and contingent events as plot elements in the story of the nation. Hayden White, *Metahistory: The Historical Imagination in Nineteenth-Century Europe* (Baltimore: Johns Hopkins University Press, 1975), 7.

52 Homi K. Bhabha, *Nation and Narration* (New York: Routledge, 1990), 19.

53 Benedict Anderson, *Imagined Communities: Reflections on the Origin and Spread of Nationalism* (London: Verso, 1991). Foucault explains that national formations exceed and envelop space: wrapped up in the fluid and fluctuating concept of the nation, he suggests, was the idea of it as "a sort of mass of individuals who move from one frontier to another, through States, beneath States, and at an infra State level." Michel Foucault, *"Society Must Be Defended": Lectures at the Collège de France, 1975–1976*, trans. David Macey (New York: Picador, 2003), 142. The term "population" used to be associated with territory, a community fixed in place. But as geographer Stephen Legg points out, the etymology of the word "charts the tearing away of people from place." Stephen Legg, "Foucault's Population Geog-

raphies: Classifications, Biopolitics and Governmental Spaces," *Population, Space and Place* 11 (2005): 137. Legg explains that, with modernity and industrialization, ascribed statuses fell away, people became physically and socially mobile, and the concept of population lost its territorial anchor. The population that had to be individuated, stamped, and identified for sovereign states to maintain territorial control also had to be secured ideologically to the land they found themselves on.

54 Doreen Massey, *For Space* (London: Sage Publications, 2005), 5.

55 Homi Bhabha locates the ever-present "ambivalent tensions" as effects of the "cultural temporality of the nation," a "much more transitional social reality" than the image of a social formation anchored by the past and moving in unison toward a future would suggest. Bhabha, *Nation and Narration*, 1.

56 Walter Johnson, "Possible Pasts: Some Speculations on Time, Temporality, and the History of Atlantic Slavery," *Amerikastudien/American Studies* 45, no. 4 (2000): 498.

57 Mark Rifkin, *Beyond Settler Time: Temporal Sovereignty and Indigenous Self-Determination* (Durham, NC: Duke University Press, 2017), 52.

58 Lauren Berlant, "Slow Death (Sovereignty, Obesity, Lateral Agency)," *Critical Inquiry* 33 (Summer 2007): 754.

59 J. Halberstam, *In a Queer Time and Place: Transgender Bodies, Subcultural Lives* (New York: New York University Press, 2005), 1.

60 Elizabeth Freeman, *Time Binds: Queer Temporalities, Queer Histories* (Durham, NC: Duke University Press, 2010), xxii.

61 Dana Luciano, *Arranging Grief: Sacred Time and the Body in Nineteenth-Century America* (New York: New York University Press, 2007), 9.

62 Lee Edelman, *No Future: Queer Theory and the Death Drive* (Durham, NC: Duke University Press, 2004).

63 Some have questioned the assumptions embedded in the claim of queer anti-normativity heralded by Lee Edelman and Michael Warner (Michael Warner, "Introduction: Fear of a Queer Planet," *Social Text* 29 [1991]: 3–17), as well as the suggestion that the queer white people who do not hew to assimilationist norms are somehow estranged from the white supremacist institutions that extract resources from the internally dispossessed. Jasbir K. Puar notes that attempts to render queer subjects as "exclusively transgressive" amount to a kind of unearned "sexual exceptionalism" that is nevertheless "implicated in ascendant white American nationalist formations." Puar, *Terrorist Assemblages*, 22. See also Cathy J. Cohen, "Punks, Bulldaggers, and Welfare Queens: The Radical Potential of Queer Politics?," *GLQ: A Journal of Lesbian and Gay Studies* 3, no. 4 (1997): 437–65; Sara Ahmed, *Queer Phenomenology: Orientations, Objects, Others* (Durham, NC: Duke University Press, 2006); José Muñoz, "Cruising the Toilet: Leroi Jones/Amiri Baraka, Radical Black Traditions, and Queer Futurity," *GLQ: A Journal of Lesbian and Gay Studies* 13, no. 2–3 (2007): 353–67; Andrea Smith, "Queer Theory and Native Studies: The Heteronormativity of Settler Colonialism," *GLQ: A Journal of Lesbian and Gay Studies* 16, no. 1–2 (2010): 41–68; Wiegman and Wilson, "Queer

Theory without Antinormativity"; Andrea Long Chu and Emmett Harsin Drager, "After Trans Studies," *TSQ: Transgender Studies Quarterly* 6, no. 1 (2019): 103–116.

64 The regulation of marriage—who can marry whom, and under what conditions— typifies what Foucault calls "biopower," which targets phenomena, like reproduction and marriage, that "occur within a population that exists over a period of time." Biopower is wrapped up in racist projects, and in this context best thought of as a reflection of nation rather than state. (Foucault sometimes refers to biopower as an element of state power emerging in the nineteenth century, but for the purposes of this thought experiment of distinguishing nation and state, distribution and recognition, I situate biopolitical techniques of power organized around the produc- tion of life [some lives] as an element of national imperatives.) Articulated through mechanisms of biopower directed toward a population, racism becomes "a way of separating out the groups that exist within a population . . . a way of establishing a biological type caesura within a population that appears to be a biological domain." Racism is deployed to ensure the "improvement of the species or race" and protect it from "biological threats." Reproducing the race (making live) is accompanied by "indirect murder" (letting die): "exposing someone to death, increasing the risk of death for some people." Foucault, *Society Must Be Defended*, 254–55.

65 Hannah Arendt, *The Origins of Totalitarianism* (New York: Harcourt, Brace, Jova- novich, 1973), 378.

66 Nira Yuval-Davis, *Gender & Nation* (Los Angeles: Sage Publications, 1997). Mi- chael Shapiro explains this double-coding thus: "Citizenship is located both in a legal, territorial entity, which is associated with the privileges of sovereignty and the rights of individuals, and in a cultural community where it is associated with a history of shared ethnic and social characteristics." Shapiro describes how "the symbolic maintenance of the nation-state requires a management of historical narratives as well as territorial space." Michael J. Shapiro, "National Times and Other Times: Re-thinking Citizenship," *Cultural Studies* 14, no. 1 (2000): 80–81. See also Jacqueline Stevens, *Reproducing the State* (Princeton, NJ: Princeton Uni- versity Press, 1999).

67 Agamben, *Homo Sacer*, 128. Butler puts it thus: "the category of the stateless is reproduced not simply by the nation state but by a certain operation of power that seeks to forcibly align nation with state, one that takes the hyphen, as it were, as a chain." Spivak and Butler, *Who Sings the Nation-State?*, 12.

68 Ruth Wilson Gilmore, *Golden Gulag: Prisons, Surplus, Crisis, and Opposition in Globalizing California* (Los Angeles: University of California Press, 2007), 28.

69 Devon W. Carbado, "Racial Naturalization," *American Quarterly* 57, no. 3 (2005): 638.

70 Marilyn Strathern, *Reproducing the Future: Anthropology, Kinship, and the New Reproductive Technologies* (Manchester: Manchester University Press, 1992), 3.

71 Cooper, *Family Values*; Robert O. Self, *All in the Family: The Realignment of American Democracy since the 1960s* (New York: Hill and Wang, 2012).

72 Susan Pearson, "'Facts Which Might Be Embarrassing': Illegitimacy, Vital Regis- tration, and State Knowledge," in *Intimate States: Gender, Sexuality and Gover-*

nance in Modern U.S. History, ed. Margot Canaday, Nancy F. Cott, and Robert O. Self (Chicago: University of Chicago Press, 2021).

73 Cassius Adair has shown how racial markers on driver's licenses were used in the early decades of the twentieth century to regulate Black mobility during the Great Migration. Cassius Adair, "Licensing Citizenship: Anti-Blackness, Identification Documents, and Transgender Studies," *American Quarterly* 71, no. 2 (2019): 569–94. Jesse Bayker has explored how the gender of some Black people we might now label transgender was policed through identity documents. For example, before the Civil War, free Black people were expected to produce "freedom papers" issued by local officials that established their identity as free persons. Those documents typically indicated an individual's gender and name. There was no general expectation that white people carry identification. As a result, individuals such as Baltimore resident Mary Ann Waters, assigned male at birth, could not produce papers attesting to her name and the gender she lived in. When she was arrested in 1851 on suspicion of petty theft and her assigned sex at birth was discovered, Waters was held in jail as a presumed escaped enslaved person. Jesse Bayker, "Before Transsexuality: Transgender Lives and Practices in Nineteenth-Century America" (PhD diss., Rutgers University, 2019): 32–24.

74 Rahul Rao, "Global Homocapitalism," *Radical Philosophy*, no. 194 (December 2015): 44.

75 For American studies scholar Roger Lancaster, the typical academic account of homonormativity "reflects a fantasy version of gay life. No one in the real world would want to take on the full weight of anti-normativity, which implies social exclusion (the *No Future* version of queer life expounded by Lee Edelman). No one wants to inhabit this existential queer position—a pure and terrifying unassimilable abjection—cooked up in the heyday of queer theory, the better to dramatize the force of sexual stigma. Or better yet, we should say: these positionings continue to have appeal for academics, who are often relatively well-off at elite universities, who have the leisure to pose and play at abjection. Their work distills a schizophrenic desire: they want to run free with the wolves while howling in protest against their exclusion from society. But the authors are in fact very far removed from the lives of the most oppressed and marginalized, who they take as their models and who they purport to represent." Roger Lancaster, "Of All the Things to Say about Mayor Pete," *Nonsite.org* (blog), June 10, 2019, https://nonsite.org. For a longer discussion of queer studies' relationship with class inequality, see Matt Brim, *Poor Queer Studies: Confronting Elitism in the University* (Durham, NC: Duke University Press, 2020).

CHAPTER 5. INCARCERATION, IDENTITY POLITICS, AND THE TRANS-CIS DIVIDE

1 Gina Barton, "Prisoner Sues State over Gender Rights," *Milwaukee-Wisconsin Journal Sentinel*, January 23, 2005, www.jsonline.com.

2 Associated Press, "Transgendered Inmates Push for State-Funded Sex-Change Surgery," *USA Today*, August 19, 2006, http://usatoday30.usatoday.com.

3 "VA Doc Recommends State Pay for Inmate's Gender-Reassignment Surgery," Queerty, July 6, 2012, www.queerty.com.

4 Ryan Smith, "Tax Dollars at Work: Will State Pay for Wife-Killer's Sex Change?," CBS News, December 1, 2009, www.cbsnews.com.

5 For example: Massachusetts Senate Bill S.1812, "An Act relative to the appropriate use of public funds," 2009–2010 session (prohibiting public funds for "sex reassignment surgery," hormones, or laser hair removal), https://malegislature.gov; California Senate Bill 1079, 2011–2012 session (defining gender-affirming surgery as medically unnecessary), www.leginfo.ca.gov; South Carolina General Assembly Bill 108, 2015–2016 session (prohibiting "sexual reassignment surgery" but allowing hormone therapy if the individual was on hormones before they were incarcerated), www.scstatehouse.gov; Arizona House Bill 2293, 2017–2018 session ("medical and health services do not include gender reassignment surgery"), www.azleg.gov; Michigan House bill 6524, 2017–2018 session ("a prisoner who receives gender reassignment surgery at his or her request is responsible for the entire cost of the treatment"), www.legislature.mi.gov; Alaska House Bill 5, "An Act prohibiting the expenditure of state money on gender reassignment medical procedures," 2019–2020 session, www.akleg.gov.

6 John Gramlich, "America's Incarceration Rate Is at a Two-Decade Low," Pew Research Center, May 2, 2018, www.pewresearch.org. While the incarceration rate was at a twenty-year low, in 2016 there were still 6.7 million people in the US under some kind of criminal justice supervision. Sentencing Project, "Fact Sheet; Prisons and People in Prisons," August 2017, www.sentencingproject.org.

7 Darren Rosenblum, "'Trapped' in Sing-Sing: Transgendered Prisoners Caught in the Gender Binarism," Michigan Journal of Gender and Law 6 (2000): 499–571; Sydney Tarzwell, "The Gender Lines Are Marked with Razor Wire: Addressing State Prison Policies and Practices for the Management of Transgender Prisoners," Columbia Human Rights Law Review 38 (2006): 167–220; Spade, Normal Life; Elias Vitulli, "Racialized Criminality and the Imprisoned Trans Body: Adjudicating Access to Gender-Related Medical Treatment in Prisons," Social Justice 37, no. 1 (2010–11): 53–68; J. Sumner and L. Sexton, "Same Difference: The 'Dilemma of Difference' and the Incarceration of Transgender Prisoners," Law & Social Inquiry 41, no. 3 (2016): 616–42.

8 Department of Justice, "Prisons and Jails Standards, United States Department of Justice Final Rules," May 17, 2012, https://bja.ojp.gov.

9 Bureau of Prisons, US Department of Justice, "Transgender Offender Manual," May 11, 2018, www.bop.gov.

10 Statement of Interest of the United States at 2, Diamond v. Ward, No. 5:20-cv-00453-MTT (M.D. Ga, April 21, 2021).

11 According to an investigative report by NBC News, of the 4,890 incarcerated trans prisoners in state prisons that they were able to identify—not every correctional system cooperated with their requests—only 15 were segregated according to their lived gender. Kate Sosin, "Trans, Imprisoned—and Trapped," NBC News, February 26, 2020, www.nbcnews.com.

12 Lori Sexton, Valerie Jenness, and Jennifer Macy Sumner, "Where the Margins Meet: A Demographic Assessment of Transgender Inmates in Men's Prisons," *Justice Quarterly* 27, no. 6 (2009): 835–66, https://doi.org/10.1080/07418820903419010; J. Lydon et al., "Coming Out of Concrete Closets: A Report on Black and Pink's LGBTQ Prisoner Survey" (Boston: Black and Pink, 2015), www.issuelab.org.

13 Allen J. Beck, "Sexual Victimization in Prisons and Jails Reported by Inmates, 2011–2012" (Office of Justice Programs, US Department of Justice, December 2014), www.bjs.gov.

14 Dareh Gregorian, "Dozens of Cons Eye Sex Swap," *New York Post*, July 18, 2003, 4.

15 In Black and Pink's 2015 survey of 1,100 LGBTQ prisoners incarcerated at the time of the survey, 85 percent had been placed in solitary confinement during their time in prison or jail. Lydon et al., "Coming Out of Concrete Closets." See also "'It's War in Here': A Report on the Treatment of Transgender and Intersex People in New York State Men's Prisons" (New York: Sylvia Rivera Law Project, 2007), 18, https://srlp.org.

16 Lisa Guenther, *Solitary Confinement: Social Death and Its Afterlives* (Minneapolis: Minnesota University Press, 2013); Rosenblum, "'Trapped' in Sing-Sing," 530.

17 Associated Press, "California Is First to Pay for Prisoner's Sex-Reassignment Surgery," *New York Times*, January 7, 2017, www.nytimes.com. Indeed, in at least three cases in which courts ordered correctional systems to provide gender affirming surgery, prisoners who had been denied parole were summarily granted it. Beth Schwartzapfel, "Were These Transgender Prisoners Paroled—or Just Kicked Out?" (Marshall Project, October 8, 2015), www.themarshallproject.org.

18 Douglas Routh et al., "Transgender Inmates in Prisons: A Review of Applicable Statutes and Policies," *International Journal of Offender Therapy and Comparative Criminology* 61, no. 6 (2017): 645–66. Since that article went to press, some state correction departments listed in it as having exclusions on transition-related health care have changed their policies, including Connecticut, Florida, Maine, Rhode Island, and Vermont. See also Elliot Oberholtzer, "The Dismal State of Transgender Incarceration Politics" (Prison Policy Initiative, November 8, 2017), www.prisonpolicy.org.

19 For an overview of the limited research on this question, see J. M. White Hughto et al., "Creating, Reinforcing, and Resisting the Gender Binary: A Qualitative Study of Transgender Women's Healthcare Experiences in Sex-Segregated Jails and Prisons," *International Journal of Prisoner Health* 14, no. 2 (2018): 69–88.

20 California Correctional Health Services, "Guidelines for Review of Requests for Sex Reassignment Surgery (SRS)," 2015, 3, http://transgenderlawcenter.org.

21 Chris Johnson, "Despite Harris Deal, Few Surgeries Granted to Trans Inmates in California," *Washington Blade*, November 20, 2019, www.washingtonblade.com. According to the same article, based on original investigative reporting by the *Blade*, 20 percent of such requests from trans men were allowed to go forward. In 2020, as a result of this reporting, California reformed its policy once again.

"CCHCS/DHCS Care Guide: Transgender Care Guide," February 2020, https:// cchcs.ca.gov.

22 Deborah Sontag, "Transgender Woman Cites Attacks and Abuse in Men's Prison," *New York Times*, April 5, 2015, www.nytimes.com.

23 *Kosilek v. Spencer* (District Court), 889 F. Supp. 2d 190 (D. Mass. 2012), aff'd, 740 F.3d 733 (1st Cir. 2014), reversed en banc, 774 F.3d 63 (1st Cir. 2014).

24 *Gibson v. Collier*, No. 16–51148 (5th Cir. 2019).

25 *Fields v. Smith,* 653 F.3d 550 (7th Cir. 2011).

26 *Edmo v. Corizon, Inc.*, No. 19–35017 (9th Cir. 2019).

27 See, e.g., the TGI Justice Project (www.tgijp.org), Sylvia Rivera Law Project (www. srlp.org), and the now-defunct Queers for Economic Justice.

28 Morgan Bassichis, Alexander Lee, and Dean Spade, "Building an Abolitionist Trans & Queer Movement with Everything We've Got," in *Captive Genders: Trans Embodiment and the Prison Industrial Complex*, ed. Eric A. Stanley and Nat Smith (Oakland: AK Press, 2011), 15–40; Lydon et al., "Coming out of Concrete Closets"; Spade, *Normal Life*.

29 The Williams Institute estimates that about 0.6 percent of the adult population in the United States identify as transgender. Flores et al., "How Many Adults Identify as Transgender?" A meta-analysis of large population-based samples came up with a slightly smaller number: 0.39 percent of the adult US population, or 390 per 100,000 people, identified as transgender or answered a question indicating that their gender identity was not congruent with the sex assigned at birth. Esther L. Meerwijk and Jae M. Sevelius, "Transgender Population Size in the United States: A Meta-Regression of Population-Based Probability Samples," *American Journal of Public Health* 107, no. 2 (February 2017): E1–8.

30 "Transgender Incarcerated People in Crisis," Lambda Legal, accessed August 20, 2020, www.lambdalegal.org.

31 James et al., "Report of the 2015 U.S. Transgender Survey," 190.

32 Thomas P. Bonczar, "Prevalence of Imprisonment in the U.S. Population, 1974–2001," Bureau of Justice Statistics, Special Report, August 2003, www.bjs.gov. This report predates the US Transgender Survey by fifteen years, but its analysis centers on the jump in incarceration rates since 1974. By 2001, the US incarceration rate was nearing its peak.

33 Jaime M. Grant, Lisa A. Mottet, and Justin Tanis, "Injustice at Every Turn: A Report of the National Transgender Discrimination Survey" (Washington, DC: National Center for Transgender Equality and the National Gay and Lesbian Task Force, 2011), 65, www.transequality.org.

34 S. E. James et al., "Report of the 2015 U.S. Transgender Survey," 190. Another study, of prisoners in the California prison system, found that transgender prisoners are disproportionately Black compared to the general prison population. Sexton, Jenness, and Sumner, "Where the Margins Meet," 12. See also S. L. Reisner, Zinzi Bailey, and Jae Sevelius, "Racial/Ethnic Disparities in History of Incarceration, Experiences of Victimization, and Associated Health Indicators

among Transgender Women in the U.S.," *Women Health* 54, no. 8 (2014): 657–767. The rate of incarceration for all Black people in the United States, based on US census data, was five times that of whites. Leah Sakala, "Breaking Down Mass Incarceration in the 2010 Census: State-by-State Incarceration Rates by Race/Ethnicity" (Northampton, MA: Prison Policy Initiative, May 28, 2014), www.prisonpolicy.org. On the declining difference in the racial incarceration gap, see John Gramlich, "The Gap between the Number of Blacks and Whites in Prison Is Shrinking" (Washington, DC: Pew Research Center, April 30, 2019), www.pewresearch.org. Overall, women's incarceration rates are not falling nearly as quickly as men's; in some jurisdictions, they are rising. On the difference in incarceration rates between men and women, see Wendy Sawyer, "The Gender Divide: Tracking Women's State Prison Growth" (Northampton, MA: Prison Policy Initiative, January 9, 2018), www.prisonpolicy.org.

35 Alexander, *The New Jim Crow*; Jackie Wang, *Carceral Capitalism* (Cambridge, MA: Semiotext(e), 2018).

36 Anne E. Fehrenbacher et al., "Exposure to Police and Client Violence among Incarcerated Female Sex Workers in Baltimore City, Maryland," *American Journal of Public Health* 110, no. S1 (2020): S152. On the connections—or possible lack thereof—between transphobia and the heightened vulnerability—from crime, from the police—that trans sex workers face, Mirha-Soleil Ross puts it bluntly. Looking at cases of trans sex workers who were killed by clients who didn't realize they were trans, Ross points out that transphobia can't be the only explanation for the murders of trans sex workers. "My main request is for transgender activists to stop their sinister appropriation of the abuse and violence that transsexual and transvestite prostitutes endure on every continent." Viviane Namaste, "'Activists Can't Go on Forever Acting in the Abstract.' An Interview with Mirha-Soleil Ross," in *Sex Change, Social Change*, 2nd ed. (Toronto: Women's Press, 2011), 122.

37 Gilmore, *Golden Gulag*, 70–78.

38 Loïc Wacquant, *Punishing the Poor: The Neoliberal Government of Social Insecurity* (Durham, NC: Duke University Press, 2009), 12, 19. Emphasis in original. See also Bernadette Rabuy and Daniel Kopf, "Prisons of Poverty: Uncovering the Pre-Incarceration Incomes of the Imprisoned" (Northampton, MA: Prison Policy Initiative, 2015), www.prisonpolicy.org.

39 Wang, *Carceral Capitalism*, 83. Emphasis in original.

40 Overall, however, women's incarceration rates are not falling nearly as quickly as men's; in some jurisdictions, they are rising. On the difference in incarceration rates between men and women, see Wendy Sawyer, "The Gender Divide: Tracking Women's State Prison Growth" (Northampton, MA: Prison Policy Initiative, January 9, 2018), www.prisonpolicy.org.

41 Grant, Mottet, and Tanis, "Injustice at Every Turn," 163. See also White Hughto et al., "Reinforcing and Resisting the Gender Binary," 70.

42 Reisner, Bailey, and Sevelius, "Racial/Ethnic Disparities," 759.

43 Ibid., 763.

44 James et al., "Report of the 2015 U.S. Transgender Survey," 6.

45 Certainly, as Joey L. Mogul, Andrea J. Ritchie, and Kay Whitlock point out, emphasizing the policing of queer communities is often a necessary rejoinder to "theories and scholarship that have focused almost exclusively on the dispropor- tionate and selective policing of racial 'minority' communities, presumed on a belief that these communities are monolithic when it comes to class, gender, and sexuality." Joey L. Mogul, Andrea J. Ritchie, and Kay Whitlock, *Queer (In)Justice: The Criminalization of LGBT People in the United States* (Boston: Beacon Press, 2011), 51.

46 Elías Cosenza Krell, "Is Transmisogyny Killing Trans Women of Color? Black Trans Feminisms and the Exigencies of White Femininity," *TSQ: Transgender Studies Quarterly* 4, no. 2 (2017): 226.

47 Nira Yuval-Davis, "Intersectionality and Feminist Politics," *European Journal of Women's Studies* 13, no. 3 (2006): 197.

48 C. Riley Snorton, *Black on Both Sides: A Racial History of Trans Identity* (Min- neapolis: University of Minnesota Press, 2017); Julian Gill-Peterson, *Histories of the Transgender Child* (Minneapolis: University of Minnesota Press, 2018); Emily Skidmore, "Constructing the 'Good Transsexual': Christine Jorgensen, Whiteness, and Heteronormativity in the Mid-Twentieth-Century Press," *Feminist Studies* 37, no. 2 (2011): 270–300; Che Gossett, "Blackness and the Trouble of Trans Visibility," in *Trap Door: Trans Cultural Production and the Politics of Visibility*, ed. Reina Gossett, Eric A. Stanley, and Johanna Burton (Cambridge, MA: MIT Press, 2017), 183–90; Snorton, *Black on Both Sides*; Treva Ellison et al., "We Got Issues: Toward a Black Trans*/Studies," *TSQ: Transgender Studies Quarterly* 4, no. 2 (2017): 162– 69.

49 Grant, Mottet, and Tanis, "Injustice at Every Turn," 178.

50 Ibid., 171.

51 "A Blueprint for Equality: A Federal Agenda for Transgender People" (Washing- ton, DC: National Center for Transgender Equality, 2012), 4, www.transequality. org.

52 Human Rights Campaign, "Understanding the Transgender Community," accessed September 1, 2020, www.hrc.org. Nihils Rev and Fiona Maeve Geist describe representing transgender people engaging in sex work as a symptom of failure as "a jarringly retrogressive account of trans entry into sex work given the rich history of trans sex work as a site of agency and resistance integral to the formation of trans cultures and social networks." Nihils Rev and Fiona Maeve Geist, "Staging the Trans Sex Worker," *TSQ: Transgender Studies Quarterly* 4, no. 1 (2017): 117–18.

53 For example, one publication from a mainstream advocacy organization points out, "More and more employers, for example, now have policies which ban discrimination based on gender identity; they recognize that intolerance is bad for business." "Teaching Transgender: A Guide to Leading Effective Trainings"

(Washington, DC: National Center for Transgender Equality, 2009), https://web. archive.org/web/20170524061142/http://www.transequality.org/issues/resources/ teaching-transgender-guide-leading-effective-trainings.

54 Aizura, "Of Borders and Homes," 295; Spade, "What's Wrong with Trans Rights?"

55 Judith N. Shklar, *American Citizenship: The Quest for Inclusion* (Cambridge, MA: Harvard University Press, 1991).

56 Dylan Rodriguez, *Forced Passages: Imprisoned Radical Intellectuals and the US Prison Regime* (Minneapolis: University of Minnesota Press, 2005), 170.

57 Bernard E. Harcourt, *The Illusion of Free Markets* (Cambridge, MA: Harvard University Press, 2011), 41.

58 Wang, *Carceral Capitalism*; Elizabeth Hinton, *From the War on Poverty to the War on Drugs: The Making of Mass Incarceration in America* (Cambridge, MA: Harvard University Press, 2016); Naomi Murakawa, *The First Civil Right: How Liberals Built Prison America* (New York: Oxford University Press, 2014); Andrew Dilts, *Punishment and Inclusion: Race, Membership, and the Limits of American Liberalism* (New York: Fordham University Press, 2014); Angela Y. Davis, *Are Prisons Obsolete?* (New York: Seven Stories Press, 2011); Mary Fainsod Katzenstein, Leila Mohsen Ibrahim, and Katherine D. Rubin, "The Dark Side of American Liberalism and Felony Disenfranchisement," *Perspectives on Politics* 8, no. 4 (December 2010): 1035–54; Wacquant, *Punishing the Poor*; Gilmore, *Golden Gulag*; Rodriguez, *Forced Passages*.

59 Denny Dallas, "The Clarke Institute of Psychiatry: Canada's Shame," *Transgender Forum*, April 13, 1998.

60 Andrea James, "Toronto's Clarke Institute (Now CAMH) and Eugenics," accessed September 25, 2020, www.transgendermap.com.

61 Robert Dickey, "Gender Dysphoria and Antisocial Behavior," in *Clinical Management of Gender Identity Disorders in Children and Adults*, ed. R. Blanchard and B. W. Steiner (Washington, DC: American Psychiatric Press, 1990), 196.

62 Maxine Peterson et al., "Transsexuals within the Prison System: An International Survey of Correctional Services Policies," *Behavioral Sciences and the Law* 14 (1996): 221.

63 Dickey, "Gender Dysphoria and Antisocial Behavior," 195, 197.

64 Peterson et al., "Transsexuals within the Prison System," 221.

65 Ibid., 226.

66 Brady Thomas Heiner, "The American Archipelago: The Global Circuit of Carcerality and Torture," in *Colonial and Global Interfacings: Imperial Hegemonies and Democratizing Resistances*, ed. Gary Backhaus and John Murungi (Newcastle upon Tyne: Cambridge Scholars Publishing, 2007), 85.

67 Michel Foucault, "Questions on Geography," in *Power/Knowledge: Selected Interviews and Other Writings, 1972–1977*, trans. Colin Gordon (New York: Pantheon, 1980), 68.

68 Ibid., 177.

69 Regina Kunzel, *Criminal Intimacy: Prison and the Uneven History of Modern American Society* (Chicago: University of Chicago Press, 2008), 1.

70 Dickey, "Gender Dysphoria and Antisocial Behavior," 199.

71 Massey, *For Space*, 20.

72 Ibid., 61.

73 Peterson et al., "Transsexuals within the Prison System," 226.

74 Massey, *For Space*, 20.

75 Lydon et al., "Coming Out of Concrete Closets," 37, 42; "Unjust: How the Broken Criminal Justice System Fails Transgender People" (Washington, DC: Center for American Progress, Movement Advancement Project, 2016), 101, 105, www.lgbtmap.org. One study found that transgender prisoners incarcerated for a long time are less likely to report suicide attempts if trans-related care was provided by correctional facilities in their state. Leah Drakeford, "Correctional Policy and Attempted Suicide among Transgender Individuals," *Journal of Correctional Health Care* 24, no. 2 (2018): 171–82.

76 Elizabeth A. Povinelli, *Economies of Abandonment: Social Belonging and Endurance in Late Liberalism* (Durham, NC: Duke University Press, 2011), 3.

77 Sarah Lamble, "Queer Necropolitics and the Expanding Carceral State: Interrogating Sexual Investments in Punishment," *Law Critique* 24, no. 3 (2013): 244. See also Stephen Dillon, "The Only Freedom I Can See: Imprisoned Queer Writing and the Politics of the Unimaginable," in *Captive Genders: Trans Embodiment and the Prison Industrial Complex*, ed. Eric A. Stanley and Nat Smith, (Oakland, CA: AK Press, 2011), 169–87.

78 Rodriguez, *Forced Passages*, 185.

79 *Maggert v. Hanks*, 131 F.3d 670, 672 (1997).

80 Richard Posner, "An Economic Theory of the Criminal Law," *Columbia Law Review* 85, no. 6 (1985): 1195. See also Gary S. Becker, "Crime and Punishment: An Economic Approach," in *Essays in the Economics of Crime and Punishment*, ed. Gary S. Becker and William M. Landes (Cambridge, MA: National Bureau of Economic Research, 1974), 1–54.

81 Wisconsin Legislature Representatives Scott Suder and Ted Kanavas, "'Inmate Sex Change Prevention Act' Becomes Law," press release, January 6, 2006.

82 Attorney Jennifer Levi, who has been litigating on behalf of transgender prisoners for some time as an attorney with GLBTQ Legal Advocates & Defenders, points out that media and popular criticism of proposals to provide such care to prisoners has centered, in part, on the very idea that trans prisoners should "not receive medical care that those outside prison walls may not be able to afford." Jennifer Levi, "Transgender Exceptionalism Should Not Cloud Legal Analysis" (Jurist, October 16, 2012), www.jurist.org.

83 Movement Advancement Project, "Equality Maps: Healthcare Laws and Policies," accessed September 25, 2020, www.lgbtmap.org.

84 Kellan E. Baker, "The Future of Transgender Coverage," *New England Journal of Medicine* 376, no. 19 (May 11, 2017): 1801–4.

85 *Bostock v. Clayton County*, 140 S. Ct. 1731, 1741 (2020).

86 *Asapansa-Johnson Walker v. Azar, Memorandum and Order*, No. 20-CV-2834 (E.D.N.Y. August 20, 2020), 2.

87 It's also possible that this conservative Supreme Court will allow a religious exemption for health care providers, granting them wide latitude to refuse to provide care to transgender people.

88 National Center for Transgender Equality, "ENDA by the Numbers," accessed August 16, 2014, www.transequality.org.

89 David Hudson, "President Obama Signs a New Executive Order to Protect LGBT Workers," White House Archives of President Obama, July 21, 2014, https://obamawhitehouse.archives.gov.

90 Paul Krugman and Robin Wells, *Economics*, 3rd ed. (New York: Worth Publishers, 2015), 714–15.

91 Bernard E. Harcourt, "Neoliberal Penality: A Brief Genealogy," *Theoretical Criminology* 14, no. 1 (2010): 77.

92 Harcourt, *The Illusion of Free Markets*, 41.

93 Wacquant, *Punishing the Poor*, 79.

94 Andrew Dilts, *Punishment and Inclusion: Race, Membership, and the Limits of American Liberalism* (New York: Fordham University Press, 2014), 59.

95 Elias Isquith, "Starbucks Is a National Joke: Why Its #RaceTogether Campaign Is So 'Self-Righteous,'" *Salon*, March 19, 2015, www.salon.com.

96 *Bostock v. Clayton County*, 140 S. Ct. 1731 (2020).

97 Berlant, "Slow Death."

CONCLUSION

1 Erica L. Green, Katie Benner, and Robert Pear, "'Transgender' Could Be Defined Out of Existence under Trump Administration," *New York Times*, October 21, 2018.

2 "Equality Maps: Snapshot: LGBTQ Equality by State," (Movement Advancement Project), accessed October 28, 2020, www.lgbtmap.org. On the equality maps page, use the "Gender Identity" tab to see a visual representation of gender identity policy tallies for each state.

3 Miriam Smith, *Political Institutions and Lesbian and Gay Rights in the United States and Canada* (New York: Routledge, 2008).

4 Stephen Cohen, *The Gay Liberation Youth Movement in New York: An Army of Lovers Cannot Fail* (New York: Routlege, 2007).

5 "But for" is a legal construction, aptly explained and critiqued by Kimberlé Crenshaw: "Imagine a basement which contains all people who are disadvantaged on the basis of race, sex, class sexual preference, age and/or physical ability. These people are stacked—feet standing on shoulders—with those on the bottom being disadvantaged by the full array of factors, up to the very top, where the heads of all those disadvantaged by a singular factor brush up against the ceiling. Their ceiling is actually the floor above which only those who are *not* disadvantaged in

any way reside. In efforts to correct some aspects of domination, those above the ceiling admit from the basement only those who can say that 'but for' the ceiling, they too would be in the upper room. A hatch is developed through which those placed immediately below can crawl. Yet this hatch is generally available only to those who—due to the singularity of their burden and their otherwise privileged position relative to those below—are in the position to crawl through. Those who are multiply-burdened are generally left below unless they can somehow pull themselves into the groups that are permitted to squeeze through the hatch." Kimberlé Crenshaw, "Demarginalizing the Intersection of Race and Sex: A Black Feminist Critique of Antidiscrimination Doctrine, Feminist Theory and Antiracist Politics," *University of Chicago Legal Forum*, no. 1 (1989): 151–52.

6   Before the mainstream of what we now call the LGBT rights movement consolidated into identity groups, there were few distinctions between demands for sexual and gender freedom. As the borders between non-conforming genders and sexualities were erected and consolidated around identity groups, what we now call transgender people were generally excluded from LGB movements. Shannon Price Minter, "Do Transsexuals Dream of Gay Rights? Getting Real about Transgender Inclusion," in *Transgender Rights*, ed. Paisley Currah, Richard M. Juang, and Shannon Price Minter (Minneapolis: Minnesota University Press, 2006), 143.

7   Here I follow Kate Manne in distinguishing sexism from misogyny: misogyny polices and enforces patriarchal orders, and sexism is an "ideology that has the overall function of rationalizing and justifying patriarchal social relations." Kate Manne, *Down Girl: The Logic of Misogyny* (New York: Oxford University Press, 2017), 78–79.

8   Jonathan M. Katz, "Major Companies Press North Carolina on Law Curbing Protections from Bias," *New York Times*, March 29, 2016, www.nytimes.com.

9   Robert P. Jones and Daniel Cox, "How Race and Religion Shape Millennial Attitudes on Sexuality and Reproductive Health" (Washington, DC: Public Religion Research Institute, 2015), www.prri.org.

10 Loretta Ross and Rickie Solinger, *Reproductive Justice: An Introduction* (Berkeley: University of California Press, 2017).

11 Paisley Currah, "Defending Genders: Sex and Gender Non-Conformity in the Civil Rights Strategies of Sexual Minorities," *Hastings Law Journal* 48 (1997): 1363–85; Currah, "Transgender Rights Imaginary."

12 Currah, "Gender Pluralisms."

13 Paisley Currah, "Transgender Rights without a Theory of Gender?," *Tulsa Law Review* 52, no. 3 (2017): 441–51.

14 Though it is possible to record the sex assigned at birth for epidemiological purposes and still omit sex classification on copies of the birth certificate. V. M. Shteyler, J. A. Clarke, and E. Y. Adashi, "Failed Assignments—Rethinking Sex Designations on Birth Certificates," *New England Journal of Medicine* 383, no. 25 (2020): 2399.

15 Paisley Currah, "Feminism, Gender Pluralism, and Gender Neutrality: Maybe It's Time to Bring Back the Binary," *PaisleyCurrah.com* (blog), April 26, 2016, https://paisleycurrah.com. For an important discussion on different forms of gender neutrality, see Marie Draz, "On Gender Neutrality: Derrida and Transfeminism in Conversation," *philoSOPHIA* 7, no. 1 (2017): 91–98.

16 Jay Prosser, *Second Skins: The Body Narratives of Transsexuality* (New York: Columbia University Press, 1998), 15.

17 Rita Felski, "Fin de Siècle, Fin de Sexe: Transsexuality, Postmodernism, and the Death of History," *New Literary History* 27, no. 2 (1996): 338.

18 Mary Anne Case, "Trans Formations in the Vatican's War on 'Gender Ideology,'" *Signs: Journal of Women in Culture and Society* 44, no. 31 (2019): 639–63, https://doi.org/10.1086/701498.

19 Professional athletic associations are not state actors, but their decisions to exclude athletes from competing can certainly be understood as sanctions. On the "sex testing" of female athletes, see Katrina Karkazis and Rebecca Jordan-Young, "The Powers of Testosterone: Obscuring Race and Regional Bias in the Regulation of Women Athletes," *Feminist Formations* 30, no. 2 (2018): 1–39; Brenna Munro, "Caster Semenya: Gods and Monsters," *Safundi: The Journal of South African and American Studies* 11, no. 4 (2010): 383–96. See also Siobhan Somerville, *Queering the Color Line: Race and the Invention of Homosexuality in American Culture* (Durham, NC: Duke University Press, 2000).

20 Lugones, "Heterosexism"; Sally Markowitz, "Pelvic Politics: Sexual Dimorphism and Racial Difference," *Signs: Journal of Women in Culture and Society* 26, no. 2 (2001): 389–414. Kevin Henderson lays out the connections between gender critical feminism and the racialized policing of the sex binary. Kevin Henderson, "J. K. Rowling and the White Supremacist History of 'Biological Sex,'" *Radical History Review*, July 28, 2020, www.radicalhistoryreview.org.

21 Robyn Wiegman, "Eve's Triangles, or Queer Studies beside Itself," *Differences* 26, no. 1 (2015): 50.

22 Jasbir K. Puar, "Bodies with New Organs Becoming Trans, Becoming Disabled," *Social Text* 33, no. 3 (September 1, 2015): 54.

23 In addition to the anti-transgender legislation at the state level, in 2021 twenty states led by Republication governors challenged the Biden administration's decision to construe prohibitions against sex discrimination in federal law as including gender identity. Complaint for Declaratory and Injunctive Relief, *Tennessee v. Department of Education*, No. 3:21-cv-00308 (E.D. Tenn, August 30, 2021).

BIBLIOGRAPHY

Adair, Cassius. "Licensing Citizenship: Anti-Blackness, Identification Documents, and Transgender Studies." *American Quarterly* 71, no. 2 (2019): 569–94.

Agamben, Giorgio. *Homo Sacer: Sovereign Power and Bare Life*. Stanford, CA: Stanford University Press, 1998.

Ahmed, Sara. *Queer Phenomenology: Orientations, Objects, Others*. Durham, NC: Duke University Press, 2006.

Aizura, Aren. "Of Borders and Homes: The Imaginary Community of (Trans)Sexual Citizenship." *Inter-Asia Culture Studies* 7, no. 2 (2006): 289–309. https://doi.org/10.1080/14649370600673953.

———. "Transnational Transgender Rights and Immigration Law." In *Transfeminist Perspectives in and beyond Transgender and Gender Studies*, edited by Finn Enke, 133–50. Philadelphia: Temple University Press, 2011.

———. *Mobile Subjects: Transnational Imaginaries of Gender Reassignment*. Durham, NC: Duke University Press, 2018.

Alexander, Michelle. *The New Jim Crow: Mass Incarceration in the Age of Colorblindness*. New York: New Press, 2010.

Allen, Ronald J., and Michael S. Pardo. "The Myth of the Law-Fact Distinction." *Northwestern University Law Review* 97 (2003): 1769–807.

Anderson, Benedict. *Imagined Communities: Reflections on the Origin and Spread of Nationalism*. London: Verso, 1991.

Arendt, Hannah. *On Revolution*. New York: Penguin Books, 1963.

———. *The Origins of Totalitarianism*. New York: Harcourt, Brace, Jovanovich, 1973.

Ashley, Florence. "L'in/visibilité constitutive du sujet trans: l'exemple du droit québécois." *Canadian Journal of Law and Society* 35, no. 2 (2020): 317–40.

Aultman, B Lee. "Cisgender." *TSQ: Transgender Studies Quarterly* 1, no. 1–2 (May 2014): 61–62.

Aultman, B Lee, and Paisley Currah. "Politics outside the Law: Transgender Lives and the Challenge of Legibility." In *LGBTQ Politics: A Critical Reader*, edited by Marla Brettschneider, Susan Burgess, and Christine Keating, 34–53. New York: New York University Press, 2017.

Austin, J. L. *How to Do Things with Words*. Cambridge, MA: Harvard University Press, 1962.

Bailey, Moya. "Misogynoir in Medical Media: On Caster Semenya and R. Kelly." *Catalyst: Feminism, Theory, Technoscience* 2, no. 2 (2016): 1–31.

Baker, Kellan E. "The Future of Transgender Coverage." *New England Journal of Medicine* 376, no. 19 (May 11, 2017): 1801–4.

Barnes, Jonathan, ed. *The Complete Works of Aristotle*. Princeton, NJ: Princeton University Press, 1984.

Bassichis, Morgan, Alexander Lee, and Dean Spade. "Building an Abolitionist Trans and Queer Movement with Everything We've Got." In *Captive Genders: Trans Embodiment and the Prison Industrial Complex*, edited by Eric A. Stanley and Nat Smith, 15–40. Oakland, CA: AK Press, 2011.

Bawer, Bruce. *A Place at the Table: The Gay Individual in American Society*. New York: Simon & Schuster, 1994.

Bayker, Jesse. "Before Transsexuality: Transgender Lives and Practices in Nineteenth-Century America." PhD diss., Rutgers University, 2019.

Beauchamp, Toby. *Going Stealth: Transgender Politics and U.S. Surveillance Practices*. Durham, NC: Duke University Press, 2019.

Becker, Gary S. "Crime and Punishment: An Economic Approach." In *Essays in the Economics of Crime and Punishment*, edited by Gary S. Becker and William M. Landes, 1–54. Cambridge, MA: National Bureau of Economic Research, 1974.

Berlant, Lauren. "Slow Death (Sovereignty, Obesity, Lateral Agency)." *Critical Inquiry* 33 (Summer 2007): 754–80.

Bettcher, Talia Mae. "Evil Deceivers and Make-Believers: On Transphobic Violence and the Politics of Illusion." *Hypatia* 22, no. 3 (2007): 43–65.

Bhabha, Homi K. *Nation and Narration*. New York: Routledge, 1990.

Boag, Peter G. *Re-Dressing America's Frontier Past*. Berkeley: University of California Press, 2011.

Bowker, Geoffrey C., and Susan Leigh Star. *Sorting Things Out: Classification and Its Consequences*. Cambridge, MA: MIT Press, 1999.

Braidotti, Rosi. "Becoming Woman: Or Sexual Difference Revisited." *Theory, Culture & Society* 30, no. 3 (2003): 43–64.

Brim, Matt. *Poor Queer Studies: Confronting Elitism in the University*. Minneapolis: Duke University Press, 2020.

Brown, George. "Autocastration and Autopenectomy as Surgical Self-Treatment in Incarcerated Persons with Gender Identity Disorder." *International Journal of Transgenderism* 12 (2010): 31–39.

Brown, Wendy. "Finding the Man in the State." *Feminist Studies* 18, no. 1 (Spring 1992): 7–34.

———. *Edgework: Critical Essays on Knowledge and Politics*. Princeton, NJ: Princeton University Press, 2005.

———. *Undoing the Demos: Neoliberalism's Stealth Revolution*. Brooklyn, NY: Zone Books, 2015.

———. *In the Ruins of Neoliberalism: The Rise of Antidemocratic Politics in the West*. New York: Columbia University Press, 2019.

Butler, Judith. *Gender Trouble*. New York: Routledge, 1990.

———. *Bodies That Matter*. New York: Routledge, 1993.

———. *Excitable Speech.* New York: Routledge, 1997.

———. "Merely Cultural." *Social Text,* no. 52/53 (1997): 265–77.

Butler, Roya, Andrew Dam, Sarah Eberspacher, Charlotte Kelley, and Alina Pastor-Chermak, eds. "Correctional Facilities." *Georgetown Journal of Gender and the Law* 20 (2019): 357–95.

Byrd, Jodi. *The Transit of Empire: Indigenous Critiques of Colonialism.* Minneapolis: University of Minnesota Press, 2011.

Canaday, Margot. *The Straight State: Sexuality and Citizenship in Twentieth Century America.* Princeton, NJ: Princeton University Press, 2011.

Caplan, Jane. "'This or That Particular Person': Protocols of Identification in Nineteenth-Century Europe." In *Documenting Individual Identity: The Development of State Practices in the Modern World,* edited by Jane Caplan and John Torpey, 49–66. Princeton, NJ: Princeton University Press, 2001.

Caplan, Jane, and John Torpey, eds. *Documenting Individual Identity: The Development of State Practices in the Modern World.* Princeton, NJ: Princeton University Press, 2001.

Carbado, Devon W. "Racial Naturalization." *American Quarterly* 57, no. 3 (2005): 633–58.

Case, Mary Anne. "Trans Formations in the Vatican's War on 'Gender Ideology.'" *Signs: Journal of Women in Culture and Society* 44, no. 31 (2019): 639–63. https://doi.org/10.1086/701498.

Chu, Andrea Long. "On Liking Women." *n+1* 30 (August 2018). www.nplusonemag.com.

Chu, Andrea Long, and Emmett Harsin Drager. "After Trans Studies." *TSQ: Transgender Studies Quarterly* 6, no. 1 (2019): 103–16.

Clarke, Jessica A. "They, Them, and Theirs." *Harvard Law Review* 132 (2019): 894–991.

Clarkson, Nicholas L. "Terrorizing Transness: Necropolitical Nationalism." *Feminist Formations* 32, no. 2 (2020): 163–82.

Clymer, Jeffory. *Family Money: Property, Race, and Literature in the Nineteenth Century.* New York: Oxford University Press, 2012.

Cohen, Cathy J. "Punks, Bulldaggers, and Welfare Queens: The Radical Potential of Queer Politics?" *GLQ: A Journal of Lesbian and Gay Studies* 3, no. 4 (1997): 437–65.

Cohen, Stephen. *The Gay Liberation Youth Movement in New York: An Army of Lovers Cannot Fail.* New York: Routlege, 2007.

Cooper, Melinda. *Family Values: Between Neoliberalism and the New Social Conservatism.* Brooklyn, NY: Zone Books, 2017.

Cott, Nancy F. *Public Vows: A History of Marriage and Nation.* Cambridge, MA: Harvard University Press, 2000.

Cover, Robert M. "Violence and the Word." *Yale Law Journal* 95, no. 8 (1986): 1601–29.

Crenshaw, Kimberlé. "Demarginalizing the Intersection of Race and Sex: A Black Feminist Critique of Antidiscrimination Doctrine, Feminist Theory and Antiracist Politics." *University of Chicago Legal Forum,* no. 1 (1989): 139–67.

———. "Mapping the Margins: Intersectionality, Identity Politics, and Violence against Women of Color." In *Critical Race Theory: The Key Writings That Formed the*

Movement, edited by Kimberlé Crenshaw, Neil Gotanda, Gary Peller, and Kendall Thomas, Vol. 376. New York: New Press, 1995.

———. "Postscript." In *Framing Intersectionality: Debates on a Multi-faceted Concept in Gender Studies*, edited by Helma Lutz, Maria Teresa Herrera Viva, and Linda Supik, 221–33. Farnham, UK: Ashgate Press, 2011.

Crenshaw, Kimberlé, Neil Gotanda, Gary Peller, and Kendall Thomas. *Critical Race Theory: The Key Writings That Formed the Movement*. New York: New Press, 1996.

Crissman, Halley P., Christina Czuhajewski, Michelle H. Moniz, Missy Plegue, and Tammy Chang. "Youth Perspectives Regarding the Regulating of Bathroom Use by Transgender Individuals." *Journal of Homosexuality* 67, no. 14 (December 5, 2020): 2034–49.

Culler, Jonathan. *The Literary in Theory*. Stanford, CA: Stanford University Press, 2007.

———. *On Deconstruction*. Ithaca, NY: Cornell University Press, 2007.

Currah, Paisley. "Defending Genders: Sex and Gender Non-conformity in the Civil Rights Strategies of Sexual Minorities." *Hastings Law Journal* 48 (1997): 1363–85.

———. "Queer Theory, Lesbian and Gay Rights, and Transsexual Marriages." In *Sexual Identities/Queer Politics*, edited by Mark Blasius, 178–99. Princeton, NJ: Princeton University Press, 2001.

———. "The Transgender Rights Imaginary." *Georgetown Journal of Gender and the Law* 4 (2003): 705–20.

———. "Gender Pluralisms under the Transgender Umbrella." In *Transgender Rights*, edited by Paisley Currah, Richard M. Juang, and Shannon Price Minter, 3–31. Minneapolis: Minnesota University Press, 2006.

———. "The New Transgender Panic: 'Men' in Women's Bathrooms." *PaisleyCurrah.com* (blog), March 31, 2016. https://paisleycurrah.com.

———. "Feminism, Gender Pluralism, and Gender Neutrality: Maybe It's Time to Bring Back the Binary." *PaisleyCurrah.com* (blog), April 26, 2016. https://paisleycurrah.com.

———. "Transgender Rights without a Theory of Gender?" *Tulsa Law Review* 52, no. 3 (2017): 441–51.

———. "How a Conservative Legal Perspective Just Saved LGBT Rights." *Boston Review*, June 19, 2020. www.bostonreview.net.

Currah, Paisley, and Shannon Minter. *Transgender Equality: A Handbook for Activists and Policymakers*. New York: Policy Institute of the National Gay and Lesbian Task Force and National Center for Lesbian Rights, 2000.

Currah, Paisley, and Lisa Jean Moore. "'We Won't Know Who You Are': Contesting Sex Designations in New York City Birth Certificates." *Hypatia* 24, no. 3 (2009): 113–35.

Currah, Paisley, and Tara Mulqueen. "Securitizing Gender: Identity, Biometrics, and Gender Non-conforming Bodies at the Airport." *Social Research* 78, no. 2 (2011): 557–82.

Currah, Paisley, and Dean Spade. "Introduction to Special Issue: The State We're In—Locations of Coercion and Resistance in Trans Policy, Part I." *Sexuality Research & Social Policy* 4, no. 4 (December 2007): 1–6.

Currah, Paisley, and Susan Stryker. "Introduction: Making Trans Count." *TSQ: Transgender Studies Quarterly* 2, no. 1 (2015): 1–12.

Dallas, Denny. "The Clarke Institute of Psychiatry: Canada's Shame." *Transgender Forum*, April 13, 1998.

Darwin, Helana. "Challenging the Cisgender/Transgender Binary: Nonbinary People and the Transgender Label." *Gender & Society* 20, no. 10 (2020): 1–24.

Davidson, Megan. "Seeking Refuge under the Umbrella: Inclusion, Exclusion, and Organizing within the Category Transgender." *Sexuality Research & Social Policy: Journal of NSRC* 4, no. 4 (2007): 60–80.

Davis, Angela Y. *Are Prisons Obsolete?* New York: Seven Stories Press, 2011.

Davis, Heath Fogg. "Sex-Classification Policies as Transgender Discrimination: An Intersectional Critique." *Perspectives on Politics* 12 (2014): 45–60.

———. *Beyond Trans: Does Gender Matter?* New York: New York University Press, 2017.

Deleuze, Gilles. *Negotiations 1972–1990.* Translated by Martin Joughin. New York: Columbia University Press, 1995.

Dembroff, Robin. "Why Be Nonbinary?" Aeon, October 30, 2018. https://aeon.co.

Derrida, Jacques. *Limited, Inc.* Translated by Samuel Weber and Jeffrey Mehlman. Chicago: Northwestern University Press, 1988.

Dillon, Stephen. "The Only Freedom I Can See: Imprisoned Queer Writing and the Politics of the Unimaginable." In *Captive Genders: Trans Embodiment and the Prison Industrial Complex*, edited by Eric A. Stanley and Nat Smith, 169–87. Oakland, CA: AK Press, 2011.

Dilts, Andrew. *Punishment and Inclusion: Race, Membership, and the Limits of American Liberalism.* New York: Fordham University Press, 2014.

Drakeford, Leah. "Correctional Policy and Attempted Suicide among Transgender Individuals." *Journal of Correctional Health Care* 24, no. 2 (2018): 171–82.

Draz, Marie. "On Gender Neutrality: Derrida and Transfeminism in Conversation." *PhiloSOPHIA* 7, no. 1 (2017): 91–98.

Du Bois, W. E. B. *Dusk of Dawn: An Essay toward an Autobiography of Race as a Concept.* New York: Routledge, 2017.

Duggan, Lisa. *The Twilight of Equality: Neoliberalism, Cultural Politics, and the Attack on Democracy.* Boston: Beacon Press, 2003.

Edelman, Lee. *No Future: Queer Theory and the Death Drive.* Durham, NC: Duke University Press, 2004.

Ellison, Treva, Kai M. Green, Matt Richardson, and C. Riley Snorton. "We Got Issues: Toward a Black Trans*/Studies." *TSQ: Transgender Studies Quarterly* 4, no. 2 (2017): 162–69.

Eng, David J., J. Halberstam, and José Esteban Muñoz. "What's Queer about Queer Studies Now." *Social Text* 23, no. 3–4 (2005): 1–17.

Engel, Stephen M. "Developmental Perspectives on Lesbian and Gay Politics: Fragmented Citizenship in a Fragmented State." *Perspectives on Politics* 13, no. 2 (2015): 287–311.

Enke, Finn. "The Education of Little Cis: Cisgender and the Disciplining of Opposite Bodies." In *Transfeminist Perspectives*, edited by Finn Enke, 60–77. Philadelphia: Temple University Press, 2012.

———. "Collective Memory and the Transfeminist 1970s: Toward a Less Plausible History." *Transgender Studies Quarterly* 5, no. 1 (February 1, 2018): 9–29.

Fausto-Sterling, Anne. "The Five Sexes: Why Male and Female Are Not Enough." *Sciences*, April 1993.

———. *Sexing the Body: Politics and the Construction of Sexuality*. New York: Basic Books, 2000.

———. *Sex/Gender: Biology in a Social World*. New York: Routledge, 2012.

Fehrenbacher, Anne E., Ju Nyeong Park, Katherine H. A. Footer, Bradley E. Silberzahn, Sean Allen, and Susan G. Sherman. "Exposure to Police and Client Violence among Incarcerated Female Sex Workers in Baltimore City, Maryland." *American Journal of Public Health* 110, no. S1 (2020): S152–59.

Felski, Rita. "Fin de Siècle, Fin de Sexe: Transsexuality, Postmodernism, and the Death of History." *New Literary History* 27, no. 2 (1996): 337–49.

Flores, Andrew R., Jody L. Herman, Gary J. Gates, and Taylor N. T. Brown. "How Many Adults Identify as Transgender in the United States?" Los Angeles: Williams Institute, June 2016. https://www.williamsinstitute.law.ucla.edu.

Flynn, Taylor. "The Ties That (Don't) Bind." In *Transgender Rights*, edited by Paisley Currah, Richard M. Juang, and Shannon Price Minter, 32–50. Minneapolis: University of Minnesota Press, 2006.

Foucault, Michel. *The History of Sexuality, Volume I*. Translated by Robert Hurley. New York: Pantheon Books, 1978.

———. *Discipline and Punish: The Birth of the Prison*. Translated by Alan Sheridan. New York: Vintage, 1979.

———. "Questions on Geography." In *Power/Knowledge: Selected Interviews and Other Writings, 1972–1977*, translated by Colin Gordon, 63–77. New York: Pantheon, 1980.

———. *"Society Must Be Defended": Lectures at the Collège de France, 1975–1976*. Translated by David Macey. New York: Picador, 2003.

———. *Security, Territory, Population: Lectures at the Collège de France, 1977–1978*. Translated by Graham Burchell. New York: Palgrave MacMillan, 2007.

———. *The Birth of Biopolitics: Lectures at the Collège de France, 1978–1979*. Translated by Graham Burchell. New York: Palgrave MacMillan, 2008.

Fraser, Nancy. *Justice Interruptus: Critical Reflections on the "Postsocialist" Condition*. New York: Routledge, 1996.

———. "Social Justice in the Age of Identity Politics: Redistribution, Recognition, and Participation." Stanford University, 1996. www.ssoar.info.

Freeman, Elizabeth. *Time Binds: Queer Temporalities, Queer Histories*. Durham, NC: Duke University Press, 2010.

Frye, Phyllis Randolph, and Alyson Dodi Meiselman. "Same-Sex Marriages Have Existed Legally in the United States for a Long Time Now." *Albany Law Review* 64, no. 3 (2001): 1031–71.

Garfinkel, Harold. "Passing and the Managed Achievement of Sex Status in an 'Intersexed' Person." In *The Transgender Studies Reader*, edited by Susan Stryker and Stephen Whittle, 58–93. New York: Routledge, 2006.

Garriga-López, Claudia Sophía. "Transfeminism." In *Global Encyclopedia of Lesbian, Gay, Bisexual, Transgender, and Queer History*, edited by Howard Chiang, 1619–23. New York: Gale, 2019.

Germon, Jennifer. *Gender: A Genealogy of an Idea.* New York: Palgrave MacMillan, 2009.

Gill-Peterson, Julian. *Histories of the Transgender Child.* Minneapolis: University of Minnesota Press, 2018.

Gleeson, Jules, and Elle O'Rourke, eds. *Transgender Marxism.* London: Pluto Books, 2021.

Gordon, Linda, ed. *Women, The State, and Welfare.* Madison: University of Wisconsin Press, 1990.

Gossett, Che. "Silhouettes of Defiance: Memorializing Historical Sites of Queer and Transgender Resistance in an Age of Neoliberal Inclusivity." In *The Transgender Studies Reader 2*, edited by Susan Stryker and Aren Z. Aizura, 580–90. New York: Routledge, 2013.

———. "We Will Not Rest in Peace: AIDS Activism, Black Radicalism, Queer and/or Trans Resistance." In *Queer Necropolitics*, edited by Jin Haritaworn, Adi Kuntsman, and Silvia Posocco, 31–50. New York: Routledge, 2014.

———. "Blackness and the Trouble of Trans Visibility." In *Trap Door: Trans Cultural Production and the Politics of Visibility*, edited by Reina Gossett, Eric A. Stanley, and Johanna Burton, 183–90. Cambridge, MA: MIT Press, 2017.

Gotanda, Neil. "A Critique of 'Our Constitution Is Color-Blind.'" *Stanford Law Review* 44, no. 1 (November 1991): 1–68.

Gramlich, John. "America's Incarceration Rate Is at a Two-Decade Low." Pew Research Center, May 2, 2018. www.pewresearch.org.

———. "The Gap between the Number of Blacks and Whites in Prison Is Shrinking." Washington, DC: Pew Research Center, April 30, 2019. www.pewresearch.org.

Grant, Jaime M., Lisa A. Mottet, and Justin Tanis. "Injustice at Every Turn: A Report of the National Transgender Discrimination Survey." Washington, DC: National Center for Transgender Equality and the National Gay and Lesbian Task Force, 2011. www.transequality.org.

Green, Erica L., Katie Benner, and Robert Pear. "'Transgender' Could Be Defined Out of Existence under Trump Administration." *New York Times*, October 21, 2018.

Green, Jamison, and Larry Brinkin. "Investigation into Discrimination against Transgendered People." San Francisco: Human Rights Commission City and County of San Francisco, 1994.

Greenberg, Julie A. "Defining Male and Female: Intersexuality and the Collision between Law and Biology." *Arizona Law Review* 41 (1999): 266–328.

———. "When Is a Man a Man, and When Is a Woman a Woman." *Florida Law Review* 52, no. 4 (2000): 745–68.

———. *Intersexuality and the Law*. New York: New York University Press, 2012.

Grewal, David Singh, and Jedediah Purdy. "Law and Neoliberalism." *Law and Contemporary Problems* 77 (2015): 1–23.

Gross, Ariel J. *What Blood Won't Tell: A History of Race on Trial in America*. Cambridge, MA: Harvard University Press, 2008.

Guenther, Lisa. *Solitary Confinement: Social Death and Its Afterlives*. Minneapolis: Minnesota University Press, 2013.

Halberstam, J. *In a Queer Time and Place: Transgender Bodies, Subcultural Lives*. New York: New York University Press, 2005.

Hall, Ellie. "These Transgender Women Are Suing Alabama Officials So They Can Get Their Driver's Licenses Changed." *BuzzFeed News*, February 6, 2018. www.buzzfeednews.com.

Hall, Stuart. *The Hard Road to Renewal: Thatcherism and the Crisis of the Left*. London: Verso, 1988.

Hanley, Sarah. "Engendering the State: Family Formation and State Building in Early Modern France." *French Historical Studies* 16, no. 1 (1989): 4–27.

Haraway, Donna. "Monkeys, Aliens, and Women: Love, Science, and Politics at the Intersection of Feminist Theory and Colonial Discourse." *Women's Studies International Forum* 12, no. 3 (1989): 295–312.

Harcourt, Bernard E. "Neoliberal Penality: A Brief Genealogy." *Theoretical Criminology* 14, no. 1 (2010): 74–92.

———. *The Illusion of Free Markets*. Cambridge, MA: Harvard University Press, 2011.

Harris, Cheryl. "Whiteness as Property." *Harvard Law Review* 106, no. 8 (1993): 1707–91.

Hartman, Andrew. *A War for the Soul of America: A History of the Culture Wars*. Chicago: University of Chicago Press, 2015.

Hartsock, Nancy. "Foucault on Power: A Theory for Women?" In *Feminism/Postmodernism*, edited by Linda Nicholson, 157–75. New York: Routledge, 1990.

Heiner, Brady Thomas. "The American Archipelago: The Global Circuit of Carcerality and Torture." In *Colonial and Global Interfacings: Imperial Hegemonies and Democratizing Resistances*, edited by Gary Backhaus and John Murungi, 84–117. Newcastle upon Tyne: Cambridge Scholars Publishing, 2007.

Henderson, Clarence. "I Fought for Civil Rights. It Is Offensive to Compare It with the Transgender Fight." *Charlotte Observer*, May 19, 2016. www.charlotteobserver.com.

Henderson, Kevin. "J. K. Rowling and the White Supremacist History of 'Biological Sex.'" *Radical History Review*, July 28, 2020. https://www.radicalhistoryreview.org.

Hennessy, Rosemary. *Profit and Pleasure: Sexual Identities in Late Capitalism*. New York: Routledge, 2000.

Hinton, Elizabeth. *From the War on Poverty to the War on Drugs: The Making of Mass Incarceration in America*. Cambridge, MA: Harvard University Press, 2016.

Hochschild, Jennifer, and Vesla Weaver. "Policies of Racial Classification and the Politics of Inequality." In *Remaking America: Democracy and Public Policy in an Age of Inequality*, edited by Joe Soss, Jacob Hacker, and Suzanne Mettler, 160. New York: Russell Sage Foundation, 2007.

Honig, Bonnie. "Declarations of Independence: Arendt and Derrida on the Problem of Founding a Republic." *American Political Science Review* 85, no. 1 (n.d.): 1991.

———. *Emergency Politics: Paradox, Law, Democracy*. Princeton, NJ: Princeton University Press, 2009.

Hunter, Tera W. *Bound in Wedlock: Slave and Free Black Marriage in the Nineteenth Century*. Cambridge, MA: Harvard University Press, 2017.

Hutcheson, Francis. *A System of Moral Philosophy*. London: Thoemmes Press, 2006.

International Conference on Transgender Law and Employment Policy. "The International Bill of Gender Rights." In *Transgender Rights*, edited by Paisley Currah, Richard M. Juang, and Shannon Price Minter, 327–31. Minneapolis: Minnesota University Press, 2006.

Irving, Dan, and Vek Lewis, eds. "Special Issue on Trans Political Economy." *TSQ: Transgender Studies Quarterly* 4, no. 1 (February 2017).

Isquith, Elias. "Starbucks Is a National Joke: Why Its #RaceTogether Campaign Is So 'Self-Righteous.'" *Salon*, March 19, 2015. www.salon.com.

James, Andrea. "Toronto's Clarke Institute (Now CAMH) and Eugenics," n.d. www.transgendermap.com.

James, S. E., J. L. Herman, S. Rankin, M. Keisling, L. Mottet, and M. Anafi. "The Report of the 2015 U.S. Transgender Survey." Washington, DC: National Center for Transgender Equality, 2016. https://transequality.org.

Jensen, Laura. "Government, the State, and Governance." *Polity* 40, no. 3 (2008): 379–85.

Johnson, Cathy Marie, Georgia Duerst-Lahti, and Noelle H. Norton. *Creating Gender: The Sexual Politics of Welfare Policy*. Boulder, CO: Lynne Rienner Publishers, 2007.

Johnson, Chris. "Despite Harris Deal, Few Surgeries Granted to Trans Inmates in California." *Washington Blade*, November 20, 2019. www.washingtonblade.com.

Johnson, Walter. "Possible Pasts: Some Speculations on Time, Temporality, and the History of Atlantic Slavery." *Amerikastudien/American Studies* 45, no. 4 (2000): 485–99.

Jordan-Young, Rebecca. *Brain Storm: The Flaws in the Science of Sex Differences*. Cambridge, MA: Harvard University Press, 2011.

Jordan-Young, Rebecca, and Katrina Karkazis. *Testosterone: An Unauthorized Biography*. Cambridge, MA: Harvard University Press, 2019.

Kapitan, Alex. "The Radical Copyeditor's Style Guide for Writing about Transgender People," 2020. www.radicalcopyeditor.com.

Karkazis, Katrina. *Fixing Sex: Intersex, Medical Authority and Lived Experience*. Durham, NC: Duke University Press, 2008.

Karkazis, Katrina, and Rebecca Jordan-Young. "The Powers of Testosterone: Obscuring Race and Regional Bias in the Regulation of Women Athletes." *Feminist Formations* 30, no. 2 (2018): 1–39.

Katri, Ido. "Transgender Intrasectionality: Rethinking Anti-discrimination Law and Litigation." *University of Pennsylvania Journal of Law and Social Change* 20, no. 1 (2017): 51–79.

———. "Trans Bodies, Gay Sexuality, and the Disphoric State between Them." In *Enticements: Queer Legal Studies*, edited by Brenda Cossman and Joseph C. Fischel. New York: New York University Press, forthcoming.

Katyal, Sonia K. "The Numerus Clausus of Sex." *Chicago Law Review* 84 (2017): 389–494.

Katzenstein, Mary Fainsod, Leila Mohsen Ibrahim, and Katherine D. Rubin. "The Dark Side of American Liberalism and Felony Disenfranchisement." *Perspectives on Politics* 8, no. 4 (December 2010): 1035–54.

Katznelson, Ira. *When Affirmative Action Was White*. New York: W. W. Norton & Company, 2005.

Kessler, Suzanne. *Lessons from the Intersexed*. New Brunswick, NJ: Rutgers University Press, 1998.

Kessler, Suzanne, and Wendy McKenna. *Gender: An Ethnomethodological Approach*. Hoboken, NJ: John Wiley and Sons, 1978.

Korte, Gregory. "Judge in Texas Blocks Obama Transgender Bathroom Rules." *USA Today*, August 22, 2016. www.usatoday.com.

Koyama, Emi. "The Transfeminist Manifesto." In *Catching a Wave: Reclaiming Feminism for the 21st Century*, edited by Rory Dicker and Alison Piepmeier, 244–59. Boston: Northeastern University Press, 2003.

Krell, Elías Cosenza. "Is Transmisogyny Killing Trans Women of Color? Black Trans Feminisms and the Exigencies of White Femininity." *TSQ: Transgender Studies Quarterly* 4, no. 2 (2017): 226–42.

Krugman, Paul, and Robin Wells. *Economics*. 3rd ed. New York: Worth Publishers, 2015.

Kunzel, Regina. *Criminal Intimacy: Prison and the Uneven History of Modern American Society*. Chicago: University of Chicago Press, 2008.

Labuski, Christine, and Colton L. Keo-Meier. "The (Mis)Measure of Trans." *TSQ: Transgender Studies Quarterly* 2, no. 1 (2015): 13–33.

Lamble, Sarah. "Queer Necropolitics and the Expanding Carceral State: Interrogating Sexual Investments in Punishment." *Law Critique* 24, no. 3 (2013): 229–53.

Lancaster, Roger. "Of All the Things to Say about Mayor Pete." *Nonsite.org* (blog), June 10, 2019. https://nonsite.org.

Lane, M., G.C. Ives, EC Sluiter, and et al. "Trends in Gender-Affirming Surgery in Insured Patients in the United States." *Plastic Reconstructive Surgery Global Open* 6, no. 4 (1738e): April 16, 2018.

Laqueur, Thomas. *Making Sex: Body and Gender from the Greeks to Freud*. Cambridge, MA: Harvard University Press, 1990.

Legg, Stephen. "Foucault's Population Geographies: Classifications, Biopolitics and Governmental Spaces." *Population, Space and Place* 11 (2005): 137–56.

Llewellyn, Karl N. "Remarks on the Theory of Appellate Decision and the Rules or Canons about How Statutes Are to Be Construed." *Vanderbilt Law Review* 3, no. 3 (1950): 395–406.

Levi, Jennifer. "Transgender Exceptionalism Should Not Cloud Legal Analysis." *Jurist*, October 16, 2012. www.jurist.org.

———. "Telling Our Transgender Stories—Words, Pictures, Medical and Social Narratives—Is the Medium Still the Message?" Gay and Lesbian Advocates and Defenders, 2015.

Lipskey, Michael. *Street Level Bureaucracy: Dilemmas of the Individual in Public Service*. 2nd ed. New York: Russell Sage Foundation, 2010.

Loeb, Elizabeth. "Cutting It Off: Bodily Integrity, Identity Disorders, and the Sovereign Stakes of Corporeal Desire in U.S. Law." *WSQ: Women's Studies Quarterly* 36, no. 3–4 (2008): 44–63.

López, Ian Haney. *White by Law: The Legal Construction of Race*. Revised ed. New York: New York University Press, 2006.

Lu, Kailas M., and E. F. Rothman. "Prevalence and Types of Gender-Affirming Surgery among a Sample of Transgender Endocrinology Patients prior to State Expansion of Insurance Coverage." *Endocrine Practice* 23 (2017): 780–86.

Luciano, Dana. *Arranging Grief: Sacred Time and the Body in Nineteenth-Century America*. New York: New York University Press, 2007.

Lugones, María. "Heterosexism and the Colonial/Modern Gender System." *Hypatia* 22, no. 1 (2007): 187–209.

Lydon, J., K. Carrington, H. Low, R. Miller, and M. Yazdy. "Coming out of Concrete Closets: A Report on Black and Pink's LGBTQ Prisoners' Survey." Boston: Black and Pink, 2015. www.issuelab.org.

MacKinnon, Catherine A. *Toward a Feminist Theory of the State*. Cambridge, MA: Harvard University Press, 1991.

Malkin, M. L., and C. DeJong. "Protections for Transgender Inmates under PREA: A Comparison of State Correctional Policies in the United States." *Sexuality Research & Social Policy* 16 (2019): 393–407.

Man, Paul de. *Allegories of Reading*. New Haven, CT: Yale University Press, 1982.

Manion, Jen. *Female Husbands: A Trans History*. New York: Cambridge University Press, 2021.

Manne, Kate. *Down Girl: The Logic of Misogyny*. New York: Oxford University Press, 2017.

Markowitz, Sally. "Pelvic Politics: Sexual Dimorphism and Racial Difference." *Signs: Journal of Women in Culture and Society* 26, no. 2 (2001): 389–414.

Martin, Biddy. *Femininity Played Straight*. New York: Routledge, 1996.

Marx, Karl. "On the Jewish Question." In *The Marx-Engels Reader*, edited by Robert Tucker, 26–46. New York: Norton, 1978.

Massey, Doreen. *For Space*. London: Sage Publications, 2005.

McKenna, Wendy, and Suzanne J. Kessler. "Transgendering: Blurring the Boundaries of Gender." In *Handbook of Gender and Women's Studies*, edited by Kathy Davis, Mary Evans, and Judith Lorber, 342–55. London: Sage Publications, 2006.

Meerwijk, Esther L., and Jae M. Sevelius. "Transgender Population Size in the United States: A Meta-regression of Population-Based Probability Samples." *American Journal of Public Health* 107, no. 2 (February 2017): E1–8.

Méndez, Xhercis. "Notes toward a Decolonial Feminist Methodology: Revisiting the Race/Gender Matrix." *Trans-Scripts* 5 (2015): 41–59.

Merrill, Thomas W., and Kathryn Tongue Watts. "Agency Rules and the Force of Law: The Original Convention." *Harvard Law Review* 116, no. 2 (2002): 467–592.

Mettler, Suzanne. *Dividing Citizens: Gender and Federalism in New Deal Public Policy.* Ithaca, NY: Cornell University Press, 1998.

Meyerowitz, Joanne. *How Sex Changed: A History of Transsexuality in the United States.* Cambridge, MA: Harvard University Press, 2002.

Mies, Maria. *Patriarchy and Accumulation on a World Scale: Women in the International Division of Labor.* London: Zed Books, 1986.

Miller, Pavla. *Transformations of Patriarchy in the West, 1500–1900.* Indianapolis: Indiana University Press, 1998.

Mills, Charles W. *The Racial Contract.* New York: New York University Press, 1997.

Mink, Gwendolyn M. "The Lady and the Tramp: Gender, Race, and the Origins of the American Welfare State." In *Women, the State, and Welfare,* edited by Linda Gordon, 92–122. Madison: University of Wisconsin Press, 1990.

———. "Ending Single Motherhood." In *The Promise of Welfare Reform,* edited by Keith Kilty and Elizabeth A. Segal, 155–68. New York: Haworth Press, 2006.

Minter, Shannon Price. "The United States of Chaos: The Uncertain Status of Transsexual Marriages under Current U.S. Law & a Proposed Standard for Future Cases." National Center for Lesbian Rights, 2002.

———. "Do Transsexuals Dream of Gay Rights? Getting Real about Transgender Inclusion." In *Transgender Rights,* edited by Paisley Currah, Richard M. Juang, and Shannon Price Minter, 141–70. Minneapolis: Minnesota University Press, 2006.

———. "'Déjà vu All Over Again': The Recourse to Biology by Opponents of Transgender Equality." *North Carolina Law Review* 95, no. 4 (2017): 1161–204.

Mitchell, Timothy. "Society, Economy, and the State Effect." In *State/Culture: State-Formation after the Cultural Turn,* edited by George Steinmetz, 76–97. Ithaca, NY: Cornell University Press, 1999.

Mogul, Joey L., Andrea J. Ritchie, and Kay Whitlock. *Queer (In)Justice: The Criminalization of LGBT People in the United States.* Boston: Beacon Press, 2011.

Moreau, Julie. "Idaho Must Allow Transgender People to Change Birth Certificate Sex, Court Rules." *NBC News,* March 8, 2018. www.nbcnews.com.

Morgan, Jennifer L. *Laboring Women: Reproduction and Gender in New World Slavery.* Philadelphia: University of Pennsylvania Press, 2004.

Mottet, Lisa. "Modernizing State Vital Statistics Statutes and Policies to Ensure Accurate Gender Markers on Birth Certificates: A Good Government Approach to Recognizing the Lives of Transgender People." *Michigan Journal of Gender and Law* 19, no. 2 (2013): 373–470.

Muñoz, José. "Cruising the Toilet: Leroi Jones/Amiri Baraka, Radical Black Traditions, and Queer Futurity." *GLQ: A Journal of Lesbian and Gay Studies* 13, no. 2–3 (2007): 353–67.

Munro, Brenna. "Caster Semenya: Gods and Monsters." *Safundi: The Journal of South African and American Studies* 11, no. 4 (2010): 383–96.

Murakawa, Naomi. *The First Civil Right: How Liberals Built Prison America*. New York: Oxford University Press, 2014.

Nagle, Angela. *Kill All Normies*. Alresford: Zero Books, 2017.

Namaste, Viviane. "'Activists Can't Go on Forever Acting in the Abstract.' An Interview with Mirha-Soleil Ross." In *Sex Change, Social Change*, 2nd ed., 117–37. Toronto: Women's Press, 2011.

———. *Sex Change, Social Change: Reflections on Identity, Institutions, and Imperialism*. 2nd ed. Toronto: Women's Press, 2011.

New, Holly. "How to Change Information on DMV Documents." Text. New York DMV, July 31, 2015. https://dmv.ny.gov.

New York Academy of Medicine Committee on Public Health. "Change of Sex on Birth Certificates for Transsexuals." *Bulletin of the New York Academy of Medicine* 42, no. 8 (1966): 721–24.

Nietzsche, Fredrich. *On the Genealogy of Morals*. Translated by Douglas Smith. New York: Oxford University Press, 2009.

Norton, Laura H. "Neutering the Transgendered: Human Rights and Japan's Law No. 111." In *The Transgender Studies Reader*, edited by Susan Stryker and Stephen Whittle, 591–603. New York: Routledge, 2006.

Novak, William J. "The Concept of the State in American History." In *Boundaries of the State in US History*, edited by James T. Sparrow, William J. Novak, and Stephen W. Sawyer, 325–49. Chicago: University of Chicago Press, 2015.

Oberholtzer, Elliot. "The Dismal State of Transgender Incarceration Politics." Prison Policy Initiative, November 8, 2017. www.prisonpolicy.org.

Oh, Reginald. "On Account of Race or Color: Race as Corporation and the Original Understanding of Race." *Albany Law Review* 72, no. 4 (Winter 2009): 1029.

Olsen, Otto H., ed. "Brief for Homer A. Plessy, Plessy v. Ferguson." In *The Thin Disguise: Turning Point in Negro History. Plessy v. Ferguson—a Documentary Presentation (1864–1896)*, 98. New York: Humanities Press, 1967.

Padula, William V., and Kellan Baker. "Making Health Insurance Work for Transgender Americans." *LGBT Health* 4, no. 4 (August 2017): 244–47.

Pape, Madeline, Katrina Karkazis, J. R. Latham, and Stacey A. Ritz. "Resisting and Remaking Sex in the Petri Dish, the Clinic, and on the Track." *Catalyst: Feminism, Theory, Technoscience* 6, no. 2 (2020): 1–17.

Pascoe, Peggy. *What Comes Naturally: Miscegenation Law and the Making of Race in America*. New York: Oxford University Press, 2009.

Pateman, Carole. *The Sexual Contract*. Stanford, CA: Stanford University Press, 1988.

Pateman, Carole, and Charles Mills. *The Contract and Domination*. New York: Polity Press, 2007.

Pearson, Susan. "'Facts Which Might Be Embarrassing': Illegitimacy, Vital Registration, and State Knowledge." In *Intimate States: Gender, Sexuality and Governance in Modern U.S. History*, edited by Margot Canaday, Nancy F. Cott, and Robert O. Self. Chicago: University of Chicago Press, 2021.

Plemons, Eric. *The Look of a Woman: Facial Feminization Surgery and the Aims of Trans- Medicine*. Durham, NC: Duke University Press, 2017.

Posner, Richard. "An Economic Theory of the Criminal Law." *Columbia Law Review* 85, no. 6 (1985): 1193–231.

Povinelli, Elizabeth A. *Economies of Abandonment: Social Belonging and Endurance in Late Liberalism*. Durham, NC: Duke University Press, 2011.

Prosser, Jay. *Second Skins: The Body Narratives of Transsexuality*. New York: Columbia University Press, 1998.

Puar, Jasbir K. *Terrorist Assemblages*. Durham, NC: Duke University Press, 2007.

———. "Bodies with New Organs Becoming Trans, Becoming Disabled." *Social Text* 33, no. 3 (September 1, 2015): 45–73.

Puri, Jyoti. *Sexual States: Governance and the Struggle over the Antisodomy Law in India*. Durham, NC: Duke University Press, 2016.

Rabuy, Bernadette, and Daniel Kopf. "Prisons of Poverty: Uncovering the Pre-incarceration Incomes of the Imprisoned." Northampton, MA: Prison Policy Initiative, 2015. www.prisonpolicy.org.

Rao, Rahul. "Global Homocapitalism." *Radical Philosophy*, no. 194 (December 2015): 38–49.

Raymond, Janice. *The Transsexual Empire: The Making of a She-Male*. New York: Teachers College Press, 1994.

Reed, Adolph, Jr. *Class Notes: Posing as Politics and Other Thoughts on the American Scene*. New York: New Press, 2000.

Reisner, S. L., Zinzi Bailey, and Jae Sevelius. "Racial/Ethnic Disparities in History of Incarceration, Experiences of Victimization, and Associated Health Indicators among Transgender Women in the U.S." *Women Health* 54, no. 8 (2014): 657–767.

Repo, Jemima. *The Biopolitics of Gender*. New York: Oxford University Press, 2016.

Rev, Nihils, and Fiona Maeve Geist. "Staging the Trans Sex Worker." *TSQ: Transgender Studies Quarterly* 4, no. 1 (2017): 112–27.

Rifkin, Mark. *Beyond Settler Time: Temporal Sovereignty and Indigenous Self-Determination*. Durham, NC: Duke University Press, 2017.

Robin, Corey. *The Reactionary Mind*. New York: Oxford University Press, 2011.

Rodriguez, Dylan. *Forced Passages: Imprisoned Radical Intellectuals and the US Prison Regime*. Minneapolis: University of Minnesota Press, 2005.

Roediger, David R., and Elizabeth D. Esch. *The Production of Difference: Race and the Management of Labor in U.S. History*. New York: Oxford University Press, 2012.

Rosenblum, Darren. "'Trapped' in Sing-Sing: Transgendered Prisoners Caught in the Gender Binarism." *Michigan Journal of Gender and Law* 6 (2000): 499–571.

Ross, Loretta, and Rickie Solinger. *Reproductive Justice: An Introduction*. Berkeley: University of California Press, 2017.

Rothstein, Richard. *The Color of Law: A Forgotten History of How Our Government Segregated America*. New York: Liveright, 2018.

Routh, Douglas, Gassan Abess, David Makin, Mary K. Stohr, Craig Hemmens, and Jihye Yoo. "Transgender Inmates in Prisons: A Review of Applicable Statutes and Policies." *International Journal of Offender Therapy and Comparative Criminology* 61, no. 6 (2017): 645–66.

Ruiz, Rebecca. "The Line in Loretta Lynch's Defense of Transgender Rights That Made Everyone Cry." *Mashable*, June 10, 2016. http://mashable.com.

Rule, James B, Douglas McAdam, Linda Stearns, and David Ugulow. "Documentary Identification and Mass Surveillance in the United States." *Social Problems* 31, no. 2 (December 1983): 222–34.

Sakala, Leah. "Breaking Down Mass Incarceration in the 2010 Census: State-by-State Incarceration Rates by Race/Ethnicity." Northampton, MA: Prison Policy Initiative, May 28, 2014. www.prisonpolicy.org.

Saks, Eva. "Representing Miscegenation Law." *Raritan* 8, no. 2 (1988): 39–69.

Salamon, Gayle. *Assuming a Body: Transgender and Rhetorics of Materiality*. New York: Columbia University Press, 2009.

Savage, Mike, and Anne Witz, eds. *Gender and Bureaucracy*. Cambridge: Blackwell, 1992.

Sawyer, Wendy. "The Gender Divide: Tracking Women's State Prison Growth." Northampton, MA: Prison Policy Initiative, January 9, 2018. www.prisonpolicy.org.

Schilt, Kristen. *Just One of the Guys? Transgender Men and the Persistence of Gender Inequality*. Chicago: University of Chicago Press, 2010.

Schmitt, Carl. *Political Theology*. Translated by George Schwab. Chicago: University of Chicago Press, 2005.

Schroeder, L.O. "Renaissance for the Transsexual: A New Birth Certificate." *Journal of Forensic Sciences* 18, no. 3 (July 1973): 237–45.

Schuller, Kyla. *The Biopolitics of Feeling: Race, Sex, and the Science of the Nineteenth Century*. Durham, NC: Duke University Press, 2018.

Schwartzapfel, Beth. "Were These Transgender Prisoners Paroled—or Just Kicked Out?" Marshall Project, October 8, 2015. www.themarshallproject.org.

———. "DOJ Tells Prions to Put Safety First in Housing Transgender Inmates." *Marshall Project*, March 29, 2016. www.themarshallproject.org.

Scott, James C. *Seeing Like a State*. New Haven, CT: Yale University Press, 1998.

Sears, Alan. "Queer Anti-Capitalism: What's Left of Lesbian and Gay Liberation?" *Science and Society* 69, no. 1 (January 2005): 92–112.

Sears, Clare. *Arresting Dress: Cross-Dressing, Law, and Fascination in Nineteenth-Century San Francisco*. Durham, NC: Duke University Press, 2014.

Sedgwick, Eve Kosofsky. *Epistemology of the Closet*. Berkeley: University of California Press, 1990.

Self, Robert O. *All in the Family: The Realignment of American Democracy since the 1960s*. New York: Hill and Wang, 2012.

Serano, Julia. *Whipping Girl: A Transsexual Woman on Sexism and the Scapegoating of Femininity*. 2nd ed. Berkeley: Seal Press, 2016.

Sexton, Lori, Valerie Jenness, and Jennifer Macy Sumner. "Where the Margins Meet: A Demographic Assessment of Transgender Inmates in Men's Prisons." *Justice Quarterly* 27, no. 6 (2009): 835–66.

Shapiro, Michael J. "National Times and Other Times: Re-Thinking Citizenship." *Cultural Studies* 14, no. 1 (2000): 79–98.

Sharswood, George, Henry Roscoe, and Thomas Colpitts Granger. *A Digest of the Law of Evidence in Criminal Cases*. Philadelphia: T. & J. Johnson, 1840.

Shibley Hyde, Janet, Rebecca S Bigler, Daphna Joel, Charlotte Chucky Tate, and Sari M. van Anders. "The Future of Sex and Gender in Psychology: Five Challenges to the Gender Binary." *American Psychologist* 74, no. 2 (March 2019): 171–93.

Shklar, Judith N. *American Citizenship: The Quest for Inclusion*. Cambridge, MA: Harvard University Press, 1991.

Shteyler, V. M., J. A. Clarke, and E. Y. Adashi. "Failed Assignments—Rethinking Sex Designations on Birth Certificates." *New England Journal of Medicine* 383, no. 25 (2020): 2399–401.

Silva, Denise Ferreria da. *Toward a Global Idea of Race*. Minneapolis: University of Minnesota Press, 2007.

Singer, T. Benjamin. "From the Medical Gaze to Sublime Mutations." In *The Transgender Studies Reader*, edited by Susan Stryker and Stephen Whittle, 601–20. New York: Routledge, 2006.

———. "Umbrella." *TSQ: Transgender Studies Quarterly* 1, no. 1–2 (2014): 259–61.

Skidmore, Emily. "Constructing the 'Good Transsexual': Christine Jorgensen, Whiteness, and Heteronormativity in the Mid-Twentieth-Century Press." *Feminist Studies* 37, no. 2 (2011): 270–300.

———. *True Sex: The Lives of Trans Men at the Turn of the Twentieth Century*. New York: New York University Press, 2017.

Slobodian, Quinn. *Globalists: The End of Empire and the Birth of Neoliberalism*. Cambridge, MA: Harvard University Press, 2018.

Smith, Andrea. "Queer Theory and Native Studies: The Heteronormativity of Settler Colonialism." *GLQ: A Journal of Lesbian and Gay Studies* 16, no. 1–2 (2010): 41–68.

Smith, Miriam. *Political Institutions and Lesbian and Gay Rights in the United States and Canada*. New York: Routledge, 2008.

Smith, Rogers. "Beyond Tocqueville, Myrdal and Hartz: The Multiple Traditions in America." *American Political Science Review* 87, no. 3 (1993): 549–66.

Snorton, C. Riley. *Black on Both Sides: A Racial History of Trans Identity*. Minneapolis: University of Minnesota Press, 2017.

Snorton, C. Riley, and Jin Haritaworn. "Trans Necropolitics: A Transnational Reflection on Violence, Death, and the Trans of Color Afterlife." In *The Transgender Studies Reader 2*, edited by Susan Stryker and Aren Z. Aizura, 66–76. New York: Routledge, 2013.

Somerville, Siobhan. *Queering the Color Line: Race and the Invention of Homosexuality in American Culture*. Durham, NC: Duke University Press, 2000.

Sontag, Deborah. "Transgender Woman Cites Attacks and Abuse in Men's Prison." *New York Times*, April 5, 2015. www.nytimes.com.

Spade, Dean. "What's Wrong with Trans Rights?" In *Trans Feminist Perspectives in and beyond Transgender Studies*, edited by Finn Enke, 184–202. Philadelphia: Temple University Press, 2011.

———. *Normal Life: Administrative Violence, Critical Trans Politics, and the Limits of Law*. 2nd ed. Durham, NC: Duke University Press, 2015.

Spillers, Hortense J. "Mama's Baby, Papa's Maybe: An American Grammar Book." *Diacritics* 17, no. 2 (1987): 65–81.

Spivak, Gayatri Chakravorty, and Judith Butler. *Who Sings the Nation-State?* New York: Seagull, 2007.

Star, Susan Leigh, and Geoffrey C. Bowker. "Enacting Silence: Residual Categories as a Challenge for Ethics, Information Systems, and Communication." *Ethics and Information Technology* 9 (2007): 273–80.

Stevens, Jacqueline. *Reproducing the State*. Princeton, NJ: Princeton University Press, 1999.

Stoltenberg, John. "#GenderWeek: Andrea Was Not Transphobic." *Feminist Times*, 2014. https://web.archive.org/web/20160317032310/http://www.feministtimes.com/%e2%80%aa%e2%80%8egenderweek-andrea-was-not-transphobic.

Stone, Sandy. "The Empire Strikes Back: A Posttranssexual Manifesto." In *Body Guards: The Cultural Politics of Gender Ambiguity*, edited by Julia Epstein and Kristina Kraus, 280–304. New York: Routledge, 1991.

Strathern, Marilyn. *Reproducing the Future: Anthropology, Kinship, and the New Reproductive Technologies*. Manchester, UK: Manchester University Press, 1992.

Stryker, Susan. "My Words to Victor Frankenstein above the Village of Chamounix." *GLQ: A Journal of Lesbian and Gay Studies* 1, no. 3 (1994): 237–54.

———. *Transgender History: The Roots of Today's Revolution*. 2nd ed. New York: Seal Press, 2017.

Stryker, Susan, and Talia Mae Bettcher. "Introduction: Trans/Feminisms." Edited by Susan Stryker and Talia Mae Bettcher. *TSQ: Transgender Studies Quarterly* 3, no. 1–2 (2016): 5–14.

Sumner, J., and L. Sexton. "Same Difference: The 'Dilemma of Difference' and the Incarceration of Transgender Prisoners." *Law & Social Inquiry* 41, no. 3 (2016): 616–42.

Tarzwell, Sydney. "The Gender Lines Are Marked with Razor Wire: Addressing State Prison Policies and Practices for the Management of Transgender Prisoners." *Columbia Human Rights Law Review* 38 (2006): 167–220.

Taylor, Jami K., Daniel C. Lewis, and Donald P. Haider-Markel. *The Remarkable Rise of Transgender Rights*. Ann Arbor: University of Michigan Press, 2018.

Torpey, John. *The Invention of the Passport: Surveillance, Citizenship, and the State*. Cambridge: Cambridge University Press, 2000.

Vade, Dylan. "Expanding Gender and Expanding the Law: Toward a Social and Legal Conceptualization of Gender That Is More Inclusive of Transgender People." *Michigan Journal of Gender and Law* 11, no. 2 (2005): 253–316.

Valentine, David. *Imagining Transgender: An Ethnography of a Category*. Durham, NC: Duke University Press, 2007.

Valverde, Mariana. *Law's Dream of a Common Knowledge*. Princeton, NJ: Princeton University Press, 2003.

———. "Genealogies of European States: Foucauldian Reflections." *Economy and Society* 36, no. 1 (2007): 159–78.

Vitulli, Elias. "Racialized Criminality and the Imprisoned Trans Body: Adjudicating Access to Gender-Related Medical Treatment in Prisons." *Social Justice* 37, no. 1 (2010–11): 53–68.

Wacquant, Loïc. *Punishing the Poor: The Neoliberal Government of Social Insecurity*. Durham, NC: Duke University Press, 2009.

Wang, Jackie. *Carceral Capitalism*. Cambridge, MA: Semiotext(e), 2018.

Warner, Michael. "Introduction: Fear of a Queer Planet." *Social Text* 29 (1991): 3–17.

Weber, Max. *Charisma and Disenchantment: The Vocation Lectures*. Edited by Paul Reitter and Chad Wellmon. Translated by Damion Searls. New York: New York Book Review Classics, 2020.

Weiss, Jillian Todd. "The Gender Caste System: Identity, Privacy, and Heteronormativity." *Law and Sexuality* 10, no. 1 (2001): 123–86.

West, Candace, and Don H. Zimmerman. "Doing Gender." *Gender & Society* 1, no. 2 (1987): 125–51.

White, Hayden. *Metahistory: The Historical Imagination in Nineteenth-Century Europe*. Baltimore: Johns Hopkins University Press, 1975.

White Hughto, J. M., K. A. Clark, F. L. Altice, S. L. Reisner, T. S. Kershaw, and J. E. Pachankis. "Creating, Reinforcing, and Resisting the Gender Binary: A Qualitative Study of Transgender Women's Healthcare Experiences in Sex-Segregated Jails and Prisons." *International Journal of Prisoner Health* 14, no. 2 (2018): 69–88.

Whyte, Jessica. *The Morals of the Market: Human Rights and the Rise of Neoliberalism*. Brooklyn, NY: Verso, 2019.

Wiegman, Robyn. "Eve's Triangles, or Queer Studies beside Itself." *Differences* 26, no. 1 (2015): 48–73.

Wiegman, Robyn, and Elizabeth A. Wilson. "Queer Theory without Antinormativity." *Differences* 26, no. 1 (2015): 1–25.

Wilson, Bianca D. M., Alexandria-Grissell H. Gomez, Madin Sadat, Soon Kyu Choi, and M. V. Lee Badgett. "Pathways into Poverty: Lived Experiences among LGBTQ People." Williams Institute, 2020. https://williamsinstitute.law.ucla.edu.

Wilson Gilmore, Ruth. *Golden Gulag: Prisons, Surplus, Crisis, and Opposition in Globalizing California*. Los Angeles: University of California Press, 2007.

Wolff, Tobias Barrington. "Civil Rights Reform and the Body." *Harvard Law & Policy Review* 6 (2012): 201–31.

Wuest, Jo. "The Scientific Gaze in American Transgender Politics: Contesting the Meanings of Sex, Gender, and Gender Identity in the Bathroom Rights Cases." *Politics & Gender* 15, no. 2 (2019): 336–60.

Wynter, Sylvia. "Unsettling the Coloniality of Being/Power/Truth/Freedom: Towards the Human, after Man, Its Overrepresentation—an Argument." *CR: The New Centennial Review* 3, no. 3 (2003): 257–337.

Yang, T seming. "Choice and Fraud in Racial Identification: The Dilemma of Policing Race in Affirmative Action, the Census, and a Color-Blind Society." *Michigan Journal of Race and Law* 11, no. 2 (2006): 367–471.

Young, Ezra. "Demarginalizing Trans Rights." In *Deploying Intersectionality: Legal, Intellectual, and Activist Interventions,* edited by Kimberlé Crenshaw. New York: New Press, 2021.

Young, Iris Marion. *Justice and the Politics of Difference.* Princeton, NJ: Princeton University Press, 1990.

Yuval-Davis, Nira. *Gender & Nation.* Los Angeles: Sage Publications, 1997.

———. "Intersectionality and Feminist Politics." *European Journal of Women's Studies* 13, no. 3 (2006): 193–209.

INDEX

Page numbers in *italics* indicate Tables.

ABOUT THE AUTHOR

Paisley Currah is Professor of Political Science and Women's and Gender Studies at Brooklyn College and the Graduate Center of the City University of New York. With Susan Stryker, he was the founding editor of *TSQ: Transgender Studies Quarterly*, the flagship journal of transgender studies.